James Croil

A historical and statistical Report of the Presbyterian Church of

Canada

In Connection with the Church of Scotland, for the year 1866. Second Edition

James Croil

A historical and statistical Report of the Presbyterian Church of Canada
In Connection with the Church of Scotland, for the year 1866. Second Edition

ISBN/EAN: 9783337162610

Printed in Europe, USA, Canada, Australia, Japan

Cover: Foto ©ninafisch / pixelio.de

More available books at **www.hansebooks.com**

A

HISTORICAL AND STATISTICAL

REPORT

OF THE

PRESBYTERIAN CHURCH OF CANADA,

IN CONNECTION WITH

THE CHURCH OF SCOTLAND,

FOR THE YEAR 1866.

SECOND EDITION.

PRINTED BY ORDER OF THE SYNOD.

Montreal:
PRINTED BY JOHN LOVELL, ST. NICHOLAS STREET.
1868.

To Messrs. THOMAS PATON, WILLIAM DARLING, JAMES JOHNSTON, ALEXANDER BUNTIN, JOHN RANKIN, JAMES S. HUNTER, JOHN L. MORRIS, and GEORGE STEPHEN, the Committee appointed by the Synod, at Ottawa, in 1865, to manage the Schemes of the Church; to the Reverends DR. MATHIESON, DR. JENKINS, and ANDREW PATON, who were associated with them; and to the memory of the late Mr. JOHN GREENSHIELDS, who was the Convener of the Committee, this Report is respectfully DEDICATED.

PREFATORY NOTICE.

THIS Second Edition embraces, more or less fully, all the *corrigenda et addenda* with which the Author has been supplied during the three months that the Report has been before the public. It is gratifying to be able to state, that the alterations made are neither numerous nor such as to vitiate, in any important particular, the general accuracy of the first edition.

It is worthy of remark that the sum of $3,265.75, given on page 144 as the total amount of contributions to the Home Mission Fund for 1866, refers only to the *Synodical* Home Mission. In addition to this each Presbytery supports a *local* Home Mission. That of Toronto expends annually about $1000 within its bounds. In the Presbytery of Montreal the sum of $642 was thus expended last year; and in that of Glengary about $450. At the least $3000 is annually contributed for Presbyteries' Home Missions, and to this should properly be added the sum of $1,651, styled "additional," under the heading of "salary" (page 122), and which is fully explained at the foot of page 143. These, added to the sum first mentioned, give an aggregate of $7,906 as the ordinary annual contributions of the Church from all sources for Home Mission purposes.

The omission of full particulars regarding the "Indian Orphanage Scheme and Juvenile Mission" is acknowledged with regret. This most interesting scheme was commenced in 1856, at the instance of Mr. John Paton of Kingston; and its success has been very marked and cheering. Its operations are carried on chiefly through the instrumentality of the Scottish Ladies' Association for Female Education in India, and towards its support the Churches in Nova Scotia and New Brunswick have extended their hearty co-operation. There was contributed to this Mission, chiefly through the Sabbath Schools of the Church, the sum of $854 for the year ending 1st June, 1867; the number of Indian orphan children clothed, supported, and educated by our young friends at that date being 34; while means have been provided and application made for the appropriation of five others.

On page 128, the number of Ministers in charges is stated to be 107; on page 129, calculations regarding stipend assume the number of Ministers to be 108, including two assistant Ministers. The seeming discrepancy is accounted for by the fact of the Minister of Goderich having resigned early in 1866, and, as no salary is stated in the tables to have been promised him by the people for that year, in the calculation reference to his name was dropped.

A clerical error occurs in the addition of the column "Total Salary promised," in the Presbytery of Montreal: in the case of St. Gabriel congregation, Mr. Campbell having been inducted in December, 1866, the salary promised to him should not have been included in the calculations made on page 129; hence the alteration now made, that "the average salary *promised* to each minister, from all sources, was $750, instead of $738, as stated in the first instance."

The name of the Rev. John B. Mowat, unaccountably omitted in the list of Professors of Queen's College—page 159—will be found in its proper place in this edition.

By the suspension of the Commercial Bank, which occurred in October last, the investments of our Church and College have been seriously affected. By the recent amalgamation of the Commercial with the Merchants' Bank of Montreal, the actual loss is ascertained to be two-thirds of the original investments. The Church has thus lost $84,366, and the College, $21,332. An appeal made to the Church at large by the Temporalities' Board, to provide for at least the first year's deficit of revenue, has been cheerfully responded to, the sum of about $8,500 having been received for this purpose.

The announcement by the Government of Ontario of their intention to withdraw the annual grant of $5,000 hitherto enjoyed by Queen's College is fraught with grave consequences to the future of thatInstitution.

" The Presbyterian," a monthly Magazine and Journal of Missionary intelligence published by the Lay Association of Montreal, has now entered on its twenty-first year. This periodical has been the means of circulating a large amount of information regarding the Christian Church in all parts of the world. The prudence and ability with which it has been conducted have earned for it a high rank in Canadian literature and have placed the Members of our own Church under lasting obligation to those disinterested friends who at different times have been connected with its management. Many of them are now beyond the reach of our thanks, but these honoured names are held in gratefulr cmembrance.

A publication so useful and interesting—so well fitted to advance the interests—so indispensable, indeed, to the progress and prosperity of the Church, ought to have a wide circulation. It should be read in every family.

I feel very thankful that this humble attempt to illustrate the rise and progress of the Church of Scotland in Canada has met with a reception more favourable than I had dared to anticipate, and my best acknowledgments are hereby tendered to the kind friends who have shewn their appreciation of the importance of the work by furnishing corrections, and thus adding to its value as a trustworthy record of the past history of the Church.   J. C.

1st April, 1868.

INTRODUCTORY.

THIS Report will be found to contain historical facts of interest, and it embraces statistical returns, more or less complete, from every Congregation of the Church. It had been easy to produce a more flattering and highly coloured statement, but this would not have advanced the end contemplated—the welfare of the Church. I have been careful to exaggerate nothing, " nothing extenuate, nor set down aught in malice;" my single aim has been to render what follows thoroughly reliable. Notwithstanding what is advanced in respect of inadequate support to ministers and missions—this is deplored in all Churches—on the whole, we have reason to " thank God and take courage." Our Church occupies an honoured position among the Churches of Canada, and has a large number of warmly attached adherents, who are able and willing to do all that may reasonably be asked of them if the proper means are employed to enlist their prac tical sympathies.

For the information herewith submitted I am mainly indebted to the Ministers and Office-bearers of the Church. I thank them, every one, as well for their great personal kindness as for their willing co-operation with me. Dr. Mathieson laid me under special obligations by placing at my disposal valuable manuscripts, and supplying details that could not have been otherwise obtained. Mr. Dobie gave me the benefit of his experience as Convener of the Committee on Statistics. The Professors of Queen's College kindly supplied all the information given about that Institution, and Mr. McKerras, Synod Clerk, besides assisting in other ways, furnished me with the histories in M. S., bearing date 1833, of most of the Congregations then existing, of which I am only sorry that the limited space at my disposal prevented me from making more copious extracts. I thank the Very Reverend Principal Snodgrass, for his *great patience* in carefully revising these pages for the Press, for his corrections and reproofs, and for access to the well-filled shelves of the Library of Queen's College. The following works may be mentioned as possessing a historical interest in connection with the Church : Letters, by the Rev. William Bell, and by his son, the Rev. Andrew Bell, published in 1824; The Canadian Magazine, in 4 volumes, 1823-25; the Canadian Review, 2 vols., 1824-25 ; The Canadian Miscellany, the first periodical published in the interests of the Church of Scotland in Canada, and of which only six numbers appeared in 1828, the copy in the library being the only one I have seen ; the Christian Examiner and Presbyterian Review, 4 vols., 1837-40, which was conducted by the late Dr. McGill, then of Niagara ; A Retrospect of 36 years' Missionary Labour, by J. Carruthers, 1861. Each of these supplied its quota of material. The printed Minutes of Synod, from 1831 to the present time; A Digest of the Minutes of Synod of the Canada Presbyterian Church, by the Rev. Alexander F. Kemp, together with the Minutes of the United Synod of Upper Canada from 1831 until their union with us in 1840, have all been carefully examined, as well as the 20 volumes of the Presbyterian, commencing with 1848. In addition to these sources of information, the older records of all the Presbyteries have been examined and placed under contribution. While every precaution that seemed possible was taken to ensure correctness of detail, it is more than likely that some slight inaccuracies may have crept in. The writer will esteem it a kindness if parties observing such will furnish him with the corrections for a second edition, which is sure to be required.

To avoid repetition, figures in brackets have been introduced which indicate the numbers of the Congregations in connection with which additional particulars are to be obtained. The Alphabetical List at the close, supplies, so far as is known to the writer, the names of all who have been Ministers of the Church during the last 100 years; their nationality; the dates of ordination; the charges in which they officiated, and the Universities at which they were educated. If additional names or dates occur to any reader I hope to be informed of them.

It is regretted that from want of full information, the Churches in the Maritime Provinces are not included in this Report; it is intended, however, to publish some account of them in separate form hereafter.

It only remains for me here to express my devout acknowledgments, to a kind Providence that permitted not the slightest accident to befall me in all my journeyings.

But for one event I should look back upon the time spent in this work with unmingled pleasure. That event was the death of him who, I may say it without disrespect to any other, was at once the originator and the principal promoter of a plan for furthering the interests of the Church of which he had long been a useful, active, and consistent member, and at the same time a most liberal supporter. He, who of all others was most sanguine as to the results of the Agency, only saw the work begun. I shall never forget the date of my visit to Ottawa, for there this heart-rending telegram reached me, " Montreal, 23rd March, 1867, MR. GREENSHIELDS died this morning."

The necessity for re-writing the whole of the historical portion of the Report, added to the time required for authenticating the statements contained in it, has delayed its publication until now.

JAMES CROIL.

MORRISBURG, ONT., 1st December, 1867.

CHURCH AGENT'S REPORT,

FOR THE YEAR 1866.

In the month of February, 1865, your Committee saw fit to offer me the appointment of Agent for the Schemes of the Church, and, in March following, I commenced a personal visitation of each Congregation. The nature and extent of the work preclude the possibility of entering into minute details; besides, having already, in the pages of " the Presbyterian," gone over, though in a very hurried and imperfect manner, a considerable portion of the field, it seems unnecessary to burden this Report with topographical description and incident of travel. Though thus shorn of what might have proved in some degree interesting or amusing, it is hoped that the plain facts submitted may not be without a present value, and furnish as well *mémoires pour servir* for the future historian. The Statistical Tables annexed, and the brief historical sketch given of each Congregation, may, for our present purpose, sufficiently illustrate the progress and position of the Church.

Our Congregations, 126 in number, are scattered over a distance, from East to West, of, in round nnmbers, 700 miles. The actual distance travelled in reaching them has been close upon 12,000 miles. That this should have been traversed in little more than a year, without inconvenience or bodily fatigue worth mentioning, is in itself a significant fact and speaks well for the means of communication in our new country. That it was done at an expense so small as scarcely to be entitled nominal is due very much to the liberality of the Grand Trunk Railway authorities, who, during the whole time, provided me with a free pass over all their lines of Railway in Canada, and also to the kindness of friends everywhere who provided transport from place to place as occasion demanded.

It may be proper to state the plan and purpose of these visits, which, though slightly varied according to circumstances, were essentially the same in all. Each minister, previous to my coming, was requested to call a meeting of his Congregation, and the managers were asked to furnish a statement of their receipts and disbursements, for all purposes, for the then past year. Latterly, printed Schedules were made use of and with good effect. Commending and encouraging where there appeared even the smallest room for doing so, pointing out in a friendly way apparently defective management, and, receiving from some, hints likely to be of service to others, I placed before each Congregation the present position and requirements of the Church at large—explained the nature and object of its various Schemes, the urgent need of more liberal support—suggesting, as the best mode of attaining this end, thorough organization and systematic management. It gives me pleasure to state that in every quarter I was well received. I must not, however, leave your Committee under the impression that your Agent drew crowded audiences. The meetings were, for the most part, thinly attended. In this, perhaps, I may have been considered in some places rather *fastidious*, yet, in view of the object to be accomplished, and the improbability of a like effort being soon repeated, my regrets must be acknowledged to have been reasonable. I believe that in every case the Ministers used their influence to secure a full attendance, but they will bear me out in the remark that in this they failed, and from this cause much of our labour has been lost. In 35 instances I addressed Congregations on the Sabbath. When time permitted I visited as many families as possible, and conversed with elders and managers. In a few cases each household, in Congregations numbering from 70 to 80 families, was visited : the results, however, were so entirely satisfactory as to make amends for time spent and personal inconvenience incurred. Where the Minister's salary was found to be either inadequate or irregularly paid, my chief efforts were turned in that direction.

Grouped into Presbyteries, the Congregations will be noticed separately, in the order of visitation. The number prefixed to each corresponds with those of the statistical table, to which reference, in all cases, is invited in order fully to understand the condition of each Congregation.

I. PRESBYTERY OF NIAGARA.

This is in point of numbers the smallest Presbytery in the Church, having within its bounds only 163 families. There are but four Ministers on its roll and it is with difficulty that they secure a quorum for the transaction of business. It has no Mission stations, nor means of instituting such. It was formerly a part of the Hamilton Presbytery and was constituted in 1863.

1. DUNDAS.

The town of this name is beautifully situated at the head of the Bay of Burlington, five miles from Hamilton. It has a population of 5000, and is noted for its manufactures. In the year 1825, the Rev. George Sheed, a licentiate from Aberdeen, came as tutor to the family of the Hon. James Crooks, and at the request of the people, officiated regularly every other Sabbath, in a free Church then recently opened, during the first twelve months of his residence among them. Having returned to Scotland, he received ordination in the spring of 1827, and was soon after inducted as the Minister of Ancaster and Flamboro, over which he continued to be pastor till his death in 1832. The Rev. Mark Y. Stark, a graduate of Glasgow University, was appointed in 1833. It is said that Dr. Candlish had been designated to this charge, and that, having meantime accepted an appointment in Edinburgh, Mr. Stark came in his stead, at the instance of the Glasgow Colonial Society. Mr. Stark left the Church in 1844, and died at Dundas, in January, 1866. He was greatly respected. The Rev. Andrew Bell, became Minister of Dundas and Ancaster in 1847. He was translated to L'Orignal in 1852, and died there (see 119) in 1856. Mr. Kenneth McLennan was ordained and inducted in 1853. He removed to Paisley in 1857, and is now Minister of Whitby (45). The Rev. James Herald, the present incumbent, and who came to Canada as a Missionary from the Colonial Committee in 1857, was inducted to Dundas in June, 1858.

The property consists of a small stone Church, and a good brick manse, with two acres of land. There is a preaching station at Flamboro West, five miles distant. At Ancaster, formerly in connection with the charge, there is a good Church, in which, however, there has not been regular service for some years.

2. NIAGARA.

The town of Niagara, formerly Newark, and once the seat of government for Upper Canada, has a population of 2000. It has been declining for some years past: consequently, our Congregation has not increased of late, but rather diminished.

The Session Records date from 1st October, 1794, at which time the Rev. John Dunn was Minister. He is believed to have been a licentiate of the Presbytery of Glasgow, and officiated to a Presbyterian Congregation in Albany for some time. After preaching two years at Stamford and Niagara, he abruptly relinquished his pastoral duties, confessing, it is said, that he could no longer preach doctrines which he himself did not believe. He entered into business, and lived for some years in Niagara as a merchant. While in pursuit of traffic, in the year 1803, the vessel in which he sailed (the "Speedy," carrying 10 guns) foundered in Lake Ontario, and all on board perished.

The Rev. John Young, formerly of Montreal (see 80), succeeded Mr. Dunn, in 1802, but did not remain long. In 1804, Government made a grant to the Congregation of a block of four acres in the town, upon which a frame Church was built, seated for 300, at an expense of £625. About this time the Rev. John Burns, a Minister of the Scotch Secession Church came from the State of New York, and was engaged to preach every third Sabbath at Niagara. He continued to do so until the war broke out in 1812, when the whole town was laid in ashes by the Americans. On the return of peace, in 1815, Mr. Burns resumed his Ministerial duties teaching at the same time the District School. He died in 1824. His successor, Mr Thomas Creen, from the North of Ireland, ministered for a few months with considerable popularity, but was soon induced to accept of ordination from the Bishop of Quebec, and to exchange the small and very uncertain income which the Presbyterian Congregation could afford, for the £200 sterling a year granted to each Episcopal Missionary by the Society for promoting Christian knowledge. In course of time he became Rector of Niagara, and held that position till his death, which took place a few years ago. After Mr. Creen, a Mr. Johnston, also from Ireland, officiated at Niagara for a short time. In 1827, the Rev. Thomas Fraser, formerly of the Relief Church, Dalkeith, Scotland, was placed over the charge. At the end of one year he left and connected himself with the Dutch Reformed Church in the States. Subsequently, he became the Minister of Lanark, C. W. (101). The Rev. Robert McGill from Ayrshire followed in 1829, and remained until 1845 when he was called to Montreal to fill the charge of St. Paul's, then vacant by the death of Dr. Black. During his Ministry, in 1831, the present Church was erected. He also built the manse. In 1838 he received a call to a Congregation in Glasgow, which, however, he declined. He died in Montreal, in 1856, (82). The Rev. John Cruickshank, formerly of Brockville, and now the parish minister of Turriff, in Banffshire, accepted a call to the charge in 1846 and held it till 11th April 1849. In 1850, Mr. John B. Mowat was ordained and inducted. He remained until 1857 when he was appointed to the chair of Oriental Languages and Biblical Criticism in Queen's College. The Rev. Charles Campbell, the present Minister, was inducted in 1858. The Church is of brick—a large substantial edifice. The manse, which is also of brick, is an excellent building and was purchased from Dr. McGill, with a legacy of $3000 left to the Congregation by the late John Young, in his life time a merchant in Niagara.

3. CLIFTON.

This charge dates from 1857, in which year the Rev. George Bell, formerly of Simcoe, was inducted. The village of Clifton, about two miles below the Falls of Niagara, is the terminus of the Great Western Railroad. The Congregation, being chiefly composed of employés of the Company, is necessarily fluctuating. Though not large, it is well organized. The Church, a handsome structure of brick, was built in 1856, when hopes were entertained of a large increase to the population. A large amount of debt, about $4,500, incurred in its erection, and which has since had a depressing effect on the Congregation, has now been liquidated through the self-denying liberality of the people themselves added to the generosity of many friends in Canada, and a donation from the Colonial Committee of £200 stg. There is neither glebe nor manse. Adjoining the Church, however, a tasteful residence has been erected by the Minister, which, it is hoped, the Congregation may be in a position to purchase before long.

4. SALTFLEET AND BINBROOKE.

The Rev. George Cheyne was ordained by the Presbytery of Strathbogie in 1831 " to the office of the Ministry in the British Provinces of N. America, wherever Providence may order his lot." He settled at Amherstburgh where he remained a number of years, and became the Minister of Saltfleet and Binbrooke in September, 1843. In the following year he left the Church, and is now the Canada Presbyterian Minister of the place. Mr. Wm. Johnson was ordained and inducted in 1852. He removed to L'Orignal in 1857; and thence to Arnprior, and Lindsay (36). The Rev. Hugh Niven, from Scotland, was inducted in 1857.

There is a small frame church at Saltfleet, a poor manse and five acres of good land. At Binbrooke, ten miles distant, there is also a Church. For further details, *vide* the Statistical Table.

II. PRESBYTERY OF HAMILTON.

This Presbytery held its first meeting, by appointment of Synod, on the first Monday of October, 1836. Up to 1861 it included in its jurisdiction the whole of the Province west of the City of Hamilton, as well as the Peninsula lying to the east of it. In this, there are now four Presbyteries, viz., Hamilton, Niagara, Guelph and London. Like the first Presbytery noticed, it is too small. There is not, there cannot be, inducement to begin, nor encouragement to carry on, those Missionary enterprises, which, for some time to come, must be a distinguishing feature of an active and useful Presbytery in Canada.

5. HAMILTON.

The City of Hamilton has a population of about 25,000. Though several efforts have been made to establish a second Congregation, at present there is but one in connection with the Church of Scotland. The Rev. Alexander Gale, from Aberdeen, and formerly of Lachine (72), was the first who officiated statedly here. He was inducted in November 1833, and preached in the Court House until the first Church was erected. It was thrice enlarged. In January, 1845, the Rev. Alexander McKid, formerly of Bytown, became Minister of the charge. In 1848 he was translated to Goderich, (15). The Rev. Daniel McNee, a native of Perthshire, succeeded in 1850, and demitted the charge in 1853. In October of that year was inducted the Rev. Robert Burnet, who is still Minister. The present St. Andrew's Church was opened for worship in 1857. It cost $56,000. There is still a debt remaining on it of about $30,000. It is the finest Ecclesiastical edifice in connection with the Church in the Western Province. There is an excellent manse. The heavy debt with which the property is burdened has been much against the interests and the prosperity of the Congregation.

6. NELSON AND WATERDOWN.

The two Congregations which constitute this charge are about five miles apart, that at Waterdown being five miles from Hamilton. The surrounding country is well settled and well cultivated. The scenery is picturesque, and the charge, though somewhat scattered and by no means large, is yet, in many respects, a desirable one. The Rev. William King, a licentiate of the Synod of Ulster, and who came to Canada from Pennsylvania, in 1822, organized a Congregation at Nelson soon after his arrival. He commenced to preach at Waterdown in 1830, and continued his ministrations in both places until 1852, when declining health compelled him to demit the charge. He was connected with the United Synod of Upper Canada, and, along with seventeen others of that Synod, was received into the Church in 1840. He was much respected. He died on the 13th of March, 1859, in the 69th year of his age. The Rev. George MacDonnell, now of Fergus (25), succeeded Mr. King, in 1852. Dr. Skinner was the next minister. Originally pastor of the Secession Church at Partick, Scotland, he emigrated to Lexington, Virginia, where he officiated for 13 years; thence he removed to London, C. W., and became Minister of Nelson and

Waterdown in 1855. He died, minister of this charge, 24th March, 1864, of erysipelas—æt. 60. He was esteemed an able and eloquent preacher. The Rev. Adam Spenser, was inducted in January, 1866, but, at the Meeting of Synod following, the appointment having been ruled to be irregular, it was cancelled. Since then Mr. Henry Edmison has been harmoniously settled. There is a good frame Church at Waterdown, a comfortable manse, and five acres of glebe. A new brick Church is in course of erection at Nelson.

7. HORNBY AND TRAFALGAR.

The Rev. Samuel Porter was first settled at Trafalgar as a Minister of the United Synod of Upper Canada; although received in 1840, we do not find his name on the Synod's roll until 1846, as Minister of Clarke and Hope (47). The Rev. William Barr, now of Wawanosh, was appointed in 1847, and remained till 1859. The Rev. William Stewart, the present Minister, was inducted to the charge of Milton, Hornby and Trafalgar in 1861. In January, Milton was separated from the other two, and, since that time the Church there has been vacant. It had since 1832 been united with Esquesing under the Ministry of the Rev. Peter Ferguson, who retired, from age and infirmity, in 1857, and is since deceased. There is a good Church at Milton; at Hornby and Trafalgar, there are also comfortable Churches. There is a manse and five acres of glebe at Hornby.

8. SIMCOE.

The town of Simcoe, in the county of Norfolk, has a population of 2000. Here there is an excellent brick Church and manse. The Congregation, however, is small. Stated services are conducted at Lyndoch, Vittoria, and Wyndham, respectively, 11, 7, and 10 miles from head quarters. After Jabez Culver, a missionary who came to this part of the country with the U. E. Loyalists, the Rev. John Bryning, of Mount Pleasant, was the first to officiate in Simcoe, about the year 1820. Travelling over a wide extent of country, and preaching wherever he went, he was faithful and indefatigable in the work of the Ministry. He died at Mount Pleasant, September, 15th, 1853, aged 84. The Rev. Thomas Scott, now

.of Plantagenet, was ordained and inducted as Minister of Simcoe and Vittoria, in June, 1844. He remained but a short time. After him came one John Dyer, a singular man—a sailor and popular orator—a great preacher, who drew crowded audiences from far and near, and built a number of good Churches. He received license from the Presbytery of Hamilton in September, 1846, but it was withdrawn in April following. Like a meteor, he shone for a little while, and, meteor-like, he disappeared. No man knoweth of his sepulchre unto this day. The Rev. George Bell was inducted in 1848, and remained till January, 1857, when he was translated to Clifton. The Rev. Martin W. Livingstone, the present Minister, formerly of the U. P. Church at Musselburgh, in Scotland, was inducted in May, 1858.

9. BRANTFORD.

The town of this name occupies a fine site on the left bank of the Grand River—a noble stream. The population is between eight and nine thousand. From small materials we have been endeavouring during a number of years to build up a Congregation. It is hard to make bricks without straw! Mr. Whyte, now of Arthur, officiated here for some time as a Missionary. After him, the Rev. David Stott, from New Brunswick, was appointed, first as a Missionary, afterwards, as Minister of the charge, and receiving his support from the Colonial Committee. He succeeded in building a small church—a very small church—too small even for his own small congregation, and which was soon afterwards sold to a congregation of Negroes, who never paid for it, and never will. The Episcopalians of Brantford having built a new church, their old one was offered for sale ; Mr. Stott, or his Congregation, bought it for $500. But the conditions of sale required that it should be removed to another site ; the building being large, that cost a deal of money, and long time to do it. So long indeed was the poor old Church a-being dragged through the streets, that, for some weeks, a proverb was rife in Brantford that the Presbyterians were bringing "the Church" to every man's door ! Removing, refitting, repairing, interest upon all, converted the original $500 into as many pounds—the present measure of their indebtedness. The Rev. John S. Burnet,a Missionary from the Colonial Committee, and now assistant minister of Corn-- wall, succeeded Mr. Stott: three years more he laboured and laboured faithfully, but the prospect of establishing a Congregation is still remote. A lot of two acres of land within the town limits, a gift from MR. TEKARIHOGEA, *alias* Captain John Brant, belongs to the Congregation, but at present it is unsaleable.

III. PRESBYTERY OF LONDON.

This Presbytery, formed out of that of Hamilton, was constituted for the first time on the 3rd of July, 1856. Having met the Presbytery in session, I afterwards visited within its bounds thirteen Congregations and several mission stations. These, being mostly near lines of Railway, are easy of access.

10. LONDON.

This City has a population of 12,000. Of these, the census of 1861 gave to Presbyterians 1552, and to the Church of Scotland, 736. The city is well planned, substantially built, is a centre of considerable business, and surrounded by a fertile and beautiful agricultural country. From small beginnings the Congregation has made considerable progress. In 1842, three acres of land were granted by government for the use of a Presbyterian Congregation. The Free Church being first organized, applied for a deed, and having obtained it, settled a minister in 1851. Meanwhile, occasional services were given by the Presbytery to our few remaining adherents. In October, 1853, the Rev. Dr. Skinner accepted a call from them and was inducted. An attempt made at this time to recover the Church property ended in our having to pay the costs in Chancery. Dr. Skinner resigned in 1855 and became Minister of Nelson and Waterdown. The Rev. Francis Nicol, formerly of Newfoundland, succeeded him in 1859, and is now the Minister. The Congregation, numbering at the time of Mr. Nicol's arrival about 40 families, then worshipped in the Mechanic's Hall. There was neither Church nor site. Government was again applied to and a valuable piece of ground granted. On this a very fine edifice, octagonal in outward form, was built in 1860 ;

it cost—minus the spire—$10,000. The debt incurred at the time of building is now reduced to about $3000, and systematic efforts are being made to cancel it. On the whole, prospects are brightening.

11. GLENCOE.

This is a newly organized Congregation, 30 miles west from London, on the line of the G. W. Railway. They have not yet succeeded in getting a Minister, but they deserve one. With praiseworthy liberality, they have built a neat brick Church which was paid for without extraneous aid, seven of their number having contributed about $185 each. There is no manse as yet, but the people are prepared to provide one as soon as a Minister is settled. They have been supplied during several summers by Missionaries. The majority of the Congregation speak Gaelic.

12. CHATHAM.

Chatham, C. W., is a town of 4000 inhabitants, on the G. W. Railway, 60 miles from London and 40 from Windsor. It is the centre of a rich agricultural country. In its early days the Presbyterians applied to Government for ten acres of land within the town limits, and got it. The Church, manse, and grave-yard occupy about two acres, the remainder is fued and yields at present $300 a year. The Church, a brick building quite unworthy of the town, was erected in 1841. It was occupied by the Free Church Congregation until 1851. In that year, the Rev. John Robb, formerly of Chambly, was inducted. Failing health compelled him to resign in 1858: that same year, on the 22nd June, he died. The Rev. John Rannie, from Aberdeen, the present Minister, was appointed in September, 1859. There is a good manse and the property is free from debt. Stated services are conducted in a school house, ten miles distant.

13. NORTH EASTHOPE.

The Township * of this name embraces a fine agricultural district,

(*) For the benefit of those unaccustomed to Canadian terms, it is proper to explain that a " Township " is a subdivision of a County and is usually ten miles square.

and is noted for the substantial, even elegant, stone houses of the farming population. The Congregation is not large, but it is compact, and the people are all well to do. There is neither manse nor glebe, the Minister residing in a neat cottage, built on his own farm. The Congregation cannot justly be complimented on their Church, which is not in keeping with the "ceiled houses" of the farmers. This was formerly a branch of the charge of Stratford, and the Rev. William Bell, who was Minister of both, has, since 1857, restricted his labours to the Congregation under notice.

14. STRATFORD.

Twenty-six years ago the site of Stratford was an unbroken solitude! Now it has a population of 4000 and is rapidly increasing. Occupying the point of intersection of the Grand Trunk with the Buffalo and Lake Huron Railway, it has become a place of some importance. It is prettily situated, on " the Avon"—of course. The town is not conspicuous for fine churches. The Kirk, though neither large nor handsome, is the best looking in the place. The Rev. Daniel Allan was ordained and inducted to the charge of Stratford and Woodstock 21st November, 1838. In 1844, he "went out," protesting. Mr. Bell, now of N. Easthope (13), was inducted in 1848, and finished the Church edifice which his predecessor had commenced. The Rev. William Miller from South Ronaldshay, Scotland, entered upon the charge in 1857. In his time a vexatious lawsuit arose in connection with the Church property. He resigned in 1863. Dr. George, formerly Professor of Moral Philosophy in Queen's College, assumed the pastorate in 1864. The Congregation is increasing. The church is now too small. There is a brick house on the property, but it is not suitable for a manse. There is no glebe.

15. GODERICH.

It is difficult to conceive of a finer situation than that of Goderich. I visited it three times, in May, July, and November. The place itself, its surroundings, and its history, are invested with a kind of romance! Octagonal in plan, its broad streets diverge, with mathematical precision, from the Court House,- a handsome free-stone structure in the centre. Covering a large area, it has a population of 3000. From the elevated plateau on which it stands—100 feet above the water—there is a magnificent view of Lake Huron. On the distant horizon glorious sunsets are seen, and, at certain seasons of the year, wonderful *Mirages*. The roads in the vicinity are the best in the Province : the land is unsurpassed in fertility : the climate is salu-brious. Yet, strange to say, one fourth, or thereabouts, of the shops and houses were, at the time of my visit, closed and tenantless ! Stranger still, it is alleged, the Railway has done it all. Each of the little villages, of Clinton, Seaforth, and others, has tapped the stream of traffic that once flowed toward the shipping port of Gode-rich. To this, in some measure, may be ascribed the decline of our congregation.

In 1859, it was stated to have had 112 families; in 1866, after diligent search, I found but 82. It was vacant when I was there, by the resignation of the Rev. Alexander McKid : since then, Mr. Camelon, of Port Hope, has been inducted. Mr. McKid was minis-ter of Bytown from 1844 to 1846, when he removed to Hamilton. He was inducted the first minister of Goderich, in June, 1848. £150 was received from the C. R. Fund to aid in the erection of a manse. By some fatal mis-management, the fine building, which cost about £700, has passed out of our hands, and there is now no manse. Fortunately, there is no debt remaining ; the church, and the land adjoining, are valuable.

16. BAYFIELD.

The town of Bayfield is smaller than Goderich but equally beau-tiful. It is on the Lake Shore, 12 miles south of the County Town and connected with it by a good gravel road. There is a neat brick church, finely situated : erected in 1862. The Colonial committee having granted £25 stg., the balance of debt incurred has been provided for by the congregation. There is neither manse nor glebe. There is a small branch of the congregation at Varna, 7 miles east from Bayfield on the Seaforth road—the finest road on which I have travelled—There is no church there ;—once they attempted to build one, of grout and gravel, but it fell down, and courage fled. Bayfield was formerly a branch of Goderich. The

Rev. Hamilton Gibson, its first stated Minister, formerly of Galt, C. W., was inducted, 21st November, 1860.

17. WAWANOSH.

The centre of this township is nine miles North from Goderich, and at one time it formed a part of that congregation. It is probably one of the finest townships in the County of Huron in an agricultural point of view. The congregation is very small. There is neither manse nor glebe. The Rev. Mr. Barr, residing on a farm of his own, gave a site, on which was erected, in 1862, a neat frame church, which is free of debt. Ten acres of *swamp* were given years ago by the Canada Company for *a burying ground!* Mr. Stewart, afterwards of Woodstock, was settled here for a few years before Mr. Barr, who was inducted 28th September, 1859.

18. EAST WILLIAMS.

There is here a large Gaelic-speaking congregation, on the line of G. T. R., and 27 miles from London, which, though vacant at the time of my visit, has since been supplied with a minister, skilled in the language of Ossian. The Rev. Duncan McMillan, a native of Islay, and formerly of Caledon, came here in 1859. In his time a log church was built. He left at the secession of 1844. A long vacancy ensued. In 1855 was inducted the Rev. Robert Stevenson, a native of Kilwinning, formerly belonging to the church of the "Antiburghers." Remaining 10 years in Williams, he demitted the charge in 1865. The Rev. John M. McLeod, from Scotland, was inducted on the 16th of January, last.

Some time ago, a lot of 100 acres of land was given by the Canada Company for church purposes. This was sold, and the proceeds were applied to the erection of the present frame church. There is a good brick manse prettily situated on a lot of 5 acres of land, purchased with the grant of £150 from the Clergy Reserves Fund. There is no debt on the church property.

19. NORTH DORCHESTER.

This is a small charge comprising 40 families, scattered over a large area, and first organized, in 1853, by the Rev. William Mc-

Ewan, formerly of Belleville, who having ministered to them for ten years, was compelled, through age and infirmities, to retire.

The Rev. James Gordon, formerly of Markham, was inducted in October, 1865. The place of worship—a frame building on the gravel road, 5 miles from London—of right belongs to the Canada Presbyterian Church. There is a glebe of ten acres of good land, purchased with the C. R. grant, on which a manse is in course of erection.

20. WESTMINSTER.

The church of Westminster is twelve miles south from London, and six from the Minister's residence. There is no manse. Mr. James McEwan was inducted first minister of this charge, in October, 1854. In 1856 a good brick church was erected at a cost of £800. It is now free of debt. For further particulars, *vide* the statistical table.

21. SOUTHWOLD.

This charge having been for some time a mission station of the London Presbytery, the Rev. Donald Ross, formerly of Vaughan, was inducted its first stated minister, in 1865. Remaining 9 months he was translated to Dundee, C. E. In October, 1866, Mr. Ewan McCauley was ordained and inducted. A very neat brick church (St. Columba) was erected, in 1865, in the thriving village of Fingal, 25 miles south from London. It cost $1600; about $200 of debt only remaining on it. A glebe of ten acres with a comfortable manse has recently been purchased, although not yet paid for. This is a beautiful part of the country and the prospects of the congregation are encouraging.

22. WOODSTOCK AND NORWICH.

Our cause appears to have gone down in Woodstock, the town, meanwhile, progressing, until now it has some 5000 inhabitants. I have no satisfactory explanation to offer in this case: it seems to be a place of which more might have been made. There is a valuable acre of land in the centre of the town, and a good frame Church which has been unoccupied for some years. There *was* a manso, erected with the aid of £150 from the C. R. fund, but it has long since passed out of our hands. The Rev. Daniel Allan had the pastoral oversight of the congregation in 1844, when he left the Church. There are now three congregations of the Canada Presbyterian Church in the town. Mr. Frederick P. Sym was inducted to the charge of St. Andrew's Congregation in September, 1852. He resigned in 1855, and was succeeded, in October, 1866, by the Rev. James Stuart, formerly of Wawanosh, who retired from the ministry in 1861, since which time Woodstock has been vacant. At Norwichville, about 8 miles eastward, a remnant of the former congregation has rallied and erected a very neat frame church, and the people there are not without hope of securing and supporting a minister. The church at Norwichville is burdened with a debt of about $500, towards the liquidation of which the Colonial Committee have promised a grant of £25, on condition that the balance is otherwise provided for.

MISSION STATIONS IN THE LONDON PRESBYTERY.

WIDDER, in the township of Bosanquet, WESTWOOD, in Williams and KIPPEN in the same neighbourhood, are at present occupied as Mission Stations. At Widder there may be about 20 families, at Westwood about 15. There is no church property in either place. At Westwood, however, Mr. Elliot, of Toronto township, has promised to give 50 acres of valuable land, close to the Railway Station, so soon as a congregation shall be organized. At Kippen it is expected that a church will be built this summer, and there is every prospect of a large congregation being immediately formed. The Colonial Committee's Missionary, Mr. Daniel McDougall, has been mainly instrumental in carrying on the work in this quarter.

IV. PRESBYTERY OF GUELPH.

The first meeting of this Presbytery was held at Guelph, by appointment of Synod, July 3d, 1860. One of the newest, it is also one of the most interesting fields in the church. Besides Mission Stations, it has now 11 organized congregations, of which 8 have been formed within the last ten years. Including the counties of Bruce and Grey, with parts of Wellington, Waterloo, and Huron, it embraces a large portion of the Western Peninsula. From Guelph to the Georgian Bay, the distance is 84 miles, and, westerly, to Lake Huron, the distance is about the same. This whole region was purchased from the Canadian Government, in 1825, by the Canada Company, then formed at the instance of John Galt, the Novelist. At that time it was an unbroken wilderness. The whole of it was soon after surveyed, and mapped out into Townships and farms. Roads having been constructed, rivers bridged, grist and saw mills erected, the sites of future towns and villages were chosen. The result has been perhaps unequalled in the annals of colonization. Lands formerly considered dear at 25 cents an acre, were readily bought up by settlers at from 7s. 6d. to 10s., and are now worth from $20 to $40 per acre. The counties of Bruce and Grey, then inhabited by wolves and bears, and other wild denizens of the forest, have now a population of more than 100,000 ! " Old Scotch Wilson,"—a worthy Elder of the Kirk—the first white settler—is still alive, and well remembers the time when he travelled on foot 60 miles through the woods to reach his present residence, carrying his blanket and " rations" on his shoulder, meeting not a human being, and guided only by " THE BLEEZE! " From the window of his home—looking over fine cleared fields—he now sees a town of 3000 inhabitants, and hears the scream of the railway whistle, reminding him that from his adopted home in the " Far west," he may reach his native village of Helensburgh, on the bank of the Clyde, in twelve days !

23. GUELPH.

The seat of Presbytery, and county town of Wellington, is one of the most flourishing towns in Canada West. The Speed, a pretty little river, flows through it, and its population numbers about 5000. Here we have a large, influential, and well organized congregation. In 1832, the Canada Company granted a site in the centre of the town on which a frame Church was soon afterwards erected. It was subsequently sold to the corporation for £1750, and is now the site of the Town Hall. In 1858, the present beautiful stone Church was erected at a cost of $18,000. There is a debt of $4,400 still remaining on it. Government granted 200 acres of land near Woodstock for a glebe : this was exchanged with the Canada Company for 118 acres near Guelph, which have since become very valuable. 68 acres have been sold, 8 acres have been set apart for a glebe, and 48 acres, in " park lots," valued at $6000, remain to be sold. The Rev. James Smith, who became its first minister, in 1832, ceased to be a minister of the church in 1844. He died at Puslinch, 28th January, 1853. The Rev. Colin Grigor formerly of L'Orignal, was inducted, in February, 1848. Remaining nine years he resigned the charge and was subsequently settled at Plantagenet. The Rev. John Hogg, formerly a minister of the U. P. Church at Dumfries, Scotland, and, in that connection, some time at Hamilton, C. W., and also at Detroit, U. S., was appointed to Guelph, in 1858, and is still the minister.

24. WOOLWICH.

This is a small charge in the Township of the same name, about twelve miles from Guelph. Though nominally embracing 40 families, only about 20 of these are Presbyterian. A number of others, chiefly Episcopalian, attend regularly and contribute to the support of ordinances. There are two well conducted Sabbath Schools, one, meeting in the church, the other, at a distance of two miles, is superintended by Mr. Chambers, with marked efficiency and success. The Rev. Alex. Ross, formerly of Aldborough, was first settled as minister of this charge, in 1823. In 1846, he removed to Gwillimbury, and died at Bradford, in 1857. With the exception of occasional services from Mr. Smith, of Galt, the charge remained vacant until the induction of its present worthy minister, the Rev. James Thom, formerly of Three Rivers, in 1854. There is a small stone manse and 3½ acres of valuable land.

25. FERGUS.

The town of Fergus, containing about 2000 inhabitants, is finely situated on the Grand River, which, at this point, affords an immense water power. It is surrounded by a rich agricultural country, settled about thirty-five years since by emigrants from Scotland. The congregation is large and well equipped. It dates from 1835, when the first Church was opened for worship. With a munificence that well deserves to be recorded and imitated, it was erected at the sole expense of the late Mr. Ferguson of Woodhill, and made over in a free gift to the congregation. Though considered at the time a spacious and even handsome edifice, it became in course of time too small for the congregation, and measures taken for the erection of a larger and a better one resulted in the present beautiful church, which was opened for worship in December, 1862. It is built of the fine free-stone of the country, is of Gothic design and finished with great taste. I believe it cost only $8800. In 1836, a grant of 171 acres of land was received from the Government, although the deed for it was not obtained till 1845. The sale of this realized the sum of $5100, which was applied to the building of the new church. The congregation subscribed $2500. The balance of $1600 is as yet unprovided for. There is an excellent stone manse, but there is no glebe. The first minister of the charge, was Mr. Alexander Gardiner from Aberdeen, who was ordained and inducted, 22nd February, 1837, and who died here after a brief illness, 13th December, 1841. Mr. Bayne, of Galt, preached occasionally during the vacancy that followed. The Rev. George Smellie, who was inducted, in 1843, left the church, in 1844, and, with him, a great majority of the congregation. He is still minister of the C. P. Church of Fergus. The Rev. Hugh Mair, D.D., originally a seceding minister from Scotland, was placed over the charge on the 2nd of February, 1848. He had been for 13 years minister of Johnstown, in the State of New York, in connection with the " Old School." He died there while on a visit to his friends, 1st November, 1854. His remains were interred at Johnstown, and in the vestibule of the church at Fergus there is a marble tablet to his memory, and one also to that of A. D. Fordyce, Esq., long a Ruling Elder and active member of the church. The Rev. George MacDonell, the present minister, formerly of Nelson and Waterdown, was inducted to Fergus in May 1855. He was ordained in 1840 by the Presbytery of Lancashire, as minister of St. Luke's Church, Bathurst, N. B., where he was for eleven years.

26. ARTHUR.

The Rev. John Whyte has been settled here since March, 1857,

and is the first minister of Arthur. He was licenced by the
Presbytery of Ayr in 1849, and was assistant to Dr. Menzies of
Maybole for a year. He came to Canada in 1850, and in the
following year was inducted to Brockville, where he remained four
years. A neat brick Church was built in the village of Arthur in
1854. The Colonial Committee assisted in its erection with a grant
of $300. There is neither manse nor glebe. Repeated failures of
crops have hindered the prosperity of the congregation. As appears
from the statistical table, their contributions are small.

27. MOUNT FOREST.

This congregation was rendered vacant by the resignation of its
first minister, the Rev. John Hay, in June, 1866. He had been
inducted in January, 1861. In 1858 he came to Canada, a
missionary from the Colonial Committee, and proved eminently
useful and acceptable in many of the Mission Stations within the
bounds. He had intended returning to Scotland, but died after a
short and severe illness at Kincardine, 31st July, 1866, in the
39th year of his age. The village of Mount Forest is a thriving
place with 1500 inhabitants. The congregation is small, but,
under good management will probably increase. There is a small
frame church but no manse. The Rev. J. Allister Murray, for
some years Minister of Bathurst, N. B., has recently been inducted to the pastoral oversight of the congregation.

28. PRICEVILLE.

This charge is of recent formation, having been for a good many
years a Mission Station, and supplied during the summer months
by students in Divinity. It is now a large congregation and has
been fortunate in obtaining the services of a young and active
minister, gifted with Gaelic, Mr. Donald Fraser, who was ordained
and inducted 15th August, 1867. The little village of Priceville
is situated ten miles east from Durham in a rough hilly country,
and the people are chiefly of Celtic origin. There is a good frame
church, furnished with an accessory that very few of our country
Churches have, and which all should have, a good bell to summon
the Congregation to worship. There are five acres of land, but
no manse.

29. Owen Sound.

The town of this name is a rising place situated on an arm of the Georgian Bay. The circumstances which led to the formation of the charge are peculiar, and were stated to me in substance as follows.—Early in 1865 a portion of " Knox Church" congregation, in connection with the Canada Presbyterian Church, petitioned our Presbytery for supply. Mr. Jardine, a missionary student of Queen's College, was sent to them, and a large congregation attended his ministrations. In the end of the year a call was presented to Mr. Jardine which he declined, and, in the meantime, the church, a well finished frame building and nearly new, was transferred to trustees in connection with the Church of Scotland, who assumed the debt, amounting to $719. Nine months elapsed, and the hopes of the people to get a minister had become well-nigh exhausted. In their " straits," and to them most unexpectedly, the Rev. Duncan Morrison of Brockville seems to have been sent by Providence ; as one of the elders remarked,—" man's extremity is often God's opportunity." Mr. Morrison was inducted in October, 1866, and the work of consolidating this new charge has since then progressed satisfactorily. In connection with it, at Derby, seven miles distant, there is a Mission Station, which, it is believed, will soon become self-supporting.

30. Leith and Johnson.

This charge presents another evidence of the success attending the mission work of the Presbytery. The two congregations named having been supplied by missionaries for some years, were in 1864 united into one charge under their present minister, Mr. Alex. Hunter, who was ordained and inducted on the 27th of October in that year. At the village of Leith, which is beautifully situated on Owen Sound, a tasteful brick church was erected in 1865, at a cost of $1300. As yet there is no manse, but a good site for one has been secured. The affairs of the congregation appear to be carefully and wisely managed.

31. Kincardine.

The town of Kincardine is finely situated on Lake Huron shore. It has a population of about 2000 and is rapidly increasing. As it is noted for its genial climate and the fertility of the adjacent country, it must become an important place. The congregation is already large and is steadily increasing. The Revs. Messrs. McKid of Goderich, and Mowat, then of Niagara, first visited Kincardine some twelve years ago and conducted worship in Mr. McPherson's saw mill. That gentleman, soon after, erected a good church at his sole expense and presented it under a model deed to the congregation. Mr. Alexander Dawson was ordained and inducted the first minister of the charge, in September, 1863. There is neither manse nor glebe. Several outlying stations have been statedly supplied by Mr. D. with Sabbath Services ; some of these will soon become self-supporting congregations. Since the above was written the charge has become vacant by the resignation of the incumbent, who has joined the Canada Presbyterian Church. The congregation, however, has not forsaken " its first love."

32. PAISLEY.

This is yet another mission charge, to which the Rev. Kenneth McLennan, formerly of Dundas and Ancaster, and now of Whitby, was inducted in 1857. In October, 1859, he had the satisfaction of seeing a comfortable and commodious church opened for worship and the nucleus of a good congregation formed. He was translated to his present charge in 1860. From that time until 1866, Paisley remained vacant, when the present minister, Mr. Matthew W. McLean, was ordained and inducted on the 15th of August. It is now in a flourishing condition.

33. GALT.

The rising and prosperous town of Galt has a population of 3500. The Grand River flows through the centre of it, affording unlimited power and giving motion to much machinery. It is beautiful for situation. The Kirk is well represented, and we have a large, well-ordered, prosperous, and increasing congregation. At an early period in its history the late Mr. Dickson chose a fine site, erected a handsome church at an expense of £1000, named it St. Andrew's, and handed it over to the Congregation for half its cost ! In 1844 the Church property was claimed by the large majority who " went out." A long and vexatious Chancery suit followed and heavy expenses were incurred, the minority, however, were confirmed in the possession of it. Mr. Dickson also gave 7½ acres of land for a glebe, on which a stone manse was erected. It is finely situated, overlooking the river and the town. During last summer a large addition was made to it.

The Rev. William Stewart, from Kenmore, Scotland, was the first Minister settled in 1832. His name does not appear on the Synod's Roll after 1834. Dr. Bayne succeeded in 1836. In 1844 he became the leader of the Free Church party and his connection with the Church of Scotland ceased. During the stormy interregnum that followed, Dr. Liddell, then Principal of Queen's College, seems to have been mainly instrumental in piloting those that remained through their difficulties and securing them in the possession of their Church property. Mr. Dyer, the sailor, and orator of "high degree" — an enthusiast — a sensationalist — altogether a very extraordinary man, whom we have already met with at Simcoe— appeared for a little time to bask in the sunshine of popularity, and then mysteriously vanished. So popular was he that, in September, 1846, he received two calls, one from Galt, signed by 153 persons, and another from Fergus, signed by 51, both of which were regularly moderated in. Both, however, fell to the ground, for a fama spread abroad, and poor Dyer became the subject of a libel. Having written a farewell letter to the Congregation of Galt, he left precipitately ; he is supposed to have resumed his avocation as a sailor, and to have been drowned at sea. In November, 1848, the Rev. John Malcolm Smith, an ordained Minister of the Church of Scotland, was inducted. In 1850 he was appointed to the Chair of Classical Literature and Moral Philosophy in Queen's College. In his stead the Rev. Hamilton Gibson, now of Bayfield, came in November of that year. He remained nine years. Mr. Robert Campbell, now of St. Gabriel's, Montreal, was ordained and inducted to Galt the 10th of April, 1862, and was translated to his present charge in December, 1866. Soon after this, the Congregation gave a call to the Rev. James B. Muir of Lindsay, their present Minister, who was inducted in March following.

V. PRESBYTERY OF TORONTO.

This, the largest of our Presbyteries, has a frontage on Lake Ontario of one hundred miles. It embraces 26 organized Congregations—nearly one fourth part of the whole Church. I had several opportunities of meeting this Presbytery in session—of being benefitted by its counsels, encouragement, and co-operation, as well as of observing the orderly conduct, and harmony of its proceedings. Perhaps it has now reached the limits beyond which its efficient management might become onerous and difficult; but as this consideration falls more naturally under the notice of the Synod's Committee, charged with preparing a scheme for the redistribution of charges in the Western Presbyteries, it need not be further referred to in this report. It is one of the four Presbyteries into which the Church of Scotland was originally divided in 1831. At that time, in all Canada, to the West of Toronto, we had only six Ministers,—now there are 42. I commenced to visit the Congregations in this Presbytery on the 4th of September, and was occupied, with little intermission, until the 22nd of November, labouring during a considerable portion of that time under great disadvantages from the state of the roads and weather.

34. PORT HOPE.

The town of Port Hope—one of the prettiest places in Canada—situated on Lake Ontario, 94 miles west from Kingston, has a population of 5000. It was taken up by the Presbytery of Toronto in 1859 as a mission station,—then, without a place of worship, without manse, without organization of any kind ; now, there is a well finished brick church, a comfortable manse, and, including the station at Knoxville, nine miles inland, a congregation of 70 families. Each Lord's day there are two regular services in the town, and one at 3 p. m. in the country. The Church cost $3500, of which the Colonial Committee gave £75 stg. It is free of debt. The manse recently purchased for $1000, is good value for the money. Mr. David Camelon was ordained and inducted first Minister of the charge, on the 12th of December, 1859. Having received a call to Goderich, he was translated to that place during the present year, and Port Hope has thus become vacant.

35. PETERBORO.

The town of Peterboro, 30 miles north of Port Hope, is reached by Railway : it, too, has a thriving population of 5000, and owes its prosperity chiefly to the lumber business which is extensively carried on. Early in the history of Peterboro a grant of two acres of land was made by the Government to the Presbyterians for church purposes. Of this, one acre is in the neighbourhood of St. Andrew's Church and affords ample room for a manse—yet to be built. The other is partly fued, yielding at present $126 per annum.

The Rev. John M. Roger, from Kincardine O'Neille, in Scotland, was inducted first Minister of the charge, the 10th of November, 1833. In 1844, he, and most of the Congregation seceded, and, with the consent of the minority, retained the use of the Church until 1857, when the dissentient portion of the Congregation erected for themselves a new Church in which Mr. Roger still officiates. In 1858, the Rev. James Douglas, an ordained Minister from the Colonial Committee, was inducted to the charge of St. Andrew's. He resigned in 1864. On the 20th of January, 1867, was inducted Mr. D. J. Macdonnell, son of the respected Minister of Fergus. The Congregation has been fortunate in its choice, and its prospects are now very encouraging.

36. LINDSAY.

This place is thirty miles west from Peterboro, with which it is connected by railway, and is the county town of Victoria. It has a population of 3000 and is rapidly improving. The county buildings, erected at a cost of $70,000, are among the neatest in the Province. Fronting the Court House is St. Andrew's Church, a beautiful Gothic structure, built of white brick in 1863. There is no manse nor glebe. The Rev. Mr. Tweedie of the United Presbyterian Church, who resided at Manilla in this neighbourhood, officiated also in Lindsay for some years. After his time, the field being neglected, other denominations obtained an early and strong footing. The Presbytery gave occcasional supply until 1861, when a call was given to the Rev. William Johnson, of Arnprior, who was inducted on the 6th of April in that year. On the 19th July, 1864, from ill health, Mr. J., resigned the charge. The Rev. James B. Muir, an ordained Minister from Scotland, was inducted on the 31st of May, 1865. Mr. M. is the son of a parish schoolmaster, and was for two years assistant-minister at Kilbirnie, Scotland. Two years he officiated within the bounds of the Presbytery of the north of England, and was ordained to the ministry at Hexham, Northumberland. He came to Canada in 1864. The Congregation of Lindsay, which under him made satisfactory progress, became vacant by his translation to Galt on the 28th March, 1867.

37. BROCK.

This is a country charge, the Township bearing the same name and consisting of very fine land, was settled 30 years ago by emigrants from Inverness, Islay, and Mull. There is a pretty good frame church, an excellent manse, and 20 acres of glebe. The Rev. James Lambie, after his settlement at Pickering, made frequent visits to this part of the country. Mr. Peter Watson came as a Missionary in 1855. The first Minister who was settled in the charge was the Rev. John Campbell, a native of Canada, now of Markham, and who had been a Minister in the United States for two years. His induction took place on the 10th September, 1856. He resigned in March, 1866, from which time it remained vacant until the induction of the Rev. Archibald Currie, formerly of Cote St. George, 11th July, 1867.

38. ELDON.

The Township of this name was settled forty years ago by Highlanders from Inverness and Argyle-shires, and embraces a large extent of very fine land. The church, which was built in 1846, has recently undergone repairs and embellishment, and is now comfortably seated for 500 persons. There is a good manse. The glebe is very valuable, comprising 200 acres of land, one-half of which is in a good state of cultivation. The Rev. John McMurchy, the first Minister of the Congregation, was a native of Killearn, Cantyre, Scotland. He came to Canada in 1841, was inducted to Bradford in the following year, and translated to Eldon in 1844. Much respected for warmth of heart, " a man of independent mind " he went in and out among his attached Highland Congregation till his death, which occurred suddenly, from heart disease, 22nd September, 1866. The Rev. Neil McDougall, a native of Oban, Argyleshire, who had been for three years stationed at Indian Lands (95), was inducted 19th June, 1867.

In connection with this there is a branch Congregation at Balsover, recently erected into a separate charge, but which has not yet succeeded in obtaining a Minister. Mr. Duncan McCrae of this place, in a spirit deserving of the highest commendation, erected at his own expense a beautiful Church, and made it over in a free gift to the Congregation. There is a glebe of 15 acres, and the Congregation numbers about 70 families.

39. THORAH.

In the Township of this name, adjoining Eldon, there is another large Gaelic-speaking Congregation. It was first settled in 1832. The Rev. William Jenkins, of Markham, was then the only Presbyterian Minister in this section of country (42). To him many of the settlers carried their children for baptism, a distance of fifty miles. The late Mr. Lambie visited them frequently, but they had no stated Minister until the induction of the present incumbent, the Rev. David Watson, who was here ordained to the Ministry, 31st August, 1853. Previous to his settlement several ineffectual attempts had been made to secure a pastor, and more than once the people had been duped by designing men that came among them pretending that they were Ministers in regular standing with the Church.

St. Andrew's Church, which is a plain substantial stone building, seated for 500, was erected in 1840. An excellent brick manse was built in 1855, and the glebe consists of 100 acres of good land.

40. GEORGINA.

Beautiful lake Simcoe washes the shore of the Township of Georgina. The Congregation, which is an offshoot from Thorah, became a separate charge in 1865. Its progress has been satisfactory. In the village of Sutton there is a brick Church of Gothic design, erected in 1863. It is named " Knox Church." About the same time

c

a frame building known as " Cooke's Church " was erected at a distance of five miles : in both of these services are held every Sabbath. There is a glebe lot of 100 acres which was allocated to this Congregation from what is known as the " Seton Fund " of the Presbytery. Mr. John Gordon was ordained and inducted to this charge on the 21st of February, 1865, and is still Minister.

41. Uxbridge.

This charge has for its centre a village of the same name, situated about twenty-eight miles south from Georgina. The first Minister seems to have been the Rev. William Brown, from the Presbytery of Ahoghill, Ireland, who was inducted 23rd June, 1847. In 1850 he was suspended from the Ministerial office. In 1853, he died, and was buried in Uxbridge Church-yard. The Rev. William Cleland, a licentiate of the Irish Presbyterian Church, and for four years Minister on Long Island, New York, was admitted by the Synod in 1853, and inducted in August, 1854. Since my visit steps have been taken for the erection of a New Church, which, fortunately for them and for me, renders disparaging allusion to the old one unnecessary. There is a valuable glebe of 200 acres, five miles from the manse, in the Township of Scott. Formerly there existed a branch of the Congregation in that place. Seven years ago it was reported to the Convener of Statistics,—" it is proposed to build one, if not two Churches this year." Delays are dangerous! The manse is very comfortable, and occupying a conspicuous site on the summit of Quaker Hill, overlooks a large extent of fine rolling country.

42. Scarboro.

In the Township of Scarboro, bordering on Lake Ontario, and about ten miles from Toronto, there is one of the largest and strongest Congregations in Western Canada. This part of the country began to be settled by emigrants from the South of Scotland so early as 1799. The Rev. Mr. Jenkins, from the Synod of New York, was the first, and, for many years, the only Presbyterian Clergyman. While employed as a Missionary among the Oneida Indians in New York State, he first visited Canada about the year 1820, and soon after accepted an appointment from the Associate Synod of Scotland, to labour in the Ministry in the Townships of York, Vaughan, Markham, and Scarboro. He resided at Markham, and preached once a fortnight at Scarboro, in an unfinished frame building near the site of the present Church. To him came, as assistant, the Rev. James George, a native of Scotland, and who was ordained to the Ministry by the Associate Reformed Presbytery of NewYork, September 21st, 1831. He took the pastorate of the Scarboro Congregation about the year 1833, and, on the 4th of August, 1834, he and his Congregation connected themselves with the Church of Scotland in Canada. He was translated to Belleville in October, 1847, and in May, 1848, was re-translated to Scarboro, where he remained till 6th September, 1853, when, having been appointed to the chair of Logic and Moral Philosophy in Queen's College, he demitted the charge. Dr. George retired from the College in 1862, and became Minister of Stratford, where he now is. The Rev. James Bain, formerly a Minister of the Secession Church at Kirkaldy, Scotland, was received by the Presbytery of Toronto, in 1853, and inducted to this charge in October, 1854. A fine brick Church was built in 1849. There is a good manse and a glebe of 7½ acres, in addition to which the Minister enjoys the interest of money invested, which was realized from the sale of lands procured through the Seton Fund.

In connection with this Congregation a very beautiful frame Church was erected in the Township of Markham, in 1864. It was built without extraneous aid and is named St. John's. Mr. Bain officiates in it regularly.

43. MARKHAM.

The Rev. Mr. Jenkins, above mentioned, and who connected himself with the then Presbytery of Upper Canada, was settled here in 1820 (see 42), and seems to have retired about the year 1834. His labours were highly appreciated. In the autumn of 1836, Mr. Alexander Gardiner, from Aberdeen, was sent as a Missionary by the Glasgow Society and officiated about six months, when he accepted a call to Fergus (25). The Rev. George Galloway, a superior young man and a distinguished student of Aberdeen, was ordained and inlucted 4th February, 1840. He died at Markham village on the 11th of November, 1344. Mr. Angus McIntosh having officiated for a short time here, as Missionary, received a call to Thorold in 1842, which he accepted. He left the Church in 1844. The Rev. James Stuart, formerly a Missionary at Frampton, C. E., became Minister of Markham in 1849 ; in 1854 he was translated to Wawanosh. Mr. James Gordon, who was ordained and inducted in September, 1854, was translated to N. Dorchester in 1865. The Rev. John Campbell (37), the present incumbent, succeeded in March, 1866. There is an old weather-beaten frame Church near the village. The manse is undergoing enlargement and needful repairs, and there is a glebe lot of 100 acres situated in the Township of Georgina which was obtained through the Seton Fund.

There are two branch Congregations in connection with the charge.—(1) Stouffville, a small village seven miles north, where there are less than a dozen families belonging to the Church, who, nevertheless, have recently built a very neat little place of worship. (2) The other is at Cashel, about a like distance in a southerly direction, where a small Church was erected a good many years ago.

44. PICKERING.

This is a double charge. The section in front is at Duffin's Creek, and near the line of Railway ; the stronger half meets for worship about nine miles inland. Both have stone Churches, neither of them models of architecture, yet they are comfortable and commodious. There is a manse—much too small—and 25 acres of good land. There is a glebe, besides, of 100 acres, which is rented at present for $70 per annum. There is also the sum of $800 invested for the benefit of the Minister. Add to these that the Township of Pickering is one of the very best in Canada, and its farmers wealthy, surely they have "a goodly heritage !" These Congregations were organized by the late Rev. James Lambie, who came to Canada in 1840, and was ordained to the Ministry in the following year. A marble slab in the grave yard at Duffin's Creek, records truly what sort of man he was, thus it reads: "In memory of the Rev. James Lambie, who died September 16th, 1847, aged 42. He was a native of Tarbolton, Ayrshire, Scotland, and was the first Minister settled in the Scotch Congregations in Pickering and Whitby, to both of which he was pastor. He was a man of admirable common sense ; of a clear and profound judgment ; of great and varied attainments as a scholar ; of simple and earnest piety ; an edifying preacher, and a most self-denying and laborious servant of Christ."

The Rev. Peter McNaughton, formerly of Vaughan, and now residing there, succeeded Mr. Lambie in 1848. He resigned the charge and all connection with the Church, 21st November, 1855. He was followed by the Rev. Samuel McCaughy in September, 1856, who demitted the charge in November, 1859. The Rev. Walter R. Ross, who was inducted on the 6th of February, 1861, is now Minister.

45. WHITBY.

From the time of Mr. Lambie's death, this charge remained vacant until the 12th of December, 1860, when the Rev. Kenneth McLennan, formerly of Paisley, was inducted. Since then its pro gress has been, if not rapid, yet steady and encouraging. The town of Whitby has a population of about 4000, and has many points of attraction. The surrounding country is beautiful and highly cultivated. St. Andrew's Church is a very fine Gothic structure. It was erected in 1859, at a cost of $12,000, and of this sum Mr. Laing, a merchant in the place, contributed more than one half. Recently a large and well finished house has been purchased for a manse. There is no glebe.

46. BOWMANVILLE.

In 1840, the Rev. Thomas Alexander, then Minister of Cobourg, reported to the Presbytery of Kingston, that he had dispensed the Communion to upwards of 100 persons at Bowmanville, but no Minister of our Church seems to have been settled prior to the Rev. John H. McKerras, who was ordained and inducted in September, 1853. In October, 1866, having received the appointment of Professor of Classical Literature in Queen's College, he demitted the charge, which is now vacant. There is a frame Church, neither large nor handsome, and a good manse with four acres of valuable land attached. A lot of land, obtained through the Seton Fund, having been sold for $1,360, this sum was invested and yields $95 per annum. There is a branch of the charge at Orono, nine miles distant, but there is no Church there. Together they number 60 families and 90 Communicants. The town of Bowmanville has 3000 inhabitants, and the neighbourhood is picturesque and very productive; the roads are excellent. It is altogether a very desirable place of residence.

47. CLARKE.

This is a double charge in the Township of the same name, ten miles east from Bowmanville. There are two frame Churches about five miles apart, in both of which are conducted regular Sabbath Services and Sabbath Schools. It was first organized in 1846, by the Rev. James Lambie, at which time the Rev. Samuel Porter, formerly at Trafalgar (7), was inducted its first minister. He retired from the Ministry in 1861. Mr. James S. Mullan, the present incumbent, was ordained and inducted 31st December, 1861. The affairs of the Congregation are systematically managed. There is a glebe of 5½ acres of eligible land, and preparations are being made to erect a manse.

48. TORONTO.

The City of Toronto was founded in 1794, under the name of York. " Muddy little York," it was contemptuously styled in those days. It has now a population of nearly 50,000. Though its situation is rather low, yet its wide umbrageous streets, its splendid public buildings, and other characteristics, give to it the appearance of a very fine city. The Presbyterian population is divided, according to the census of 1861, thus :—The Church of Scotland, 2893 : The Free Church, 2480 : United Presbyterians 1231. The last two having united in 1861, made the numbers of the *Canada Presbyterian Church* 3711. It is the seat of Knox College and the stronghold of that Church. In 1866 they had five Congregations in the city, reporting a membership of 1465 Communicants. We have at present but one Congregation, that of St. Andrew's.

The Rev. James Harris, a young preacher from Ireland, was the first Presbyterian Minister of the city. He organized a Congregation in 1821, and was instrumental in building a Church, from which beginning grew up " Knox Congregation," now the largest Presbyterian Congregation in the Province, having a membership of 563, and of which the Rev. Alexander Topp is now Minister. Mr. Harris is still living, and resides, without charge, at Eglinton. The design to form a Congregation in connection with the Church of Scotland appears to have been first entertained by some members of the Legislative Assembly when in York during the Session of 1830. One of these,* the late Hon. William Morris of Perth, a gentlemen who proved himself an unwearied and successful advocate of the Church of Scotland in Canada, has left on record the following incident which had its weight in influencing him to urge the erection of a Scotch Church in York. He was walking on the morning of a Sabbath by the ruins of the former Parliament House before repairing to the Episcopal Church ; and, while musing on the want of Divine ordinances by a minister of his own Church, he bethought himself of the practicability of obtaining the ruined building from Government and converting it into a place of worship. With these thoughts he returned from his walk, and, as he entered the Episcopal Church, somewhat late, the Clerk was just giving out the following lines of the 132nd Psalm :

> " I will not go into my house; nor to my bed ascend ;
> No soft repose shall close my eyes, nor sleep my eyelids bend :
> Till for the Lord's design'd abode I mark the destin'd ground ;
> Till I a decent place of rest for Jacob's God have found."

The words came home to him like an oracle. The very next day a meeting of parties favourable to the proposal was held, at which the Hon. Francis Hincks presided, and Mr. Wm. Lyon McKenzie was secretary. A site was purchased in the centre of the town for £450, on which was forthwith erected the Church which now bears the name of St. Andrew's, and which was opened for worship on the 19th of June, 1831. The Rev. William Rintoul was the first who preached within its walls. Having arrived from

---

* I have given this statement as I found it, in the hand-writing of the Rev. Mr. Rintoul ; information since received, however, from other reliable sources, also associates the names of the late Chief Justice McLean, of Toronto, and the late Hon. Peter McGill, of Montreal, with the incident mentioned in the text.

England only a few days before the opening of the Church he was on that occasion introduced to his ministry by the Rev. Robert McGill of Niagara. The garrison of York, consisting of the 79th Regiment of Highlanders, composed his first Congregation. The population of York, which was the Provincial Metropolis and the principal military station in Upper Canada, is stated to have been at that time 5179. The sacrament of the Lord's supper was first dispensed in the Church to 112 communicants on the 30th of October, 1831. Mr. Rintoul resigned in May, 1834, and was appointed superintendent of Missions. He became Minister of Streetsville in 1835, where he remained till 1844, when he left the Church. He was inducted to St. Gabriel St. Church, Montreal, in 1850, of which he continued to be Minister till his death in 1852. The Rev. Wm. T. Leach, from Edinburgh, succeeded Mr. Rintoul in Toronto, 15th July, 1835. In 1842 he removed to York Mills. On the 15th of November in that year, he, and the Rev. Wm. Ritchie of New-Market, tendered their resignations to the Presbytery, intimating at the same time their intention, for reasons given, of joining the Church of England. Their reasons not having been considered satisfactory, they were severally served with libel, and both solemnly deposed, the former on the 27th of December, 1842, the latter on the day following. Mr. Leach, who was ordained to the Ministry by the Presbytery of Haddington in June, 1833, now resides in Montreal, a Minister of the Church of England, and also a professor in McGill University. Mr. Ritchie is now the Episcopalian Minister of Georgina. The Rev. John Barclay, from Ayrshire, was inducted to this charge 6th December, 1842. In 1855, the Senatus Academicus of the University of Glasgow, his *Alma Mater*, conferred upon him the degree of Doctor in Divinity. As Clerk of the Presbytery of Toronto, as a Trustee of Queen's College, and as a member of the Temporalities Board, Dr. Barclay has, during many years, rendered signal services to the Church.

St. Andrew's Church is seated for 1000. The Congregation own some valuable property in the city, and have, besides, 200 acres of land, and an investment of $1,200. There is no manse, but $80 per annum is paid to the Minister in lieu thereof.

49. Chinguacousy.

The township bearing this name was early settled. It lies a little to the west of Toronto and embraces a fine tract of land. The Rev. Thomas Johnson, a native of Ahoghill, Co. Antrim, was inducted to the pastorate here by the United Synod of U. C. in 1834. Having received licence in his native county in 1822, he came to Canada in 1827, and was minister of Earnestown for four years. He was received by the Synod in 1840. In 1844 the majority of his congregation seceded and retained possession of the Church property, but Mr. Johnson continued to be a staunch supporter of his adopted Church, and contended manfully with the difficulties which the defection of his congregation entailed upon him, until 1862, when the infirmities of old age compelled him to relinquish the charge. He continued, however, to preach frequently. He died on the 30th of August, 1866, having presided in public worship for the last time on the Sabbath previous, only four days before his death. He was much respected. In 1862 the log Church in which the congregation had worshipped for many years was replaced by a very neat brick edifice. There is a manse in the village of Edmonton, but there is no glebe. The Rev. George Law, formerly a Missionary in Nova Scotia, was inducted on the 10th of December last. The congregation is small, numbering only 32 families. These, however, with praiseworthy liberality have subscribed the sum of $400 for stipend. It is entirely a rural charge.

50. Caledon and Mono.

In the Townships bearing these names there are three congregations, respectively 16, 11 and 8 miles apart, which were united into one charge under Mr. William Hamilton, who was ordained the 31st of July, 1866. The Rev. Duncan McMillan, now Free Church Minister of Lobo, had been Minister of Caledon from 1831 until 1839, and the Rev. Alexander Lewis, now residing in Mono, was for many years the Presbyterian bishop of a wide extent of the surrounding country. He had been ordained to the ministry in Nova Scotia in 1822, and, coming to Canada in 1837, joined the United Synod of U. C., which in 1840 became incorporated with the Church of

Scotland in Canada. He retired from the charge of Mono in 1865, in the 74th year of his age and the 48th of his ministry. There is a good stone Church at Caledon, an old log Church at Mono East, and a new one at Mono West. The glebe comprises 100 acres of poor land. There is no manse.

51. ORANGEVILLE.

The village of Orangeville has a population of 1500 and is surrounded by a tolerably good country. There is a stone Church, "Bethel" by name, built in 1859. There is a manse with one acre of land in the village. The congregation was organized in 1837 by Mr. Lewis. The Rev. William E. McKay, formerly of Camden, was inducted in July, 1859, as the first minister of the charge, and is still the incumbent.

52. ERIN.

The township of Erin was settled chiefly by Highland Scotch. The land is hilly, but of good quality. This congregation was also organized by Mr. Lewis, in 1860, and worships in what is termed a "Union Church." Mr. Donald Strachan, a catechist, has been supplying services during the last two summers, and with much acceptance ; the people are very "willing," and contributed last summer $300 for six months services. There is no Church property.

53. TOSSORONTIO AND MULMUR.

The Townships in which this charge lies are north from Erin, and present the appearance of a new, rough, and hilly district. The valleys are rich, but the general aspect of the country, while confessedly romantic, is not prepossessing in an agricultural point of view. It formed a part of Mr. Lewis' diocese from 1837 till 1853, when the Rev. Archibald Colquhoun was inducted to the charge of Mulmur. He retired on his commutation allowance in 1861, and resides in Mulmur. Mr. Alexander McLennan was ordained and inducted to the pastoral care of these two congregations, 2nd July, 1862. There is a neat frame Church at Rosemount, in Tossorontio, and one similar in size and design at Mulmur, where there is a glebe of 100 acres. The manse is uninhabitable.

54. Nottawasaga.

At the present time Nottawasaga is said to be the best wheat-growing township in Canada. It has a frontage on the Georgian Bay, and is altogether a beautiful section of country. The price of land in favoured localities has gone up to $50, and even as high as $100 per acre. Agricolas has grown rich. A certain one whom I met with had a short time before received $5000 in cash for his wheat crop. Upon the good old principle of titheing, $500 of this would have been given for the service of Him who gave the whole. How much, is it supposed, does this modern representative of Christianity, in the finest wheat growing Township of Canada,—a man "who thanks God he was born a Presbyterian," who, " please God, intends to die a Presbyterian," whose love for the Church of Scotland, to hear him talk, is, as was that of David to Jonathan, " wonderful! passing the love of women." How much per annum does this prosperous farmer dole out for the support of a faithful and laborious minister of the Gospel ? Publish it in Gath ! FOUR " ALMIGHTY DOLLARS." Tell it in Askelon, that he refused, point blank, to become a subscriber to " The Presbyterian" at one dollar a year ! There were two good frame Churches in the Township, but one has recently been destroyed by fire. The Congregations are both large and are scattered over a wide area.

Each of them could easily support a Minister and pay him $1000 a year ; and no country Minister should have less than that, unless it might be in the South Sea Islands, where food costs nothing and raiment can almost be dispensed with. There is an excellent glebe of 100 acres, valued at $3000. There is no manse. The township was settled in 1834 by emigrants from Islay, Argyleshire, with a few from Cantyre and the north of Ireland—chiefly Presbyterians. Visited at long intervals by different ministers of the Presbytery, there was no pastor settled here until the Rev. John Campbell, formerly assistant Minister of St. Andrews' Church, Kingston, was ordained in June, 1853. On the 22nd September, 1864, Mr. Campbell died. He was universally respected, and his name and memory still linger like household words in the warm hearts of the Highlanders of Nottawasaga. Mr. Alexander McDonald, the present incumbent, was ordained and inducted to the charge on the 31st January, 1866 ; it being expressly understood that in two years from that time the congregations should form two charges.

55. INNISFIL AND GWILLIMBURY.

This charge is composed of three congregations widely separated. The Rev. William McKillican, afterwards of St. Thomas, was Minister of Gwillimbury from 1835 to 1839. The Rev. John McMurchy was ordained at Bradford, then a part of the charge, in January, 1842, and was translated to Eldon in 1844. The Rev. Alex. Ross, formerly of Woolwich, was appointed in 1846. He died at Bradford, 14th March, 1857, age 63. He was esteemed an able and learned man. The Rev. William McKee, the present Minister, who is a licentiate of the General Assembly of the Irish Presbyterian Church, and was for a short time connected with the Free Church in Canada, having been received by the Synod, was inducted in March, 1858. There are three places of worship. St. John's Church in the centre of the charge, and near the town of Bradford, is a neat structure ; that at the Scotch settlement is old and dilapidated, while the one at Innisfil is decidedly *infra dig.* There is no manse, but there is a lot of 18 acres of land within the town limits, which is valued at $1800. Bradford is situated on the margin of a dismal swamp through which the sluggish Holland River flows, in summer time exuding malaria as pestilential as the Pontine marshes.

56. NEWMARKET.

This takes its name from a small town on the Northern Railroad, 34 miles from Toronto. The population of the place is about 1200 ; the congregation is weak and scattered. The Church is a small brick building, and was used as a prison in 1837. The manse, not a very inviting structure, was purchased with the aid of the clergy reserve grant of £150. A Colonel Graham, about the year 1813, bequeathed 40 acres of good land for a glebe, which has become valuable. In 1834 the Rev. Henry Gordon, from

Edinburgh, became the Minister of Newmarket and King. In 1837 he was translated to Gananoque, where he now resides, a minister of the C. P. Church. He was succeeded in 1838 by the Rev. William Ritchie, a minister of the Church of Scotland, formerly in Demerara. He left in 1842 and joined the Church of England (see 48). Twelve years' vacancy ensued, after which the Rev. John Brown, who is now the Minister, was inducted 30th August, 1854. He is a native of Scotland, was for some years assistant to Mr. Henderson of Tranent, and, subsequently, was for two years a Missionary in Florida.

The vicinity of Newmarket is chiefly settled by Quakers, known variously as " orthodox," " heterodox," and " Hicksite" Quakers. Besides these there are the " DAVIDITES !" whose views are a queer mixture of Deism, Quakerism, and Universalism. At Sharon they have two temples ; the greater is a gorgeous, ill-shapen edifice, adorned with a cupola and a variety of ornaments *in tin*. In this strange rites are celebrated on the recurrence of certain festivals. They take their name from old David Wilson, now deceased, and to whom posterity will most likely assign a place in the list of deluded fanatics. There are other " ites" and " isms," excrescences of Christianity innumerable, in the neighbourhood of Newmarket, and, from all I could learn, the state of religion and morality in the community is at a low ebb. In the middle of fields, on Yonge Street, long considered the garden of Canada, I observed huge mounds of wheat straw that had not been housed nor threshed, but, blasted with mildew and weevil, it had been thrown on heaps to rot. The prophet Haggai must have witnessed some such sight, under some such circumstances, when he gave utterance to the words, " Ye looked for much, and lo, it came to little. Why ? saith the Lord of Hosts. Because of mine house that is waste, and ye run every man to his own house. Therefore the heaven over you is stayed from dew, and the earth is stayed from her fruit."

57. KING.

This is a section of the charge over which Mr. Gordon, now of Gananoque, was placed in 1834. The present Minister, the Rev. John Tawse, was ordained and inducted on the 8th of March, 1837.

It included at that time several preaching stations. In October, 1860, owing to failing health and strength, though with a determination not to cease from duty, even in old age, Mr. Tawse consented to the settlement of a minister in West King, by which he was in a great measure relieved from travelling. There is a good stone Church at King, but neither manse nor glebe.

58. West King.

In 1860, a large and well-finished stone Church having been erected on a piece of ground given by Mr. Ross, a member of the congregation, a call was given to Mr. James Carmichael, who was ordained and inducted on the 2nd of October in that year. A good manse has recently been built. This is a fine country charge, and the people are liberal. Mr. Carmichael officiates in Gaelic and English; he never preaches seldomer than thrice on Sabbath, often four times, and not unfrequently he delivers five sermons in one day.

59. Vaughan.

This is another large, wealthy, and liberal congregation. There are two Churches; that at Maple village is new and very neat, the other in the 7th concession is smaller and plain. There is a good manse, within five minutes' walk from a station on the Northern Railway. The glebe comprises seven acres. The Rev. Peter McNaughton came to Canada under the auspices of the Glasgow Colonial Society, having been ordained by the Presbytery of Auchterarder with a view to Eldon and Thorah, in March, 1833. Shortly after his arrival, however, he selected another sphere of labour, and was inducted to the charge of Vaughan, on the 21st of August following. In July 1844, he demitted this charge, returned to Scotland, and became Minister of the parish of Dores. In September, 1847, he was re-translated to Vaughan, and in December of the following year was translated to Pickering (see 44). The charge remained vacant until the 20th of July, 1858, when Mr. Donald Ross, now of Dundee, was ordained and inducted. He resigned in 1865. The Rev. William Aitken, the present Minister, was inducted in November, 1865. He is a native of Linlithgow, Scotland, and came to

Canada in 1864, designated by the Colonial Committee to Cobourg, where he remained one year.

The MISSION STATIONS within the bounds are numerous, and have been cared for with an assiduity and success worthy of the large and influential Presbytery of Toronto. Among these may be mentioned Purple Hill, near Cremore, where a frame Church has been erected; North Mulmur; Osprey, where the sacrament was dispensed last summer to 25 communicants; New Lowell, with about 25 families adhering to the Church; Sunnydale and Bonnytown have each a like number; and other places there are, the particulars of which escaped my notice.

VI.—PRESBYTERY OF KINGSTON.

This Presbytery met for the first time at York on the 6th of August, 1833. Sederunt, the Revs. John Machar, Kingston, James Ketchan, Belleville, and Mathew Millar of Cobourg. Notices of the first two will be found under the headings of their respective congregations. The Rev. Mathew Millar was among the first of the missionaries sent to Canada by the Glasgow Society, and is said to have been a young man of great promise. He was drowned in the Bay of Quinte. When travelling on the ice from Kingston towards Cobourg, he drove into an open part: the horse, sleigh, and body of the deceased Minister were discovered the following day. He was buried at Adolphustown, but his remains were afterwards taken up and re-interred at Cobourg. The Presbytery, having commenced with five congregations, reached its maximum in 1844, when there were eleven Ministers with charges on its roll. In 1841 occurred the second break in its ranks. The Rev. Robert McDowall, of Fredericksburgh, died. He had been sent to Canada as early as 1798 by the Classis of Albany in connection with the Dutch Reformed Church, and had laboured zealously and successfully in the Province for upwards of 40 years. In September, 1844, when the Presbytery met, Dr. Machar and Mr. Neill were then the only Ministers having charges on the roll! Since that time, although the bounds of the Presbytery have been greatly lessened, five Churches and an equal number of manses have been built. It comprises at present seven charges, besides mission stations. The Professors of Queen's College, being ordained Ministers, are, by act of Synod, members of the Presbytery and Synod. The number of such Professors is at present four.

60. PITTSBURGH.

This is a country charge, ten miles below Kingston. The Church and manse, which are new and substantially built of stone, are both tasteful and finely situated. The charge itself is of recent formation, the present Minister, Mr. William Bell, being the first. He is a son of the late Rev. Andrew Bell, and having been for a short time assistant to Dr. Machar of Kingston, he was ordained to the office of the Ministry at Pittsburgh, 6th October, 1863, on the same day that the Church was opened for worship. For many years previous to this, however, as a mission station, it had been supplied with regular services from the Professors in the College and others chiefly through the efforts of the Ladies' Missionary Association of St. Andrew's Church, Kingston. *

61. KINGSTON.

The City of Kingston is situated at the foot of Lake Ontario, and not far from the head of the far-famed Lake of the Thousand Islands. It is now the Chief Military Station of the Province of Ontario, and has a population of about 15,000. It is one of the oldest settled localities in Upper Canada, and occupies the site of the French fort of Frontenac : it was founded in 1784 and incorporated in 1838.

The Rev. John Barclay—the son of a Scottish Minister and born in the manse of Kettle, Fifeshire,—was the first pastor of St. Andrew's Church. His Ministry commenced in 1821. He was educated in Edinburgh, and was a man of great worth, eminent for his gifts and piety. The Church, which is a plain but a commodious building, was erected immediately after his arrival, and opened for worship in 1822. It is built on an acre of ground obtained from Government and deeded to certain persons named in trust, with this

---

* Since this was written Pittsburgh has become vacant by the resignation of Mr. Bell, who has been on a visit to Scotland for several months, for the benefit of his health.

specialty, "that it shall be for a Church in connection with the Established Church of Scotland, having a clergyman in communion with the same forever." Mr. Barclay died on the 26th of September, 1826, in the 30th year of his age. The Rev. John Machar succeeded him in 1827. This worthy Minister was a native of Brechin, Scotland, who studied at Aberdeen, and also at Edinburgh, under Dr. Chalmers. On receiving license he became assistant to the parish Minister of Logie, and came to Canada on the nomination of the Presbytery of Edinburgh, by whom he was ordained for this charge. He was chairman of the convention held in Kingston on the 7th June, 1831, which resulted in the first meeting of the Synod of our Church on the following day. Mr. Machar was acting Principal of Queen's College from 1846 to 1853, during which period Glasgow University conferred on him the degree of Doctor in Divinity. Having long laboured, faithfully and success fully, in his Heavenly Master's service, he departed this life the 7th of February, 1863, in the 65th year of his age, and the 35th of his Ministry. The Rev. William Maxwell Inglis, assistant Minister of St. Andrew's Church, Montreal, was chosen as Dr. Machar's successor, and inducted to the charge in August, 1863. He was born in Edinburgh, was licensed by the Presbytery of Fordyce in 1861, and he received his appointment to Montreal while he was assistant in New Gray Friars, Edinburgh. The Church occupies a fine site in the upper part of the City. The manse adjoining it is a handsome cut stone edifice, built some ten years ago through the efforts of the Ladies of the Congregation. The garden and grounds are well planned, the whole forming a very valuable property. The Congregation is large and well organized. As will be seen on reference to the statistical table, its Sabbath Schools have the largest attendance of any in the Church. Mr. John Paton, who originated the Juvenile Mission to India, and has always manifested a deep interest in it, is also superintendent of St. Andrew's Church Sabbath School.

62. ROSLIN AND THURLOW.

These are two small country Congregations, which, from being mission stations, were erected into a charge under Mr. James McCaul, who was ordained and inducted as the first Minister, 24th

August, 1864. In 1840 the Rev. James Ketchan, then Minister of Belleville, had a church built at Roslin. Subsequently, a station was opened at Melrose, and these two were formed into a charge, and a Minister of the C. P. Church set over them at two different times. Since Mr. McCaul's Ministry began, however, all the Presbyterians in this neighbourhood have united with the Church of Scotland. Through his instrumentality a good brick Church was erected at Thurlow, about seven miles from Roslin. There are several Sabbath Schools in connection with these congregations—numbering in all 180 scholars. Since the time of my visit Mr. McCaul has been translated to Melbourne, and this charge is now vacant.

63. BELLEVILLE.

In the year 1821 one acre of land was granted by Government as a site for a Presbyterian Church in connection with the Church of Scotland. The present edifice was built on that site in 1830. Though considered at the time a goodly structure, it has been thrown in the shade by some of the splendid Churches of the present day, for which Belleville enjoys an enviable distinction. In answer to a petition addressed to the Presbytery of Edinburgh, the Rev. James Ketchan was sent to this place in 1831, and became the Minister. He remained, officiating with much acceptance, until 1844, when, with leave of the Presbytery, he returned to Scotland on a visit. While there, he became connected with the Free Church and accepted a call to the charge of Mordington, in Berwickshire, where he still resides. The Rev. James George, now of Stratford, who was inducted to this charge in October, 1847, resigned in May following. From that time the Congregation remained vacant until the 13th of November, 1850, when the Rev. William McEwan was inducted. In the meantime a numerous and influential Free Church Congregation had been established, and the number of our adherents reduced to very few. Mr. McEwan resigned in 1853 and was translated to N. Dorchester (19). The Rev. Archibald Walker, a native of Renton, Scotland, and for two years Chapel Minister of Bannockburn, was ordained and inducted to Belleville 10th May, 1854. The Congregation is not large, but, according to their numbers, they are liberal. An excellent manse was erected a few years ago, and the prospects are encouraging.

64. Stirling.

While this charge was yet a mission station, Messrs. Neill of Seymour and Walker of Belleville officiated at frequent intervals. The two brothers, Messrs. John and Peter Lindsay—the former of whom has since gone to " the better country"—had each been stationed here as missionaries, but no Minister was settled prior to the induction of the present incumbent, the Rev. Alexander Buchan, in March, 1856. Then, the Church was unfinished, and there was no manse. Since that time a tasteful manse has been built, the Church has been completed, numerous improvments have been effected, and much good of a far more important kind has been accomplished, it is hoped, through the stated services which have been regularly maintained at the village of Stirling, as well as at Huntingdon, a station six miles distant. Mr. Buchan is a native of Perthshire, who having received license from the Presbytery of Dalkeith, came to Canada as a missionary from the Colonial Committee, and was ordained by the Presbytery of Quebec to the charge of Leeds and St. Sylvestre, 17th October, 1842. He returned to Scotland in 1844, and.in 1855 came again to this country under a renewed commission from the Colonial Committee. The Congregation is not large.

65. Seymour.

The Township of this name, 27 miles north from Belleville, was settled about 35 years ago, chiefly by Scotch, among whom were a number of retired officers of the army and navy. It is a pretty undulating country, and the farmers are in comfortable circumstances. The Rev. Robert Neill is the first Minister of the Congregation, and was ordained here 29th January, 1840. He is a native of Scotland, and came to Canada in 1837 at the instance of the Glasgow Colonial Society. After having filled the pulpit of St. Andrew's Church in Montreal for 6 months, he spent some time at Valcartier, and was also for 12 months assistant to Dr. Machar of Kingston. When he came to Seymour the country was quite new ; there were neither roads, churches, nor school houses. He preached at first in a store-house, with a packing box for his reading desk. The first Church edifice was opened for worship

15th November, 1840. A large and well finished stone Church has recently been completed. There is a good manse with 12 acres of valuable glebe. The Congregation is large and prosperous.

66. WOLFE ISLAND.

This Island, 21 miles long and 4 miles in width, is opposite Kingston, and distant from that city three miles. Its population is about 3600 : one-half are Roman Catholics, the remainder, Episcopalians, Presbyterians, and Methodists. In 1855 steps were first taken for the erection of a Presbyterian Church, and from that time regular services were maintained by Professors and students of Queen's College, the expenses attending the mission having been largely supplied by the members of the Congregation in Kingston, and by their good minister Dr. Machar. On the 22nd of August, 1860, Mr. George Porteous, the present minister, was ordained and inducted. The Church is comfortably seated for 200, and there is a good manse but no glebe. The Congregation, which is not large, is very much scattered.

CAMDEN, in this Presbytery, has been vacant since 1859. The Rev. Thomas Scott, its first minister, was the incumbent from June, 1848, till February, 1852, when he was translated to Williamsburgh. The Rev. William E. McKay, now of Orangeville, was also minister of this place from 1856 to 1859. There is a glebe of 50 acres at Camden, and an investment of $200, but there is neither Church nor manse. The mining regions of Madoc and Marmora are occupied by the Presbytery as mission fields.

VII. PRESBYTERY OF MONTREAL.

It is not easy to determine, precisely, when the first Meeting of he Presbytery of this name occurred. The earliest of which any record remains, however, is that held in 1803, for the ordination of Mr. Sommerville, the tenor whereof follows: "Montreal, 17th September, 1803. The former Presbytery of Montreal having been by unfortunate circumstances dissolved, the Rev. Mr. John Bethune, Minister of the Gospel at Glengarry in Upper Canada, formerly a member of the said Presbytery, and the Rev. Mr. Alexander Spark,

Minister of the Gospel at Quebec, conceiving it would be for the good of Religion to form a connection and constitute themselves into a Presbytery, did accordingly meet at Montreal, this 17th day of September, in the year of our Lord One thousand eight hundred and three, and, after prayers, the said Ministers, together with Mr. Duncan Fisher, elder, took their seats. The Rev. Mr. John Bethune was chosen moderator, the Rev. Mr. Alexander Spark, clerk. Absent, the elder from Glengarry, and the elder from Quebec. The Presbytery agreed that they shall be known and addressed by the name and style of *the Presbytery of Montreal."*

Mr. Sommerville was ordained to the office of the Ministry in St. Gabriel Street Church, by this Presbytery, at the date above mentioned, which having been done, the Court adjourned to meet on the third Monday of February following. There is no record, however, of subsequent Meetings, and it is likely that except in special cases, such as that for which it was formed, it never met. There can be little doubt that the " former Presbytery " referred to was the *first* that was constituted in Canada, and, as is remarked by Mr. Kemp, Messrs. Bethune, Spark, and Young, with their elders, must have been its members.

In the year 1818, there was formed " the Presbytery of the Canadas," composed chiefly of ministers belonging to the Associate Church of Scotland. It was dissolved at the end of two years, soon after which the United Presbytery of Upper Canada was constituted, and, in course of time, the United Synod, which continued its meetings until 1840, when its members to the number of 18, were received into connection with the Church of Scotland. The first meeting of the Presbytery, as now constituted, was held in Montreal on the 5th October, 1841, in terms of the decision of the Presbytery of Quebec, dividing the said Presbytery into two Presbyteries, namely, of Quebec and Montreal. In July, 1846, the Presbytery of Quebec ceased to exist, became incorporated with that of Montreal, and so continued until June, 1855, when it was re-organized.

Besides the Island of Montreal, and the settlements on the North Shore of the Ottawa, this Presbytery now includes that part of Canada East on the South side of the St. Lawrence lying between the St. John River, and the province line at St. Regis. Included in these limits is the Seignory of Beauharnois, six leagues square, which was granted in 1729, by the then reigning Monarch of France, to Charles Marquis of Beauharnois, at that time Governor of " La Nouvelle France," with the usual Seignorial rights. It was sold in 1763 to the Marquis de Lotbinière for about £2000 currency. In 1795, it passed into the hands of the late Hon. Edward Ellice, for £9000. And in 1839, it was transferred to a London land Company for £150,000 sterling! Mr. Ellice was thereafter a leading partner in the concern, and it is due to him and his representatives to say that they have always been kind friends of the Church. To them we are indebted for glebes at Georgetown, Ormstown, Beechridge, and St. Louis, while the Church at Beauharnois, erected many years ago by Mr. Ellice, has, together with 12 acres of valuable land, been recently handed over in a free gift to the Congregation.

67. HEMMINGFORD.

A Township and small village about 40 miles south from Montreal, give name to this charge. The Rev. John Merlin, a native of Ireland, and a minister of the United Synod of Upper Canada, was settled here in 1822. In 1841 he was received into connection with the Church of Scotland, and continued his ministrations in this place until 1855, when he retired on his commutation allowance. He died at Hemmingford, in December, 1866. The present minister, the Rev. James Patterson, was inducted in September, 1858. Having received licence from the Presbytery of Dunoon, he officiated for two years at Ardentinny before coming to Canada. The Congregation, which numbers 60 families, is well organized. The Church, built in 1843, is a stone edifice, not beautiful. A very tasteful and comfortable brick manse was erected in 1858. There is a glebe of 50 arpents.

68. RUSSELTOWN FLATS.

About ten miles west from Hemmingford we have this small and scattered congregation. The French element is in the ascendancy in this part of the country. " The Canadians," as they love to be called, are gradually ousting the " Old Countrymen." Hence, Russeltown Congregation has not increased of late, but rather fallen off in numbers. Through the instrumentality of a Mrs. Forbes, a frame Church was erected in the Township in 1826, for the use of the Protestant population. It was supplied by Ministers of various denominations until the settlement of the Rev. Archibald II. Milligan, who was inducted to the charge 13th June, 1853. At this time the Church was deeded by Mrs. Forbes. to trustees of the Church of Scotland in Canada, on condition of certain repairs, which were made accordingly. Mr. Milligan died suddenly in Montreal, 7th February, 1855. On the 21st November following, the Rev. F. P. Sym, formerly of Woodstock, became the minister, and remained until 1860, when he was translated to Beauharnois. The Rev. William Masson, the present incumbent, succeeded in October of the same year. He is a native of Morayshire, was licensed by the Presbytery of Elgin, and came to Canada in 1856. He served for two years as a missionary in the Presbytery of Hamilton, and was two years Minister of St. John's Church, in the City of Hamilton (its first and last minister). There is a good glebe of 40 arpents, and the Congregation with much spirit and liberality have commenced to build a new manse.

69. BEECH RIDGE.

This charge has its centre about ten miles from the last named, and is largely composed of Highlanders from Inverness and Ross-shires. The Rev. Thomas McPherson, now of Lancaster, became its first minister in December, 1836, and remained until 1843. Nearly 11 years of a vacancy followed, the Rev. John McDonald, the present minister, having been inducted in November, 1854. The stone Church, erected in 1831, is in good repair, and there is an excellent manse with a glebe of 40 arpents of fine land.

70. BEAUHARNOIS.

Though not large, this is an interesting and well organized charge. The town, which is prettily situated near the foot of the Cascade Rapids, on the St. Lawrence, has 1500 inhabitants, the greater part of whom are French, and this is the only Protestant Congregation in it. The Rev. Walter Roach was ordained first minister of Beauharnois, St. Louis, and Chateauguay, 21st November, 1833, these united Congregations then numbering 40 families. Born in Edinburgh, Mr. Roach was educated in his native City. As minister of these Congregations he was much respected. He died 27th August, 1849. In March, 1851, the Rev. Thomas Haig, formerly of Brockville, was inducted. He retired from the ministry in 1858, and died at Lachine in 1866. The Rev. Prosper Louis Leger, a native of La Charante, France, and a student of Queen's College, was ordained and inducted to Beauharnois, 10th March, 1859. He was beloved and respected by all, but his ministerial career was brief: he died on the 26th of November following, eight short months after his induction, in the 25th year of his age. The Rev. Frederick P. Sym (22), was inducted in July, 1860, and is still Minister.

The Church is, internally, particularly neat and confortable, and on its walls are several beautifully executed marble tablets to the memory of faithful ministers who have gone to their reward. It occupies a fine site, and was built about 35 years ago by the Seignor of Beauharnois. It has lately been made over to Trustees in connection with the Church of Scotland. There is a good manse but no glebe. In connection with the charge there is a small brick church at Chateauguay, in which the minister of Beauharnois officiates once a fortnight.

71. St. Louis de Gonzague.

This charge was separated from Beauharnois in 1850, and Mr. James T. Paul was ordained and inducted as its Minister on the 5th of June that year. In 1865 he retired on his commutation allowance: since that time it has been vacant, with the exception of such supplies as the Presbytery could send. A good many of its former members having connected themselves with other churches, it is now a weak charge. There is a good glebe, however, and, thanks to the Clergy Reserve's Manse and Glebe Fund, an excellent stone manse. The Congregation worship in a small log building which was put up for this purpose in 1842.

72. Lachine.

A Congregation was first collected at Lachine in 1818, through the labours of the Rev. Hugh Kirkland, a young Minister who came from Ireland in that year. He was inducted to the charge in January, 1818, and left in May of the following year, for the United States. In October, 1820, the Rev. William Brunton, from Scotland, began to minister to them. He resided in Montreal, and demitted his charge in 1822. The Reverends Henry Esson and Edward Black, of St. Gabriel Street Church, discharged the clerical duties of the Congregation until October, 1831, when Mr. Alexander Gale, a nephew of Mr. Esson's, arrived from Upper Canada, and was appointed by the Presbytery to act as Missionary. He was ordained and inducted the following year. In November, 1833, he left for Hamilton, C. W. Mr. John Taylor arrived from Scotland in July, 1834, and became pastor of the Congregation in October following. He resigned in 1843, and, returning to Scotland, received a presentation to the parish of Drummelzier, Peebleshire, where he died a few years ago. He was followed in Lachine by the Rev. William Simpson, the present minister, in March, 1844. Mr. Simpson is a native of Stirling, and was licensed in 1830, by the Presbytery of Old Light Burghers. He was received by the Church of Scotland in 1839, and came to Canada the following year, as a Missionary.

The Church, which was erected in 1833, has been put into a good state of repair, and is now very comfortable. There is an excellent manse, and two acres of land, including the church site, originally a gift from the heirs of the late John Grant. The Congregation is not large, but, according to their means and numbers, they are liberal.

73. Dundee.

For some years previous to the settlement of a Minister, this Congregation was much indebted to the late Rev. John McKenzie, of Williamstown, for occasional services. Mr. Duncan Moody, a licentiate of Ayr Presbytery, came to Dundee as an ordained Missionary from the Church of Scotland. He was inducted to the charge in December, 1835, and remained in it until his death, which occurred on the 5th January, 1855. He was much respected, and the Congregation flourished in his time. In 1827 the present Church was erected, which now looks a good deal the worse for wear. Steps, however, are being taken to replace it with a much larger and better one. Mr.

John Livingstone, a native of Nova Scotia, was ordained and inducted to this charge in November, 1859. He was a young man of great promise and much beloved by his congregation. He died on the 15th of August 1860, aged 27. The Rev. John Cameron, also a Nova Scotian, who had received his education at Glasgow, and had returned to his native Province as an ordained Missionary, during leave of absence, visited Canada in 1861, and was received by the Presbytery of Montreal. In June following he was inducted to Dundee. He was released from the charge in February, 1865, on his being presented to the parish of Castlehill, Campbellton, Scotland. On the 6th of March, 1866, the present minister, the Rev. Donald Ross, formerly of Southwold, and, singularly enough, also a Nova Scotian, was inducted. The prospects of the congregation are on the whole encouraging.

74. Elgin.

This was formerly a branch of the Huntingdon charge which, in 1863, was separated from it and placed under the care of the Rev. William Cochrane, an ordained Missionary from the Colonial Committee. In September, 1866, he was formally inducted as its Minister. There is a plain substantial stone church which was built in 1859. An excellent manse was erected last summer. There is no glebe. The contributions of the Congregation, for all purposes, have been very liberal.

75. Huntingdon.

The Rev. Wm. Montgomery Walker, the first Minister of the Congregation, came from Scotland. He was licensed by the Presbytery of Irvine; ordained by the Presbytery of Montreal in October, 1834; was soon after inducted to this charge, and continued to discharge the duties of its pastor with singular ability till 1844, when he received a presentation to the parish of Ochiltree, Ayrshire, of which he is still Minister. Mr. Alexander Wallace, a native of Glasgow, educated at Queen's College, was ordained and inducted in 1845. A frame Church was erected in 1833 which stood until the present large and well finished stone edifice was opened for worship in 1863. There is a glebe of 50 arpents, but as yet, no manse.

ATHELSTANE, a station four miles from Huntingdon, is a part of this charge.

76. GEORGETOWN.

This is the oldest Congregation in the county of Beauharnois, and its membership (308) is larger than that of any other country congregation in the Church. The settlement of the Township dates from 1824, and the first clergyman settled among them was the Rev. Mr. McWattie, a dissenting Minister whose services, however, appear to have been somewhat irregular and unsatisfactory. The Hon. Edward Ellice, late Seignor of Beauharnois, made a grant of 75 acres of land for a glebe, in February, 1830, on which the people erected a plain wooden place of worship. Mr. McWattie died about 1831. During the vacancy that followed, Dr. Mathieson, of Montreal, made frequent visits to this part of the country, and it is recorded that several of the couples married by Mr. McWattie, were, years after, remarried by the Dr. for the purpose of legitimatizing the children born of these unions : for, in those days, marriages by *dissenting ministers* were not recognized as legal. In August, 1831, application was made to the Glasgow Colonial Society for a Minister from the national Church. This resulted in the appointment of the Rev. Archibald Colquhoun, who was ordained by the Presbytery of Lochcarron, 14th July, 1832, and inducted to Georgetown on the 14th November following. Soon after, Mr. C. received and accepted a call to Dummer and Otanabee, where he remained until 1853, and was thence translated to Mulmur (53). Georgetown was declared vacant 4th June, 1835. In the spring of 1836 the Rev. James Creighton Muir arrived in Canada—a Missionary from the Glasgow Colonial Society. Having received a call to Georgetown, he was ordained and inducted in September of that year, and under him has grown up a large and flourishing Congregation. On the 6th of October, 1858, the Senatus Academicus of Queen's University conferred on Mr. Muir the degree of Doctor in Divinity, and, at the same time, a similar honour upon the late Rev. Alex. McGillivray of McLennan's Mountain, N. S. Although the Royal Charter, granting power to confer degrees bears date 1841, this is the first instance in which the University exercised the right, and, on this account, the honour was greatly enhanced. A fine new stone Church was erected at Georgetown in 1851 at a cost of $4800. An excellent brick manse was built in 1857, near the Church, and beautifully situated on the River Chateauguay.

77. Ormstown.

This charge, originally a branch of Georgetown Congregation, was separated from it during the incumbency of Mr. Colquhoun, in 1835. The Rev. James Anderson, a native of Cromarty, educated at Aberdeen, was its first minister. He was inducted 14th July, 1835. He died 6th April, 1861, aged 64. He was a good and useful Minister. The Rev. James Sieveright, formerly of Melbourne, succeeded in February, 1862. After an incumbency of three years he was translated to Chelsea (114). The Rev. W. C. Clark, formerly of Middleville, was inducted in April, 1865, and is now the Minister. The frame Church, erected in 1834, having served its day, it is proposed to build a new one, and for this purpose a sum of $4,000 has already been subscribed. There is a large and well finished brick manse on a fine site, and a glebe of 50 arpents. All the Presbyterians here are united, and prospects are encouraging. There is a good agricultural country in the neigbourhood, and the farmers, chiefly Lowland Scotch, are wealthy.

78. Laprairie.

The Reverends Dr. Mathieson and Dr. Black conducted regular Sabbath services at Laprairie for a number of years previous to the arrival of the Rev. David Black, who was ordained and inducted to the charge, 19th October, 1837. In 1841 he removed to Ste. Thérèse. He joined in the dissent and protest of 1844, and at that time left the Church. Having retired from active duty he now resides at Chateauguay.

The Rev. John Davidson, now of N. Williamsburgh, succeeded in 1844. Remaining till 1849 he removed to New Carlisle. The Rev. John Moffat, an ordained Missionary from Scotland, was inducted to Laprairie and Longueuil 18th November, 1858. He resigned in 1860. The Rev. John Barr who had officiated for a year previous as Missionary was inducted 3rd June, 1867. There is a good brick Church comfortably seated for 150. There is neither glebe nor manse, but vigorous efforts are being made to provide the latter.

The City of Montreal.

It seems strange that in Montreal no monument has been erected to the memory of Jacques Cartier, the first European who entered the little Indian Village of Hochelaga, in 1535. His eventful visit was fraught with important results to the future Commercial Capital of the Country, which was founded a century later and named " Ville Marie " by a French Company that had for its object " the conversion and civilization of the Aborigines." The nucleus of the infant city was a School of morality and industry " around which gathered such of the neighbouring natives as had been Christened or desired to be so." At this time the European population in Canada did not exceed two hundred souls. On the 8th of September, 1760, Montreal was finally delivered up to the British, at which time it was " a well peopled town, of an oblong form, surrounded by a wall flanked with eleven redoubts and a ditch of eight feet deep : it had also a fort or citadel which commanded the streets of the town from one end of it to the other." Fifty years later there were no wharves at Montreal, but " ships lay moored to the clayey and filthy bank of the city." No floating palaces to convey its citizens speedily and securely up and down the noble St. Lawrence. No railway linked town to town. A journey to Toronto was then a more serious matter than a voyage across the Atlantic at the present time. But now, how great the change ! Its population has reached 125,000 : its narrow dingy streets have, as if by magic, been widened and adorned with a gorgeousness of Architecture that excels in outward effect the palaces of " Genoa La Superba !" The genius of a Stephenson has given to it one of the most splendid achievements of engineering skill—the Victoria Bridge—by which this great centre of commerce is connected with all the most important points of the continent. Nor has its progress been confined to trade and commerce. The religious and charitable Institutions of Montreal are numerous and well sustained. Three-fourths of its inhabitants profess the Roman Catholic faith, yet, there are thirty-two Protestant Churches in the city. · As there has been a very

large increase since the last decennial census was taken, in 1861,
the figures which follow afford only an approximate estimate of the
relative proportions of the Protestant inhabitants,—in that year there
were about 10,000 Episcopalians, 5000 belonging to the Church of
Scotland, 3500 to the Canada Presbyterian Church, and about 3750
Methodist. The Church of Scotland is represented at present by
four Congregations, as follows.

79. St. Gabriel's, Montreal.

Previous to the close of the American Revolutionary war the Presbyterians resident in Montreal were few in number. After that,
however, they obtained yearly accessions from the old country, as
well as from the United States. For some time they were depen-
dent on the services rendered them by successive military chaplains.
One of these, the Rev. John Bethune, chaplain to the 84th Regiment, having retired from military duty, appears to have been instrumental in organizing the first Congregation in Montreal. They met
for worship in a large room that was hired for the purpose. The
first service held there by Mr. Bethune was on the 12th March,
1786, and the last, on the 6th May, 1787. Want of adequate support
is alleged to have been the reason of his leaving so soon. There
may have been another reason, however, in the fact that having
received from Government a grant of land in Glengary, which
began about this time to be pretty thickly settled by Scottish Presbyterians, Mr. Bethune very probably was led by a sense of duty,
as well as interest, to go there ; at all events he took up his residence
at Williamstown in 1787, and there continued to labour faithfully in
his Master's service until his death, which occurred on the 23rd September, 1815. [See 90). The Rev. John Young succeeded
him in Montreal. A licentiate of the Presbytery of Irvine, he had
come from Beith, Scotland, and was in 1787 settled at a place
called Curry's Bush, near Schenectady, U. S. He first visited Montreal in the year 1790 ; his second visit was in 1791. On the 18th
September in that year the Sacrament of the Lord's Supper was for
the first time administered by him, in accordance with the usages of
the Church of Scotland, in the *Recollet Roman Catholic Church*,
the use of which had been kindly allowed the Congregation while

their own Church was being built. The Recollet Fathers politely refused any pecuniary remuneration from " the Society of Presbyterians," as they were then called, but were induced to accept of a present in acknowledgement of their good offices, and which consisted of two Hogsheads of Spanish wine, containing 60 odd gallons each, and a box of candles, amounting in all to £14.2.4. Mr. Hunter, whose manuscript I have followed closely in the history of this Church, was himself a leading member of it from the very first ; he closes his account of the interesting presentation alluded to with the quaint remark,—" they were quite thankful for the same." On the 2nd of April, 1792, the site of the present ST. GABRIEL Street Church was purchased for £100, and in six months the Church was completed at a cost of about £1000. It was opened for worship 7th October, 1792. In 1791 Mr. Young and his Congregation petitioned to be taken under the care of the Presbytery of Albany, and they so remained until 1793, when they were dismissed to join a Presbytery then formed in Canada under the name of "the Presbytery of Montreal."

Mr. Young officiated for the last time in Montreal on the 2nd of August, 1802. At that time he went to Newark [now Niagara,] where he remained a short period ; he removed thence to the neighbourhood of Lake Champlain for four years ; afterwards, to Lunenburgh in Nova Scotia and, lastly, to Truro in the same Province, where he died and was buried. The Rev. Robert Forrest next came to Montreal from Scotland, viâ New York, in April, 1803. At this time he preached for five Sabbaths to the congregation, after which he went back to the States, and soon after, returned to Montreal, but not to St. Gabriel Street Church. Meanwhile, a new King had arisen who knew not Joseph ! in the person of the Rev. James Sommerville, a licentiate of the Relief Presbytery of Glasgow, who arrived in Quebec in 1802 under an engagement as a teacher of youth, and, having been ordained by the Rev. Mr. Spark and the Rev. Mr. Bethune, was inducted to this charge 18th September, 1803. Says one who knew him well : " Perhaps no other Congregation ever acted with more continued liberality towards a Minister. Even when the aberrations of mind with which he was frequently affected, rendered it necessary for him to abstain from public duties, they still continued to grant him their support and affectionate regard."

He was a warm hearted and benevolent man, and though for many years he took no active part in the duties of the pastorate, he retained his status till his death, which took place on the 2nd of June, 1837, in the 62nd year of his age. He bequeathed £1000 to be expended in the erection of a manse, for the future Minister of St. Gabriel Street Church, and £1000 for the benefit of the Natural History Society of Montreal. Mr. Forrest having been denied admittance to St. Gabriel Street Church, on his return from the States, preached for a short time in the room formerly occupied by Mr. Bethune. In the fall of 1803, he received a call from a Congregation in New York, and left Montreal. The Rev. Robert Easton, formerly Minister of Morpeth in Roxboroughshire, in connection with the Associate Reformed Synod of Scotland, succeeded Mr. Forrest in 1804. He and his Congregation continued to worship in that room until the 8th of March, 1807, when the Church in St. Peter Street was opened for worship. In 1817 the Rev. Henry Esson came as assistant and successor to Mr. Sommerville. The Rev. Edward Black who arrived in Montreal in 1822, was soon afterwards ordained and engaged as colleague with Mr. Esson in the assistantship. In 1831, when a division occurred in the Congregation, Dr. Black left with the seceding party and founded the Congregation of St. Paul's. After Mr. Sommerville's death Mr. Esson continued to be Minister of the Charge until 1844, when, having joined the Free Church, he became a Professor in Knox College, Toronto. A vexatious and protracted lawsuit followed respecting the property, which was eventually settled by compromise in 1864. The Church of Scotland agreed to pay to the other party the sum of $5800, in consideration of which we were left in undisputed tenure of the Church and manse. And thus, after a lapse of 21 years, the oldest Presbyterian Church in the Province reverted to its Auld Mother Kirk. On the first Sabbath of December, 1865, it was re-opened for worship in connection with the Church of Scotland. The Rev. Robert Campbell, formerly of Galt, was inducted to the charge 13th December, 1866. He found but a small number of adherents, the majority of the Congregation having by this time erected a new Church in another part of the City.

The work of reconstruction is, however, going on satisfactorily, and there is a good prospect that ere long a large Congregation may be established.

The Church is in good repair, and is comfortably seated for about 600 persons. The manse, on Sherbrooke street, a large cut-stone building, is valuable, and is rented at present for $480 per annum.

80. St. Andrew's, Montreal.

This Congregation branched off from St. Gabriel in the year 1803. The Rev. Robert Forrest, already mentioned (79) was its Minister, but he did not remain long. Having received a call from a congregation in New York, he left Montreal in the autumn of that year. His immediate successor, the Rev. Robert Easton, was instrumental, as we have seen, in building a second Presbyterian Church in St. Peter Street. His health failing in 1824, a Mr. Hill was employed to be his assistant. His labours, however, were of short duration, for he died suddenly of apoplexy, on the 4th of March that same year. The Rev. John Burns, M.A., was next chosen assistant to Mr. Easton ; he, having received ordination from the Presbytery of Edinburgh, began his duties in Montreal on the 11th July, 1824. At that time Mr. Easton retired upon an annuity of £150, which he received till his death, in 1851. Mr. Burns remained only about two years. In May, 1826, he resigned, and returned to Scotland. Previous to his arrival amongst them—on the 9th of July 1824—a meeting of the Congregation had been held, when they declared themselves to be " Christians in connection with the Church of Scotland," and, very soon after, it was agreed to style the Church and Congregation by the name of " St. Andrew's." About the same time the action of a majority of the Congregation who insisted upon calling a Minister of the Church of Scotland " *and none else* " having been deemed too exclusive, the minority withdrew, and formed the American Presbyterian Congregation. It was agreed, however, that they should be allowed to worship in St. Peter Street Church until they had provided a place of worship for themselves. The Rev. Alexander Mathieson, the present Minister of the charge, and the father of the Church in Canada, was licensed by the Presbytery of Dunbarton in 1823,

E

ordained by the same on the 19th of October, 1826, arrived in Montreal on the 24th of December in that year, and was inducted on the Sabbath following. At that time the Congregation comprised about 1500, of whom 250 were Communicants. The Church was seated for 760, the average attendance being 650, and its total revenues about £450. The minister's salary was £250, and the Sabbath School, believed to have been the first in our Church, numbered sixty scholars, with seven teachers. Dr. Mathieson received his degree of Doctor in Divinity from the University of Glasgow, in 1837. The present Church of St. Andrew's was opened for worship on the 12th of January, 1851. It is, without doubt, the finest Ecclesiastical structure in the Province ; Salisbury Cathedral, in England, supplied the model. Its proportions are admirable, and the interior is most elegant, and accomodates easily above 900 persons. It cost $64,000.

Mr. Robert Dobie, now Minister of Osnabruck, came from Scotland as Assistant to Dr. Mathieson, in September, 1852, under the auspices of the Colonial Committee, and remained in that position until he accepted his present charge (87). Mr. Robert Herbert Story became assistant in May, 1859. On the 20th September following he received ordination from the Presbytery of Montreal, and left in November, having received a presentation to the parish of Roseneath, Scotland. Mr. James Kerr came as assistant in May, 1860. Having remained in Montreal about a year he returned to Scotland, and resided at Bathgate. He and his young wife were passengers on board the steamship " London," which foundered in the Bay of Biscay, on her voyage to Australia, on the 11th January, 1866 ; they shared the fate of the 268 others who perished by that sad calamity.

Mr. William M. Inglis, now Minister of Kingston, was the next Assistant. He came from Scotland, and remained in Montreal till August, 1863 (61). Mr. Andrew Paton followed in November, 1864. He was born near Kirkaldy, Fifeshire, studied in Edinburgh, and was licensed by the Presbytery of Kinross in July, 1863. For a short time he was Assistant in St. George's, Glasgow, and also in Haddington, during Mr. Bell's illness. He was selected by a committee in Scotland, named by the congregation in Montreal, to procure an Assistant to Dr. Mathieson. After a year's trial he was requested to accept the appointment permanently. Having been ordained by the Presbytery of Kinross, 17th August, 1865, he was inducted as assistant and successor, 14th February, 1866.

This is the largest and wealthiest Congregation in the Church. Their contributions for all purposes during the year 1866, amounted to $10,312. In this sum is included $3000 paid for the purpose of procuring an organ. A very fine instrument built by Mr. Warren of Montreal has since been placed in the Church, at a cost of about $5000.

81. St. Paul's, Montreal.

The Rev. Edward Black, a native of the Shire of Galloway, Scotland, who came to Canada in 1822, had been shortly after his arrival ordained as colleague with Mr. Esson in St. Gabriel Street Congregation. In 1831 a division occurred ; Dr. Black left with the seceding party, organized a separate Congregation, and became their Minister. St. Paul's Church, erected in St. Helen Street, was opened for worship the 24th August, 1834. It was built entirely through Dr. Black's energy and perseverance, and chiefly by money advanced by himself for this purpose. He continued to officiate in this Church, and with much acceptance to his Congregation, until his death, which occurred on the 8th of May, 1845, in the 53rd year of his age.

The Rev. Robert McGill, formerly Minister of Niagara, succeeded Dr. Black, 5th November, 1845. On the 4th of February, 1856, he died. The memory of this excellent and pious Minister will long be cherished by this Congregation. He was a native of Ayrshire, and a licentiate of the Presbytery of Glasgow. In 1853 the University of Glasgow conferred on him the Degree of Doctor in Divinity as an acknowledgment of his learning and long continued services in the cause of Religion.

The Rev. William Snodgrass, formerly of Charlottetown, Prince Edward Island, succeeded Dr. McGill in St. Paul's the 4th November, 1856, and remained until he entered upon his duties as Principal of Queen's College, Kingston, in October, 1864. Principal Snodgrass is a native of Renfrewshire, Scotland, and an alumnus of Glasgow University. Having received license by the Presbytery of Uist, 18th August, 1852, he was ordained by the

Presbytery of Glasgow, on the 3d of September in the same year, and proceeded to Prince Edward Island in October following, under a commission from the Colonial Committee. He remained there until July, 1856. In February, 1865, he received from his *alma mater* the Degree of Doctor in Divinity.

Dr. Snodgrass was followed in this charge by its present minister, the Rev. John Jenkins, D.D. Dr. Jenkins is a native of Devonshire, England, and received his education for the Ministry at the Hoxton Theological Institution, London—now Richmond College. He was ordained in August, 1837, and proceeded at once as a Missionary to the Mysore, India, under the auspices of the Wesleyan Missionary Society of London. In 1853 he joined the Fourth Presbytery (N.S.) of Philadelphia, and for ten years was Minister of the Calvary Presbyterian Church in that city. Having returned to his native country he became a member of the Synod of the English Presbyterian Church. He was received by the Presbytery of Montreal in May, 1865, by the Synod at its first subsequent meeting, and, was inducted to St. Paul's on the 27th of June the same year. The University of New-York conferred upon him the degree of Doctor in Divinity in 1859.

Owing to the great value of the church site for business purposes, and the inconvenience of its situation to a large portion of the Congregation, it was resolved to dispose of the property. In October, 1866, St. Paul's Church was accordingly sold at public auction, for $27,440. The Sacrament of the Lord's Supper was dispensed in it *for the last time,* on Sabbath, the 20th of January, 1867, to 355 Communicants. A splendid new Church is in course of erection in Dorchester street. This Congregation stands at the head of the list of contributors to the Schemes of the Synod. There is at present no manse, but the sum of $2600 realized from property formerly held, is lodged in the Bank. Meanwhile the Minister's house rent is paid by the Congregation.

82. St. Matthew's, Montreal.

In 1858 the attention of the Presbytery was directed to the spiritual destitution of a large population residing in the neighbourhood of Point St. Charles. A Sabbath School was opened in that

year under the superintendance of Mr. W. C. Menzies, in the ticket
office of the G. T. R. It began with 17 scholars and 3 teachers.
In 1860 a mission Church was erected to seat 300 : it cost £600.
The Rev. James Stuart, a young man of high promise, was sent by
the Colonial Committee for this field, but never reached the scene of
his intended labours. He perished in the wreck of the ill-fated
" Hungarian," off Cape Sable, 20th February, 1860. The Committee
sent another missionary, the Rev. James Black, who began to labour
at Point St. Charles, 1st August, 1860. On the 4th September,
1861, he was inducted to Chatham, C.E. [83]. In 1861, the
mission station was erected into a Congregation, and, on the 24th
December in that year, Mr. William Darrach, a native of Cantyre,
Scotland, was ordained and inducted. He died on the 18th of
June, 1865, deeply regretted. He was succeeded by Mr. Joshua
Fraser, 21st September, 1865. It is a flourishing Congregation,
having 110 Church members and 180 Sabbath School scholars on
the roll.

83. CHATHAM, C. E.

This charge includes two Congregations, viz, Chatham and Gren-
ville, with a Church in each, beautifully situated on the banks of the
Ottawa. The Rev. William Mair was ordained the first Minister,
26th July, 1833. Licensed by the Presbytery of Glasgow in
1821, he officiated for six years as Sabbath lecturer in Glasgow
College, and was afterwards assistant to the late Archibald Wilson,
Minister of Cardross. There were no Churches in this part of the
country when Mr. Mair came, and the bounds of his charge he used
to define as " eighteen miles in front and as far back as I can win."
It was not long before he had two substantial stone Churches erected,
but while they were being built, he received little or nothing from
his people in the shape of stipend. After a life of self-denial such
as few ministers, now-a-days, are called on to submit to, and a long
course of faithful and zealous discharge of duty, he rested from his
labours on the 17th of October, 1860. The Rev. James Black,
from Point St. Charles Mission Church, succeeded him in September, 1861. By his instrumentality a very neat and commodious
brick manse was erected. In November, 1864, he demitted the
charge and returned to Scotland. Mr. Donald Ross, the present

Minister, was ordained and inducted on the 3rd of October, 1865.
The prospects of the Congregation are very encouraging.

VIII. PRESBYTERY OF GLENGARY.

This, one of the four original Presbyteries of the Church, held
its first meeting at Kingston, 10th June, 1831. Sederunt, Revs.
John McKenzie, Hugh Urquhart, Archibald Connell. Its congregations at that time were all within the county of Glengary. Its
present bounds correspond nearly with the limits of the old Eastern
District of Upper Canada, with the exception of the Congregations
of L'Orignal and Hawkesbury, separated from it some years since,
and, for greater convenience, attached to the Presbytery of Ottawa.
There are at present 15 organized congregations in the Presbytery,
of which 10 have Ministers. There are also several Mission Stations.
In so far as the Church of Scotland is concerned, it may truly be
said, that this is the cradle of Presbyterianism in Canada West·
Here for many years, the Rev. John Bethune lived and laboured, the
only Minister of the Church of Scotland in Upper Canada ; and the
Rev. John McKenzie, his successor, was the moderator of the first
Synod. At that time there were but three ministers in the Presbytery. Mr. McKenzie of Williamstown, Mr. Connell of Martintown, and Mr. (now Dr.) Urquhart of Cornwall. The county of
Glengary began to be settled by Scotch Highlanders immediately
after the close of the American Revolutionary war in 1783, when
bands of U. E. Loyalists, including officers and privates of the Provincial and " Continental " troops, received free grants of lands in
recognition of their services to King and country. In 1802, two
or three vessels with emigrants from Fort William, arrived at
Quebec : most of these settled in the eastern District. Some also
of the settlers sent out to the Rideau, afterwards the Bathurst
District, found their way to Glengary in 1814. Thus, U. E.
Loyalists, Dutch, German, British, but chiefly Highlanders from
Scotland, came to settle here. Many of them were Roman Catholics, and a very large number belonging to that Church is still to be
found in Glengary.

84. MATILDA.

Originally a branch of Williamsburg, this was organized as
a separate charge under the Rev. Thomas Scott, in October,

1858. He resigned in 1865 and was inducted to Plantagenet the following year. Mr. John S. Lochead, the present Minister, a graduate of Queen's College, was ordained and inducted the 21st November, 1866. There are three preaching stations, and the people are much scattered. A small frame Church was erected about the time of Mr. Scott's settlement here. There is no glebe nor manse. There is ample material for a good Congregation.

85. WILLIAMSBURGH.

The Township of this name was settled in 1784 by U. E. Loyalists, chiefly of German origin. In 1827, the Lutherans and Presbyterians conjointly erected a frame Church, distant from the St. Lawrence about six miles ; it was named St. Peter's. The Rev. Joseph Johnston, for some time Minister of Osnabruck, officiated here occasionally. The Rev. Robert Lyle, his successor, also preached at intervals. The Rev. John Dickey, a native of Ireland and a Minister of the Associate Synod of Upper Canada, was the first settled pastor. Having joined our Church with his Synod in 1840, he was inducted in 1841. He died on the 24th May, 1851. He was truly an apostolic man ; much and deservedly respected. The Rev. Thomas Scott, from Camden, C. W., succeeded him in 1852, and resigned the charge in 1858 (see 96). The Rev. John Davidson, formerly of New Richmond, C. E., was appointed in April, 1858. Mr. Davidson is a native of Paisley, and received his education in the University of Glasgow.

There is a brick manse and a good glebe of 13 acres. The old Church having served its day and fallen into disrepair, both of the Congregations worshipping in it wisely resolved to build a separate and a better place of worship. The Lutherans having first erected a large and handsome Church in 1865, the Presbyterians followed their example, and on the 3rd of March, 1867, a substantial and well finished stone edifice was opened for worship by the Very Reverend Principal Snodgrass.

86. FINCH.

The Township of this name was first settled about 45 years ago by " Lochaber-men," and others from Mull, with a few from the north of Ireland. Mr. Connell of Martintown, and Mr. McKenzie of Williamstown, gave occasional supply for many years, and had a Church erected about the year 1836. The Rev. Robert Lyle, formerly of Osnabruck, a native of Ireland, and a member of the United Synod of U. C., became Minister of Finch about the year 1838. He was deposed from the ministry in December, 1841. Mr. Donald Munro, a Missionary from Argyleshire, Scotland, sent by the Col. Com., came to Canada in 1849, and was inducted to Finch in December, 1850, where he ministered until 1864, when, owing to advanced years and infirmities, he received the sanction of Synod to retire on his commutation allowance. He died at Finch, on the 15th of February, 1867, aged 78. Mr. Hugh Lamont, the present Minister, a native of Iona, came to Canada in 1856, completed his theological course at Queen's College, was licensed by the Presbytery of Ottawa in 1864, and ordained at Finch 22nd February, 1865. The old Church looks very much like a barn. There is a good manse with two acres of land adjoining it, and a glebe of 200 acres valued at about $600. Only 15 acres of it are cleared. There has been a marked improvement in the contributions of the Congregation within the last two years.

87. OSNABRUCK.

The Township of Osnabruck, pleasantly situated on the St. Lawrence, was settled at an early period by U. E. Loyalists. In the year 1795, a frame place of worship was erected near the site of the present Church by the Lutherans and Presbyterians, conjointly. The first Ministers who officiated in it were the Rev. Samuel Schwerdfeger—a Lutheran Minister—and the Rev. John Ludewig Broeffle, a Presbyterian, both of whom officiated in the German language exclusively, and resided in the township of Williamsburgh. Mr. Broeffle was a man of good education—a kind and faithful pastor—he died in Williamsburgh in 1815, at the advanced age of nearly fourscore years. For a good many years the Presbyterian Congregation here remained vacant, enjoying, however, the occasional services of Missionaries. One of them was an Englishman— the Rev. Louis Williams—who, besides preaching, used to do a little in the way of *peddling*, and sold ribbons, trinkets and fancy goods !

There were no stores in those days! The Rev. William Taylor—a Scotchman—was settled in 1817, but after a ministry of little more then two years he accepted a call from the Scotch Congregation of Waddington, U. S., much to the regret of the people of Osnabruck. The Rev. Joseph Johnston—formerly resident in Cornwall (88)—succeeded Mr. Taylor, in 1822. After a ministry of six years or thereabouts he went to the United States. It is said that he acquired a considerable landed property in Texas, and that he died there. The Rev. Robert Lyle ministered for a period of about ten years, when he removed to the neighbouring township of Finch (86). In 1839, the Rev. Isaac Purkis, a native of Hampshire, England, a member of the United Synod of U. C. and formerly of the English Independent Church, became Minister of Osnabruck. He was received into connection with the Church of Scotland in 1841, the congregation having given in its adherence the previous year. He died after a ministry of 13 years, October 16th, 1852.

Mr. Robert Dobie—a native of Stirling, formerly Assistant to Principal Haldane, of St. Andrew's, and, for a time, to Dr. Mathieson of Montreal, was ordained and inducted to this charge on the 7th October, 1853, and is still Minister. Mr. Dobie was educated at the University of Glasgow, and College of St. Mary's, St. Andrew's, and came to Canada in September, 1852.

In 1857 a new and substantial brick Church was erected at a cost of $6000, towards which the Colonial Committee contributed £150 sterling. A suitable brick manse was before this time built, with the aid of £150 from the C. R. fund. The materials of the old Church were removed to a distance of 6½ miles and re-erected. In this Church there is fortnightly service. There is no debt on the Church property. There is a glebe of about 24 acres.

88. CORNWALL.

The Rev. John Bethune, of Williamstown, began to officiate in Cornwall soon after his arrival in Glengary (1787). This venerable and esteemed servant of God was the first, and for nearly 30 years, the only Minister of the Church of Scotland in Upper Canada. Here, as well as at Williamstown, Lancaster and Charlottenburgh, he had a church built, not long after his coming. He died in 1815 (see 90). After his death, the Rev. Joseph Johnston, a native of Ireland, and a licentiate of the Synod of Ulster, officiated and also taught the District School for some years. It is doubtful whether he was ever inducted : there is no official record to that effect extant. Mr. Bell, of Perth, in his letters from Canada (1824), speaks of him as officiating in this double capacity when he came to this country in 1817.

In 1822, the Rev. Harry Leith, from Aberdeen, came to Cornwall, and was on his arrival appointed teacher of the District School. Mr. Johnston continued his ministrations in the old church till 1823, when he removed to Osnabruck [see 87]. Mr. Leith officiated in the School House until the completion of the new Church—the present one, in October, 1826. In December of that year he received a call and presentation to the parish of Rothiemay, Scotland, which he accepted. In the beginning of January following he left Cornwall to take possession of his new charge, bearing with him the devoted attachment of his little flock and the good wishes of the whole community.

The Rev. Hugh Urquhart—a native of Rossshire, Scotland, and an alumnus of King's College, Aberdeen, was licensed by the Presbytery of Inverness, and ordained by the Presbytery of Dingwall, 5th August, 1822. He came to Canada in October of that year, and combined teaching and ministerial work in Montreal until 1827, when he received a call from Cornwall, and was inducted to the charge on the 18th of February. Mr. Urquhart taught the Eastern District School in Cornwall, until 1840, when he restricted himself to his parochial duties.

In 1857, his *alma mater* conferred on him the Degree of Doctor in Divinity. Between the years 1847 and 1857 Dr. Urquhart also filled the chair of Ecclesiastical History in Queen's College, Kingston. In the fall of 1866, the Rev. John Smith Burnet came as assistant to Dr. Urquhart, who, in the fortieth year of a laborious ministry, and in the 74th year of his age, found himself unable longer to discharge all the duties belonging to the pastorate. Mr. Burnet is a native of Dumfries, where he officiated as assistant minister for some time. He came to Canada as a Missionary from the Colonial Committee, in June, 1863. There is no manse in Cornwall ; there is a site, however, in town, and some money invested for the purpose of building a manse. There is a glebe of 100 acres of good land : and, besides, a large number of town lots, that have become valuable—yielding at present about $600 per annum, which is applied to the payment of stipend. The Congregation is now numerous and influential.

89. MARTINTOWN.

The village from which this charge takes its name lies twelve miles north from Cornwall, and has a population of about 500. This Congregation, at an early period in its history, also succeeded in securing part of the services of the late Mr. Bethune, and his pastoral relation with Martintown continued till the time of his death. In 1804, there had been erected a small frame Church for the use of a Congregation, ministered to by one Mr. Reid, a dissenter, who also taught a school. In 1811, the site—$\frac{1}{4}$th of an acre—" with the frame house or chapel"—was deeded by the said Mr. Reid, to certain parties belonging to the Church of Scotland, for the sum of £256. At this time, he went to St. Armand, C. E., and is said to have joined the Church of England in 1815. The Rev. Alexander Fletcher, a Minister of the Secession Church in Scotland, was subsequently employed for a few years, first at Williamstown, and afterwards at Martintown and its neighbourhood. In 1824 he resigned the charge, and took up his residence in Plantagenet, where he died.

The Rev. Archibald Connell, the next Minister, was born at Kilchoman, Islay, Argyleshire, 25th December, 1789, and ordained by the Presbytery of Glasgow, with a view to Martintown, 24th November, 1825; he died in August, 1836, having officiated here nearly 11 years. In his time the present Church was erected, but he did not live to see it completed. A tablet on the wall of the Church records the estimation in which Mr. Connell was held by a large and attached Congregation, and in touching terms thus alludes to his death and burial,—" within this edifice erected for the worship of God, his voice was only once heard proclaiming the tidings of salvation. Assembled with his flock under the open canopy of Heaven, to shew the Lord's death, they were driven by the inclemency of the day to seek shelter within its unfinished walls. By a remarkable coincidence, on that same day of the month—

one year afterwards—his remains were interred on the very spot where he then stood to distribute the symbols of the bread of life, and, by that solemn act, close his ministerial labours." The Rev. Dr. Mathieson preached Mr. Connell's funeral sermon the same day that he opened the Church for worship.

The Rev. Daniel Clark, a licentiate of the Presbytery of Inverness, Scotland, officiated as missionary in Martintown, for one year. In 1839, he was settled at Indian Lands, and left the Church at the division of 1844. His successor, Mr. John McLaurin, a native of Balquhidder, Perthshire, was educated at Glasgow. Having been for some time a missionary in connection with St. Columba's Church, in that City, he was ordained to this charge, 6th August, 1840. He died the 22nd of March, 1855, aged 48; much lamented by all who knew him. The Rev. Peter McVicar was inducted 23rd April, 1856. He resigned in June, 1859, returned to Scotland, and is now Minister of Manor, in Peebleshire. The Rev. James Mair, the present Minister, is a native of Aberdeenshire, and was educated at Mar. Coll. Aberdeen. He was licensed by the Presbytery of Glasgow in 1856, and, in September of that year, went to Nova Scotia, and was soon after settled at Barney's River, in that Province, where he remained nearly three years. He was inducted to Martintown, 27th September, 1860.

The Church has recently undergone extensive repairs and improvement. It is seated for 800, and is one of the best country Churches in Canada. There is, near the Church, an excellent stone manse, and a glebe of 50 acres of good land. There is a large, wealthy, and influential congregation.

90. WILLIAMSTOWN.

This was the cradle of Presbyterianism in Upper Canada. The Rev. John Bethune, as already mentioned (80) came here in 1787. Simultaneously with his coming to Glengary, there arrived emigrants from different parts of the Highlands of Scotland, as well as companies of disbanded soldiers from the United States, who, from their firm allegiance to the British Crown during the Revolutionary war, were designated "United Empire Loyalists," and to whom grants of lands were given at the close of the war in recognition of their services. While residing at Williamstown, Mr. Bethune also officiated statedly at Lancaster, Charlottenburgh, Martintown, and Cornwall. He was a man of great zeal and piety, and deservedly esteemed by all who came in contact with him. He had to contend with many difficulties, poverty, apathy, and, harder to bear than these, calumny. He never faltered in the path of duty, but laboured faithfully and affectionately over this wide district until his death, which occurred 23rd September, 1815, in the 66th year of his age, and the 44th of his ministry. His remains lie interred in the churchyard of Williamstown, where is a monument erected to his memory, by his six sons,—Angus, Norman, John, James, Alexander, and Donald. Two of these sons—" having contracted a preference for the other Church "—took orders in the Church of England. They are still living. The one, the Very Rev. John Bethune, D.D., is Dean of Montreal; the other, who for many years occupied the position of Archdeacon of Cobourg was, in 1866, consecrated Coadjutor to the late Venerable Bishop of Toronto, under the title of the Bishop of Niagara. Thus, the singular and interesting anomaly, it may almost be called, in the Church History of Canada is presented to our notice, of Presbyterianism having given two consecutive Bishops to the Episcopalian Church : the first having been a native of Scotland, and educated at Aberdeen with a view to the Ministry in the Presbyterian Church, as may be fairly inferred from the fact that shortly after his arrival in Canada proposals were made by him to accept the pastoral oversight of St. Gabriel Street Congregation in Montreal; the second, as we have just seen, being the son of a Scottish Presbyterian Minister.

The Rev. John McKenzie succeeded Mr. Bethune in 1818, and was ordained on the 23rd December in that year. He was born at Fort Augustus, Scotland, and died at Williamstown, on the 21st April, 1855, æt. 65. He was a faithful pastor, and greatly revered by his flock. That he stood well with his brother Minister is evidenced by the fact that he was chosen Moderator of the first Synod in Canada. Warmly attached to his native land, and to the Church of which he was a Minister, it may be truly said of him that, following in the steps of his Lord and master " he went about continually doing good."

On the 4th September, 1856, Mr. Peter Watson was ordained

and inducted to the charge, and is still Minister. He is a native
of Inverness-shire. The first Church in Williamstown was a wooden
one, built soon after Mr. Bethune's arrival. It was replaced by
one of stone in 1809 or '10. From weight of snow on the roof, it
fell one Sabbath morning—fortunately the Congregation had not
assembled. The present quaint-looking, but large and comfortable
stone Church was erected on the same site in 1812. It has recently
been repaired and embellished at considerable outlay, and during
last summer a massive iron fence was placed in front of it. There
is a good manse with 50 acres of land adjoining, and 75 acres at
a distance of a few miles. The congregation is large and respectable, a considerable number of them still retaining a preference
for "the Gaelic." Mr. Watson officiates in English and Gaelic
here as well as in the Church at Charlottenburgh.

91. LANCASTER.

The Township of this name has a frontage of ten miles on Lake
St. Francis. The land is for the most part very level, so much so
that at the time of the first settlements in the neighbourhood, it was
styled the "Sunken Township," and was considered almost
worthless. But the soil is naturally rich, and under judicious
management yields abundant crops. It is said to have taken its
name from the fact that a family named Falkner from Lancaster,
England, first settled here in 1776. For many years it constituted
a part of the Williamstown Congregation under Mr. Bethune, and
not until 1822 was it organized into a separate charge, the first
stated minister of which was the Rev. Alexander McNaughton,
who, having been nominated by the Glasgow Colonial Society and
ordained by the Presbytery of Paisley, 19th July, 1833, was
inducted to Lancaster in December following. On the 19th of
January, 1842, he was translated to the Parish of Colonsay, Islay,
Scotland, and was succeeded by the Rev. Thomas McPherson, the
present Minister, who is a native of Rossshire, was educated at
King's College, Aberdeen, and came to Canada in 1836. He was
first stationed at Melbourne, but after a short time he was ordained
and inducted to Beechridge, where he remained till 1843, when he
was translated to Lancaster. The old frame Church, recently taken

down, was erected in 1796, and was probably the first Presbyterian place of worship in Upper Canada. In March, 1809, a patent deed was granted by the Crown, to certain trustees, of 200 acres of land in the front concession as a glebe, " for the use of the members of the Church of Scotland, residing in the Eastern District." That land has now become valuable ; a large portion of it has been leased, in lots, for 999 years, and yields a present annual rental of $480. A well-finished stone Church—the walls of which were built some years previously—was opened for worship on the 20th of October, 1855. It cost $6,500, the whole of which was contributed by the Congregation, excepting about $200 collected in Scotland. There is a good manse. The congregation is large, and though originally all Highlanders, the Gaelic language in this, as in all the Highland Congregations in Canada, is gradually giving place to English. Mr. McPherson, however, continues to officiate in both languages at Lancaster, and also in the 4th concession Church, where services are held once a fortnight.

92. COTE ST. GEORGE.

While this Congregation remained united with Dalhousie Mills, they formed a pretty good charge ; for some years, however, from a variety of unhappy causes, they have been in a state of separation. There is no good reason why they should not now be re-united. The Church at Cote St. George, which partakes of " the barn" style of architecture, was built in 1830. In 1833, we find a Mr. John Bruce applying to the Presbytery for ordination, which was not granted—for want of a Presbyterial certificate. He resided, however, at Cote St. George, and officiated informally for some years, and then returned to Scotland. Mr. Donald Sinclair, a Scotchman, was ordained and inducted 1st June, 1843. He was released from the charge in 1846, and became Minister of the parish of Duror, Scotland. The Rev. Æneas McLean, formerly of Nova Scotia, was inducted to the charge of Cote St. George and Dalhousie Mills in 1847, and was Minister of both places until 1854. He died suddenly in Montreal, 10th June, 1855. Mr. Archibald Currie, a native of Argyleshire, was ordained and inducted to Cote St. George, alone, on the 23rd of October, 1861.

Since that time Dalhousie Mills has been dependant on the Presbytery for supply. There is a glebe at Cote St. George, purchased with aid of £75 from the Clergy Reserve fund. There is also a manse. A good brick manse was erected some years ago at Dalhousie Mills. Since the above was written, Mr. Currie has been translated to Brock, and this charge is now vacant.

93. DALHOUSIE MILLS. (See 92.)

94. LOCHIEL.

The first settlers came to Lochiel in 1796, from Glenelg in Scotland. Their first Minister was the Rev. John McLaurin, from Breadalbane, who was a student at St. Andrews, and was ordained by the Presbytery of Edinburgh, 27th October, 1819. Towards the close of that year he came to Lochiel, and at the commencement of his ministry, had a frame Church erected. He continued in the charge until the 12th of July, 1832, when he was translated to Hawkesbury and L'Orignal. During his residence at Lochiel he taught the Ottawa District School at L'Orignal, and frequently officiated there and elsewhere. The stone Church at Vankleek Hill was built under his direction. He preached in Gaelic and English, and with considerable success. He died at L'Orignal in 1833 (119). The Rev. John McIsaac was the next Minister. He was ordained with a view to Lochiel, by the Presbytery of Greenock, 30th April, 1835, and inducted on the 16th of August following. He received his education in Glasgow University, and had "the gift of tongues." Greatly to the grief of many Highland hearts in Lochiel, he returned to Scotland in 1845, and was inducted to the charge of Oban in January, 1846, where he died on the 15th of same month, 1847. In June, 1854, the Rev. John McDonald, now of Beechridge, was inducted, but his connection with this Congregation was of brief duration. Next came Mr. Donald McDonald, in September, 1856, to fill the vacancy of nearly 12 years. He remained only three years. Having resigned the charge he went to Scotland, where he was presented to Trumisgarry, thence he was translated to the parish of Sleat, in Skye, where he now is. The Rev. John Darroch, a native of Scotland, for some years resident in Virginia, and who received his theological education at Princeton, was inducted to Lochiel in 1861. He, too, after a brief incumbency resigned the charge in 1865, went to Scotland, officiated for some time as a missionary under the Colonial Committee in Ireland, and is now Minister of Portree, in the Isle of Skye. Though five times deserted, the people of Lochiel have still undiminished attachment to the Church of Scotland. There is yet a large congregation, patiently awaiting God's good time to send them a Minister who shall proclaim to them the glad tidings of salvation in the language they and their fathers learned in Caledonia, and which they still love so well.

The old Church was taken down in 1863 to make room for a large stone edifice then begun, but which is as yet unfinished. The sum of $5250 has already been expended on the new Church, and a debt of $2000 incurred. To finish it according to the original plan will require a further expenditure of from two to three thousand dollars. There is a good brick manse with five acres of land attached, and a glebe of 50 acres.*

95. INDIAN LANDS.

The Indian Lands of Glengary is a strip of two or three miles in width, running through the centre of the County, originally reserved for the benefit of the aborigines. Like most of the other Indian Reserves in Canada, this has long since passed into the hands of their white brethren. This congregation was formerly a branch of the charge of Martintown, under Mr. Connell. The Rev. Daniel Clark (89) was inducted as Minister of it, 28th August, 1839. He left the Church in 1844. Since then no Minister has been settled, although it has always been occupied as a Mission Station. During the last three years the Rev. Niel McDougall, an ordained missionary from the Colonial Committee, and now Minister of Eldon (38), has given stated supply. There is an old frame Church here, also a small manse, and 170 acres of

* While these sheets are issuing from the press, I learn that the Rev. Alexander McKay, formerly of Salt Springs, Nova Scotia, has been inducted to the charge of Lochiel. Mr. McKay was eight years in his former charge and comes among us with high testimonials.

glebe, of which 50 acres are cleared. A frame Church has recently been built in the adjoining Township of Roxboro, connected with which there are thirty-one families. In all there are eighty-six families, and with good management they might easily support a Minister.

96. PLANTAGENET.

Scattered over Plantagenet and adjoining Townships there are sixty families in connection with the Church. The charge was originally connected with L'Orignal, under the Rev. Andrew Bell. In 1857 the Rev. Colin Grigor, formerly of Guelph, was inducted. In 1859, owing to ill health, he resigned : on the 9th January, 1864, he died. The Rev. Thomas Scott, the present incumbent, formerly of Matilda, was inducted in January, 1866. This cannot be called a self-supporting congregation—the sum of $200 being all that is promised for stipend. There is a small log Church but neither manse nor glebe.

MISSION STATIONS.

Indian Lands and Dalhousie Mills, already mentioned as vacant charges, have been, in fact, for many years mission stations. Previous to Mr. McDougall's appointment, Mr. William Ferguson, M.A., a Catechist employed by the Presbytery, laboured long and faithfully at Indian Lands. Alexandria has also been occupied. The Free Church party have a good place of worship there, but, it appears, are not sufficiently numerous to support a Minister. If, by uniting all the Presbyterians within a radius of five miles, this desirable end could be accomplished, how much better that the few who refuse to entertain such a proposal should make some sacrifice of cherished predilections than that a large district of country should, year after year, and for many years, be deprived of stated gospel ordinances. This has certainly been the case at Alexandria. Mr. Ferguson has been for the last three years doing duty in Winchester Township, where we have about twenty-five families. East Hawkesbury has also been supplied with religious services by the Presbytery. This Township has four thousand five hundred inhabitants, and there is not a resident Protestant Minister of any denomination in it.

According to last census there were six hundred and thirty-five nominal adherents of the Church of Scotland in the Township.

IX. PRESBYTERY OF PERTH.

The Presbytery of Bathurst was one of the four Presbyteries into which the Province was divided in 1831. It extended from Brockville to Cobourg, embracing the whole region from these points northward to the Ottawa River. There were then only six congregations with Ministers. There are at present, within the same limits, four Presbyteries and thirty-one organized congregations. The Presbytery of Kingston branched off in 1833. The rest continued under the name of the Bathurst Presbytery until 1863, when it was considered advisable to divide it into three; these were named the Perth, Ottawa, and Renfrew Presbyteries. The Perth Presbytery has at present eight charges. The Rev. William Smart, settled at Brockville in 1811, was the first Presbyterian Minister in this part of the country; next to Mr. Henderson of St. Andrew's, he is now the oldest in the Province.

The congregations in this Presbytery were visited in the month of February, in connection with their annual missionary meetings. The attendance was good, and an excellent spirit seemingly prevails. Most of them have more or less efficiently organized missionary associations, and the result is, as may readily be supposed, highly beneficial.

97. BROCKVILLE.

Brockville is one of the most beautifully situated towns in Canada. The romantic scenery in its neighbourhood, its proximity to the Lake of the Thousand Islands, and its facilities for communication by steamers and railways, render it a very desirable place of residence. Its history begins with the present century. In the year 1808 or '9, application was made by the people of Brockville to the London Missionary Society (Independent) for a Minister. Mr. William Smart was then studying in the Missionary Seminary at Gosport, England, with the intention of going to the West Indies. This petition was the means of changing his views, and he was soon after ordained in London to the work of the ministry in Elizabethtown, U. C., and commenced his labours at Brockville in 1811. On his arrival he preached in all the settlements between Cornwall and Kingston, a distance of nearly one hundred miles, and during the absence of Mr. Easton of St. Andrew's Church, Montreal, he visited that city twice a year to administer the sacrament. About that time (1816 to '18), his congregation in Brockville had nearly all left him, and his salary was reduced to about £9 yearly! (He had, however, a small allowance from Government, in addition to what was promised by his people.) In 1816, the foundation stone of a Presbyterian Church was laid in Brockville with masonic honours. It was completed in 1817 at a cost of £1400. In 1840, Mr. Smart, with seventeen others from the United Synod of U. C., was received by the Synod of our Church. Though his name, like that of Dr. Boyd's, is not attached to the protest of the party who seceded in 1844, both of them became identified with the Free Church at that time.

In 1836, the Rev. Peter Colin Campbell came from Scotland as a Missionary, and was also settled in Brockville that year, and preached in the school-house until St. John's Church was finished. He remained until 7th March, 1842, when he was appointed Professor of Classical Literature in Queen's College, Kingston. Having received a presentation to the Parish of Caputh, Mr. Campbell returned to Scotland in 1845. He afterwards became Professor of Greek, and is now Principal of the University of Aberdeen. The Rev. John Cruickshank, formerly of Bytown (113), succeeded Mr. Campbell in Brockville in 1843. He left in 1846 for Niagara (2). The Rev. Thomas Haig was inducted in November, 1848. On the 27th February, 1851, the pastoral tie was dissolved, when he removed to Beauharnois (70). The Rev. John Whyte, now of Arthur (26), was inducted in 1851, and remained four years. After him, in October, 1856, came the Rev. Duncan Morrison, formerly of Beckwith. In 1866 he resigned the charge, having accepted a call from the congregation of Owen Sound (29). The present incumbent, Mr. Daniel McGillivray, a native of Nova Scotia, and an alumnus of Queen's College, was ordained and inducted 16th July, 1867.

St. John's Church is a neat and commodious stone edifice seated for 300. There is a stone manse not very well situated. There is no glebe. The congregation is not large, but in many respects it is a desirable charge.

98. KITLEY.

. This charge lies twenty-four miles north from Brockville on the line of Railway. The Rev. Joseph Anderson of S. Gower preached here for three or four years once a month, and organized a congregation in 1846. In 1849 a stone Church was built. The Rev. David Evans, formerly of Richmond, C. W., was inducted the first stated Minister in 1852. Age and infirmity compelled him to resign the charge in July, 1862. On the 9th of August, 1864, he died, aged 74. Mr. Donald McLean, son of the late Minister of Côte St. George, was ordained to the charge 11th February, 1863. Remaining two and a-half years, he was translated to Middleville. The Rev. William White, formerly of Richmond, the present incumbent, was inducted in September, 1866. A native of Cavan, Ireland, he went to the United States in 1852, was three and a-half years in a charge near Albany, and came to Canada in September, 1856, accredited by the Associate Reformed Presbytery of Saratoga, N. Y. There is an old frame manse, recently repaired and refitted at considerable expense, a stone Church needing repairs badly enough, and a glebe of fifty acres of good land. The congregation is not large, but they appear to be animated by a good spirit.

99. SMITH'S FALLS.

The centre of this charge—a rising village of the same name, pleasantly situated on the Rideau Canal and the Brockville and Ottawa railway—has a population of 1300. The Rev. George Romanes received a call from the inhabitants of this place in December, 1833. He remained until 1846, when he was appointed Professor of Classical Literature in Queen's College. He resigned in 1850, and went to London, England, where he now resides. The Senate of Queen's College, in 1866, conferred on him the degree of LL.D., in recognition of his great learning and eminent services to the Institution.

The Rev. Solomon Mylne, a licentiate of the Presbytery of Belfast, Ireland, came to Canada in 1849, was inducted to this charge in October, 1850, and is still the incumbent. There is a good frame Church, erected in 1836. The congregation own two town lots, a gift from Wm. Simpson, Esq., also a town lot with a small frame house on it, which was purchased with the C. R. grant of £150. There being no manse worthy of the name, the Minister resides on his private property.

100. Perth.

The country around Perth was first settled by emigrants from Lanark and Renfrewshires, in Scotland, in the year 1816. Including some discharged soldiers and half-pay officers, the settlers were for the most part weavers, but ill-adapted for encountering the difficulties incident to the settlement of a new country ; they nevertheless succeeded tolerably well. The Rev. William Bell, sent by Government in the wake of these emigrants, arrived in Perth 24th June, 1817. He found them living in small log huts, the country, at that time, as described by him, was a moral as well as a natural wilderness. Sabbath profanation, drunkenness, and other vices prevailed. He immediately took measures for the erection of a Church, which was soon finished, " with a steeple covered with tin, after the fashion of the country." Although ordained at the request of his first congregation in the Secession Church, Mr. Bell was brought up a member of the Established Church. The proposal, long entertained by himself and his Congregation, to connect themselves with the Church of Scotland, was carried into effect on the 20th October, 1835.

In the meantime, and before this took place, certain parties in Perth desirous of having an " auld Kirk Minister" had sent application to the Rev. Alex. Stuart of Douglass, in Scotland, to select a Minister of the National Church, which resulted in the ordination of the Rev. Thomas C. Wilson, who arrived in 1830. Remaining here till 1844, he returned to Scotland and is now the parish Minister of Dunkeld. Thus were two congregations established, severally known as " the first Presbyterian congregation," and the congregation of " St. Andrew's." Mr. Bell continued to be Minister of the former until his death, which occurred 16th August, 1857, in the 41st year of his ministry and the 78th of his age. He was born in Airdrie, Scotland, educated at Glasgow University, and ordained at Edinburgh in March, 1817. During his long ministry he laboured faithfully and successfully, " enduring hardness like a good soldier of Jesus Christ," and was the means of organizing nearly all the Congregations in this part of the country. Shortly before his death the two congregations in Perth united. The Rev. Wm. Bain, a native of Nairn, Scotland, the present Minister of St. Andrew's Church, came to Canada in 1834, was educated at Queen's College, and was ordained at Perth as successor to Mr. Wilson, 29th October, 1845.

St. Andrew's Church was erected in 1832. It is a large and well finished stone edifice, seated for 600. There is a good stone manse, also a valuable glebe of 200 acres, rented at present for $170, of which the Minister derives the benefit in addition to stipend. The congregation is numerous, well organized, and liberal. They have had a missionary association at work for many years, and with excellent results. As will be seen by reference to the statistical table, their collections for the Schemes are highly creditable.

101. LANARK.

The small village from which this charge derives its name is prettily situated on the river Clyde, about 11 miles from Perth. Many of the first settlers in this part of the country were from Lanarkshire, Scotland ; most of them, however, have passed away, and there are few now who remember to have " pu'ed the gowans fine" at the Cartland Craggs or about the falls of Corra Lynn. Mr. Bell, of Perth, organized the congregation on the 24th June, 1821. In March, 1822, the Sacrament of the Lord's Supper was dispensed to upwards of 40 persons. For some years the congregation enjoyed the services of the Rev. Mr. Gemmell, from Dalry, Scotland.

In 1830 the Rev. William McAlister was sent to them from Scotland. He remained until 1842, when he removed to Sarnia. In 1844 he left the Church and became Free Church Minister of Metis, C. E., where he died some years ago. The Rev. Thomas Fraser next came from the Dutch Reformed Church in the States.

He had previously been, for a short time, the Minister of Niagara (2). He retired from the ministry in June, 1861, on his commutation allowance, and now resides in Montreal. He was succeeded by the Rev. James Wilson, in June, 1862. Mr. Wilson was for three years a Missionary under the Colonial Committee in Nova Scotia, and, having returned to Scotland, was Minister of Maxwelton Chapel, Dumfries, for a short time. He then came to Canada and officiated, for a short time, in St. Joseph Street, Montreal.

The Church at Lanark is a tasteful stone edifice, built in 1860 at a cost of £1200, and is comfortably seated for 378. The Colonial Committee gave £75 stg. towards its erection, and the sum of $400, realized from the sale of glebe lands, was applied to the same purpose. There is a good stone manse and 116 acres of glebe. The congregation is prospering and its affairs are managed systematically.

102. MIDDLEVILLE AND DALHOUSIE.

This charge is situated to the north of Lanark. The Rev. Dr. John Gemmell, a native of Dalry, Ayrshire, and a member of the Associate Synod of Scotland, came to reside in the neighbourhood of Lanark about the year 1821. In 1840, he was received into connection with the Church of Scotland, and ministered in Dalhousie with much acceptance till his death in 1844. The Rev. John Robb, from the Dutch Reformed Church in the States, was settled in 1846. He died in May, 1851. Mr. William C. Clark, now of Ormstown, and for some time assistant to Mr. Fraser, of Lanark, was ordained and inducted to Middleville in October, 1858. In 1859 these two congregations became united under Mr. Clark, who, in April, 1865, was translated to his present charge. In June of that year, the Rev. D. J. McLean, formerly of Kitley, was inducted, and is still Minister.

There is a good log Church at Dalhousie, built in 1863. There is a frame Church at Middleville, where a manse was purchased in 1863, on which there remains a debt of $450. There is no glebe. Mr. McLean officiates in both Churches every Sabbath. There is a Sabbath School in each.

103. Ramsay.

The centre of this charge is the thriving village of Almonte, which has a population of 1500. It is situated on the Mississippi River, which here affords an extensive water power, that has been turned to good account by the erection of large woollen factories. Fabrics of various kinds and in large quantities are made, rivalling in texture the " tweeds " of Galashiels. Though visited occasionally by Mr. Bell, of Perth, and Mr. Buchanan, of Beckwith, there was no settled Minister in this Township until 1834, when the Rev. John Fairbairn, from Scotland, was inducted. He remained till 1842, when he returned to his native land, and having joined the Free Church, became minister of Greenlaw, in Berwickshire, where he now is. The Rev. John McMorine, a native of Sanquhar, Scotland, succeeded in January, 1846. He came to Canada in 1837 as assistant to Mr. Clugston, of Quebec, in which position he remained seven months ; thence he removed for a short time to the Presbytery of Kingston, was afterwards—in 1839—settled at Melbourne, where he remained four years, at the end of which period he resigned the charge and for a year taught the High School in Quebec. The old stone Church built about 1836, was used till lately. A handsome new one has been built in the village of Almonte. It is seated for 400. The Colonial Committee gave £50 to aid in its erection. The manse and glebe, being two miles distant, were lately sold and the proceeds have been invested. The charge is a desirable one. At Carleton Place, a thriving village, also on the Mississippi, there is a branch of the congregation where regular services are conducted .every Sabbath afternoon. The degree of Doctor in Divinity was deservedly conferred on Mr. McMorine by the Senate of Queen's University in 1865.

Since the above was written, the Church has had cause to mourn the decease of this honoured servant of the Lord, who entered upon his rest on the 22nd of May, 1867, in the 68th year of his age.

104. Beckwith.

The first settlers in the Township of Beckwith came from Perthshire, Scotland. In 1818 they petitioned the Associate Synod of Scotland for a Minister, in answer to which was sent to them the Rev. George Buchanan, who commenced his labours in August, 1822, and officiated in Gaelic and English. The next incumbent was the Rev. John Smith, from Cromarty, an ordained Minister of the Church of Scotland, who was inducted 3rd November, 1833, and died here 18th April, 1851. In October of the same year, Mr. Duncan Morrison, a native of Scotland, and an alumnus of Queen's College, was ordained and inducted to the charge. He remained till 1856, when he was translated to Brockville. Mr. McHutchison, a licentiate of the Church of Scotland, succeeded him in 1857. Having resigned the charge, he returned to Scotland in January, 1862. Mr. Walter Ross, a native of Nova Scotia, was ordained here 15th October, 1862, and is still Minister. The property consists of a stone Church, erected in 1832, a stone manse, and a glebe of 100 acres. The congregation, though not very large, is liberal. Mr. Ross officiates in Gaelic and English.

Darling Mission Station.

The Township of this name, lying to the north of Lanark, is occupied by the Presbytery as a Mission Station. It has been supplied by Catechists during several summers, and a very good log Church has been built. There is no resident Protestant Minister in this Township, which has a population of about 1200—three-fourths of whom are nominally Protestants. It is a very rough district of country, though some of the farmers, by industry and perseverance, are in comfortable circumstances.

X. PRESBYTERY OF RENFREW.

This Presbytery met for the first time by appointment of Synod, 5th August, 1863. Its bounds embrace at present six charges lying in the Valley of the Ottawa westward from Arnprior. In the Townships of Ross, Horton, McNab and Westmeath there are some tracts of fine land in a good state of cultivation : in Litchfield there are a few good farms. Of romantic scenery there is no lack, for the banks of the Ottawa and the Madawaska are everywhere picturesque, but in an agricultural point of view, the general aspect of the country is less inviting than other portions of the Province. In some places, indeed, it presents the appearance of hopeless sterility. There is a deal of poor sandy soil. Here, the landscape is disfigured by vast forests of charred leafless pines, there, by tracts of " brûlé " in which the very earth has been burned to a considerable depth. There is abundance of water power, however, and the lumber business is carried on extensively, giving renumerative employment to a large portion of the population. Though Lachlan Taylor describes the Upper Ottawa country, as " the most wretched and hopeless country inhabited by civilized men " on which *he* ever gazed : and the people, as belonging to a class among whom " *even* Methodism cannot hope to win many trophies," the Presbytery of Renfrew regard it more hopefully, and are doing what they can to supply with Christian ordinances, not only the Congregations already organized, but the settlers and " Shantiemen " living more remote amid " the ragged and rocky steeps " that have hitherto been accounted beyond the pale of civilization.

105. PAKENHAM.

The Township of this name was settled in 1823, chiefly by emigrants from Ireland. Sheriff Dickson—the Hugh Miller of Canada—built the first Presbyterian Church in 1838. It was an excellent building and stood till 1846, when it was accidentally destroyed by fire. The present stone Church—a much plainer edifice—was erected on the same site in 1847. The Colonial Committee gave £75, and the Lay Association of Montreal £25, to aid in its erection. The Rev. Alexander Mann, a native of Aberdeen and ordained by that Presbytery in 1840, was inducted in 1841 as Minister of Fitzroy, Tarbolton, Pakenham, McNab and Horton—5 townships! Three Congregations were organized in these, and each promised £30 of annual stipend. At the end of ten years, finding the work too onerous, Mr. Mann restricted his labours to Pakenham, where he has two preaching stations. There is a glebe of 25 acres of good land near the village of Pakenham, but there is no manse.

106. ARNPRIOR.

The first settlement of a Minister in this charge took place in March, 1860, when the Rev. William Johnson, formerly of L'Orignal, was inducted. He was translated to Lindsay (36) in 1861. The Rev. Peter Lindsay, the present Minister, succeeded in 1862. He is a native of Paisley, Scotland, and was ordained at Richmond, C. W., in 1853. The Church at Arnprior is a frame building, erected in 1859 by a Congregation of the United Presbyterians. In 1863 it was transferred to trustees belonging to our Church. There is now but one Presbyterian Congregation in the place. There is no manse nor glebe. On the whole the prospects of the Congregation are encouraging. The village has about 1000 inhabitants: about 50 families of these are included in this charge.

107. McNab and Horton.

The two Congregations composing this charge were originally organized by Mr. Mann, who continued to officiate to them until 1851, when the Rev. George Thompson, from Aberdeen, the present Minister, was inducted. There is a frame Church in McNab Township. A commodious stone Church was erected in the thriving village of Renfrew in 1853. The Colonial Committee aided each with a grant of £50. There is a good manse at Renfrew built in 1866, at a cost of $950, to replace one that was burned down the previous year. There is a large garden but no glebe. This is the most numerous Congregation in the Presbytery.

108. Douglas.

In Douglas and adjoining townships there are nominally 100 families connected with this charge, but they are scattered over an immense area. Mr. Canning, now of Oxford (116), was the first settled Minister, the date of his induction being October, 1859. He officiated at Douglas, Scotch Bush, Lake Dore, and Egansville. He had a small log Church built at Lake Dore. At Egansville services were conducted in a Union Church, and at Douglas, in the Townhall. Mr. John Kerr McMorine was ordained and inducted in June 1864. His labours extended over several Townships, and he had *five* regular preaching stations without a church in either of them to call his own, saving the little log Church at Lake Dore. After two years of earnest and laborious ministrations he resigned the charge, intimating to the Presbytery his intention of connecting himself with the Church of England. Consquently it has been vacant since January last. There is neither glebe nor manse. It is rather a missionary field than a charge.

109. Ross and Westmeath.

As its name implies' this charge extends over two townships : these were for many years Mission stations of the Presbytery, and enjoyed frequent visits from the late Rev. John Lindsay of Litchfield. Mr. Hugh Cameron, a native of Argyleshire, who was ordained and inducted in 1862 is now the Minister. He has no less than five preaching stations! There is a good frame Church at Ross ; towards its erection the Colonial Committee gave £30, and £25 to aid in the building of a similar one at Beachburg, Westmeath. They are both free of debt. The late Mr. Hugh Carmichael bequeathed ten acres of valuable land for a glebe. As yet there is no manse. The congregations are large but scattered.

110. Litchfield.

This charge is composed of three congregations with sessions in each, regular services being supplied to several stations besides. I am quite sure there are no two Ministers in our Church, nor, indeed, in any other Church in Canada, doing an equal amount of work and receiving for the same a smaller amount of remuneration than the Ministers of this and the last named charge. I cannot refrain from bearing testimony to their indomitable zeal and the cheerfulness with which they seem to face difficulties and discouragements which most men, now-a-days, would deem insurmountable. The Rev. John Lindsay was settled at Litchfield in 1854. He died on the 13th July, 1857. Never was pastor more beloved by his people. His name and his many endearing qualities are still fondly cherished by all who knew him—and many knew him, for he was " instant in season and out of season," proclaiming Gospel truth in settlements far remote from his own wide-spread congregation.

The Rev. Joseph Evans, now of Sherbrooke (126), came in 1861 to fill the vacancy of four years, and remained three years. Mr.

Duncan McDonald—the present incumbent, was ordained 11th January, 1865.

There are three frame Churches, all on the banks of the Ottawa. That at Cologne occupies a picturesque site, and was built chiefly by the Messrs Bryson who reside in the neighbourhood: the one at Upper Litchfield is unfinished, and the third, at Lower Litchfield, is superannuated. Near the last are three acres of land, and a log manse which has fallen into disrepair.

XI. PRESBYTERY OF OTTAWA.

This Presbytery, formerly a portion of that of Bathurst, held its first meeting by appointment of Synod on the 1st of July, 1863. It embraces nine congregations widely separated from each other.

111. HUNTLEY.

The Rev. James Sinclair, a native of Ireland, and for some time a Minister in connection with the Associate Reformed Church in the States,·the first Minister of this charge, was inducted in October, 1855. The congregation is small and divided into two branches, each having a small wooden Church. There is neither manse nor glebe.

112. RICHMOND.

The village of Richmond is distant from Ottawa City 20 miles, and is connected with it by a good macadamized road. The place has seen better days. Once it was the capital of this section of country—ahead of Bytown—now it has an air of decayed grandeur. It was named after the Duke of Richmond, a former Governor General of Canada, who died in a small log shanty in the neighbourhood, of hydrophobia, in August, 1819. The Rev. Wm. Bell mentions, incidentally, in his published letters (1824), that this congregation had given a call to the Rev. Andrew Glen, formerly at Terrebonne, as early as 1823, but I am unable to say how long he remained.

The Rev. David Evans, formerly of the United Synod of U. C., was settled here in 1841, and ministered until 1852, when he was

translated to Kitley (98). The Rev. Peter Lindsay, now of
Arnprior, succeeded him in 1853, and remained two years. The
Rev. William White, who followed in 1857, was, after an incumbency
of ten years, translated to Kitley. Mr. Elias Mullan, a licentiate
of the Presbytery, has been lately inducted.

There is a frame rough-cast Church, and a glebe of ten acres, on
which a manse has been erected. It is proposed to build a Church
at Ashton, 8 miles west, where some 20 families have expressed a
desire to co-operate in the support of a Minister. There is a fine
tract of country in this vicinity.

113. OTTAWA.

This City, now the Metropolis of the Dominion, was originally
named Bytown, in honour of its founder, Colonel By, an officer of
the Royal Engineers, sent by the Imperial Government to super-
intend the construction of the Rideau Canal, in 1819. It occupies a
noble site immediately below the Chaudiere Falls. In 1854 it was
created a city, and received its present name. Ottawa was selected
by Her Majesty Queen Victoria, in 1859, as the permanent seat
of Government for the Canadas. The New Parliament Buildings,
commenced then, and now nearly completed, are unrivalled on
the continent: they have already cost about $3,000,000. Two
years ago the Government Offices were removed to this City, and
there has been, in consequence, a large increase to the population,
which now numbers nearly 20,000. By the census of 1861 the
total population was 14,669: of these 8267 were Roman Catholics;
3351 belonged to the Church of England; 1761 were Presbyterians;
of these last, 1192 were set down to the Church of Scotland, and
569 to the Free Church. The statistics of the several Churches at
that time, however, present a somewhat different statement. The
Free Church in 1861 having, by their own shewing, a membership
of 235: the Church of Scotland, 169. In 1866 the Free Church
had two Congregations and 311 Church members. We have at present one Congregation, St Andrew's, with 197 Communicants.

St. Andrew's Church—a plain stone building, erected in 1828, is
now the oldest Protestant place of worship in the City. Its walls
were run up in a few days by a large number of workmen engaged

on the Canal, and temporarily out of employment. To meet the
wants of a gradually increasing Congregation, it was enlarged in
1854. The first Minister of the charge was the Rev. John Cruickshank, from the Presbytery of Fordyce, Banffshire, whose call bears
date, 17th September, 1829. He was inducted to the charge on
the first Sabbath of March, 1830, by the Rev. John Machar of
Kingston; the entire population of the town being then only 1809.
Mr. C. resigned in 1843 when he removed to Brockville (97).
The Rev. Alex. McKid followed in 1844 and remained two years
(15). On the 14th January, 1847, the Rev. William Durie—
formerly a Minister of the Relief Church, and who had been received
into the Church of Scotland—was inducted. After a brief incumbency of eight months, he died, on the 12th of September. The
Rev. Alex. Spence, the present Minister, received the appointment
to this charge through the Colonial Committee, and was inducted
27th July, 1848. He is a native of Aberdeenshire, and was
ordained, 22nd February, 1841, by the Presbytery of Aberdour,
as the first Presbyterian Minister of St. Vincent, West Indies,
where he remained 6½ years. The University of Queen's College
conferred upon him the degree of Doctor in Divinity in 1864.
Having received the leave of Synod to retire from the active duties
of the Ministry on his commutation allowance, Dr. Spence resigned
the charge on the 24th of October last. The Rev. Daniel Gordon
lately of Truro, Nova Scotia, a native of that Province, and who
was educated in Scotland, is now the Minister elect of this large
and important Congregation.

There is a good manse, and 178 acres of glebe land which has
recently become valuable. The Congregation is wealthy and influential. It is proposed to form a second Congregation in the
Lower Town, for which, it is believed, there is ample room.

114. CHELSEA.

The village of Chelsea, on the Gatineau, nine miles from Ottawa, is
inhabited chiefly by workmen connected with Messrs. Gilmour & Co's
extensive saw mills. The Church and Manse were built, and are
still owned by that firm, who also, with commendable liberality,
contribute $200 yearly to the Minister's salary. Having been for

several summers supplied by Missionary Students, Mr. Hugh
J. Borthwick was ordained as the first pastor in February, 1862.
He resigned in 1864. The Rev. James Sciveright, formerly of
Ormstown (76), was inducted in March, 1865. He is a native of
Aberdeen, where he commenced his theological course. He came
to Canada in 1854 and completed his curriculum of study at Queen's
College. At Ironsides, three miles nearer Ottawa, a Congregation has
recently been organized by Mr. Sciveright and joined to the charge.
Extensive works for smelting iron have been constructed there, and
a large influx of population is expected.

115. BUCKINGHAM AND CUMBERLAND.

This charge is bisected by the Ottawa river. Buckingham, on the
North side, and distant from the river about three miles, is a thriving
village of 1500 inhabitants, owing its prosperity mainly to extensive saw mills on the Rivière aux Lièvres.

Cumberland is a Township on the right bank of the Ottawa. At the
former place there is a good frame Church, and a large Congregation. There is a subtantial stone Church occupying a well selected
site at Cumberland, where are also a good manse and a glebe of 200
acres, purchased with aid of the Clergy Reserve's grant of £150,
and on which there is a debt of $600. The Rev. George Bell,
now of Clifton (3), was ordained and inducted to Cumberland,
May 30th, 1844. He remained a little over four years. The
Rev. David Shanks, formerly of Valcartier, and now of the same
place (122), was inducted in 1851 and remained three years. The
Rev. Peter Lindsay, now of Arnprior (106), followed in 1855, and
remained seven years. Mr. James C. Smith, the present Minister,
was ordained and inducted to the charge, 21st July, 1864. Services
are conducted in each Congregation every Sabbath. The crossing
of the river, at all times inconvenient, is, at certain seasons, not
unattended with danger. In other respects the charge is a very
desirable one and is well organized.

116. OXFORD.

This is a country charge, in two sections, Oxford, and Bishop's
Mills, about seven miles apart. Oxford is on the line of railway

G

between Prescott and Ottawa, 18 miles from the St Lawrence, and 37 from Ottawa City. Mr. Anderson of South Gower officiated here once a month for a number of years; but there was no settled Minister prior to the induction of Mr. Evans, now of Sherbrooke (126), who was ordained to the charge, 3rd November, 1858. Having remained three years, he was translated to Litchfield. The Rev. William T. Canning, formerly of Douglas, followed in 1862, and is still Minister. Mr. C. is a native of Ireland, and originally a Minister of the Synod of Ulster, who, previous to his reception by the Synod had officiated in the United States for a period of five years. At Oxford there is a small stone Church, a log Manse, and five acres of Glebe. A good frame Church was erected at Bishop's Mills in 1865.

117. South Gower and Mountain.

The Church at Heckston, in the Township of South Gower, is distant about seven miles from the railway station of Oxford. The Rev. Joseph Anderson, a native of the north of Ireland, and who was educated at Glasgow, commenced his ministerial labours in 1834, preaching in Mountain, Oxford, Kitley, Wilfred, Osgoode, and other Townships. He was one of the Ministers of the United Synod of U. C. who joined the Church in 1840, and continued to officiate in this charge with much acceptance until July, 1864, when advancing years and failing health compelled him to retire from the stated duties of the Ministry. He still preaches, however, frequently. There is a stone Church at Mountain; the glebe of ten acres was purchased with the Clergy Reserve grant of £150. There is no Manse. The Church at Heckston is an old, weather-beaten, shabby building. The charge, comprising 80 families, is at present vacant.

118. Spencerville.

This charge derives its name from the village, so called, on the line of railway, nine miles from Prescott. It includes a branch at Mains-ville, eight miles to the east of it, where an excellent stone Church has recently been erected. There is no glebe. A manse, however, has been purchased at Spencerville, though not yet fully paid for. At this place the Congregation meanwhile worship in the Town Hall, a large and well-finished building, which has been kindly placed at their disposal. Dr. Boyd of Prescott, who came to Canada in 1821, originated both of these Congregations. He was one of the United Synod Ministers who joined the Church in 1840; but he seceded in 1844. Some time afterwards, the Presbytery having been petitioned for supply, Mr. Peter Thompson, an ordained Missionary, was sent for a short period. More recently Mr. Morrison, lately of Brockville, paid them frequent visits. The present Minister, Mr. James B. Mullan, who had laboured for three summers as a Catechist, was ordained and inducted to the charge 23rd July, 1862. He has succeeded in forming two large Congregations. His Sabbath schools are well attended, and systematic management prevails.

119. L'Orignal and Hawkesbury.

The village of L'Orignal is pleasantly situated on the right bank of the river Ottawa, about half way between Ottawa city and St. Anne's. Hawkesbury, ten miles distant, was united with it in 1860. The Church at L'Orignal dates from 1832. On the 12th of July in that year, the Rev. John McLaurin, a native of Breadalbane, Scotland, and formerly Minister of Lochiel (94), was inducted to Hawkesbury. He taught the District school, and officiated also at L'Orignal, and died there in the spring of 1833. Mr. Colin Grigor was ordained and inducted to the charge of L'Orignal and Plantagenet, 5th June, 1844. He was translated to Guelph in 1848; thence, in 1857, he removed to Plantagenet. In 1859 he received the leave of Synod to retire on his commutation allowance. He died at Plantagenet, 9th January, 1864. The Rev. Andrew Bell, formerly of Dundas and Ancaster, was inducted to the charge of L'Orignal and Plantagenet in October, 1852. He was a man of varied attainments, an accomplished scholar, and eminent as a geologist. He was the eldest son of the late William Bell, of Perth, and was born in London, England. When a student in Glasgow he wrote a series of interesting letters for the information of intending emigrants, which were published along with his father's letters in 1824, and which received the highest encomiums from the contemporary press. He was clerk of Synod from the year 1844 till the time of his death, which took place at L'Orignal on the 27th of September, 1856. His successor in this charge was the Rev. William Johnson, formerly of Saltfleet and Binbrooke, who was translated to Arnprior in 1860, and is now on the list of retired Ministers. In August of that year, L'Orignal and Hawkesbury were united under the Presbytery of Glengary, and the present Minister, the Rev. George D. Ferguson, formerly of Three Rivers, was inducted in September following. The charge was subsequently transferred to the Presbytery of Ottawa. It embraces at present 90 families. Steps have been taken for the erection of a new Church at Hawkesbury.

XII. PRESBYTERY OF QUEBEC.

This Presbytery, formed at the first meeting of Synod in 1831, comprehended the whole of the Congregations in Lower Canada. At that time, indeed, there were but eight charges in the Lower Province having Ministers over them, including the cities of Montreal and Quebec—two in each. In 1841, there were 18 Ministers on the roll. The following year, the Presbytery of Montreal was constituted, leaving that of Quebec with only four Ministers, Messrs. Cook, Clugston, McMorine and Geggie. In 1846, the members of this Presbytery were added to the roll of that of Montreal, from which time it ceased to have a separate existence until 1856, when it was revived. In 1866, there were within its bounds, seven charges with Ministers, and a number of Mission stations.

121. QUEBEC.

This city was for many years the capital of Canada, and is still the chief sea-port and stronghold of military power in British North America. It occupies a magnificent site at the confluence of the St. Lawrence and St. Charles Rivers. In 1861, its population was 51,109, of whom 41,477 were Roman Catholics; 5,740 belonged to the Church of England; 1,258 to the Church of Scotland; 859 to the Free Church; over 1,000 were Methodists; the remainder being of different denominations. The Protestant population has not increased since then; on the contrary, it is said to be at least one thousand less now than it was even two years ago. The total population, at present, is estimated to be about 65,000, of whom not more than 8000 are Protestants.

The Rev. George Henry, a military chaplain at the time of the Conquest, was the first Presbyterian Minister who officiated in the Province. His stated ministry at Quebec, commenced so far back as the year 1765, only six years after the cession of the country to the Government of Great Britain. He presided in public worship for the last time, June 30th, 1793. He died on the 6th of July, 1795, aged 86 years. In the Quebec *Gazette*, along with the announcement of his death, occurs the following estimate of his worth :—" To the character of an able divine, he united that benevolence of heart and practical goodness which made his life a constant example of the virtues he recommended to others, and rendered him both an useful teacher of Christianity, and an ornament to society." From the year 1786 to 1789, he was relieved of half his public duty, and, from the latter date till the time of his death, of his whole duty by the Rev. Alexander Spark, then tutor in the family of Col. Caldwell, at Belmont, near the city. Mr. Spark came to Quebec in 1780, under an engagement for three years, as assistant teacher in an academy, having completed which he returned to Scotland and made application " for leave to preach the Gospel." His collegiate course had been previously completed at Aberdeen. He was accordingly licensed and ordained to the ministry by the Presbytery of Ellon, and seems to have returned to Quebec immediately thereafter. It is not certain when or how he was appointed to the charge, but having received a call signed by a number of heads of families—there being no Presbytery to induct him—" he entered on his official duties with all the formality that circumstances would permit." Until the year 1807, the Congregation met for worship in a large room in the Jesuit's barracks, which had been assigned by the Governor for their use as far back as 1767. Thereafter, war with the United States becoming imminent, and this apartment being required for military purposes, the Congregation met in the lower room of the Court House. On the 30th November, 1808, His Excellency, Sir J. H. Craig, signed letters patent making over a part of the ground on which St. Andrew's Church now stands to certain trustees.

Mr. Spark received the degree of Doctor in Divinity from his *Alma Mater*—the University of Aberdeen—in the spring of 1804. The following inscription, copied from a tablet on the wall of the Church, supplies additional particulars of Dr. Spark's incumbency: " Sacred to the memory of Alexander Spark, D.D., first Minister of this Church. He was born at Marykirk, Scotland, 7th of January, 1762; ordained pastor of the Scotch Congregation, Quebec, 1784: opened this Church for Divine Service 30th November, 1810, and died 7th March, 1819. This monument is erected by his surviving friends and members of his congregation in token of their high appreciation of his private worth, his public virtues, and his conscientious dicharge of the duties of his office."

He was a man of considerable learning and inclined to literature. His death was sudden. Having preached on Sabbath forenoon from the text (Gen. xlv. 24) " See that ye fall not out by the way,"—in which, it was thought, there appeared to be a presentiment of the separation from his flock that was so soon to follow— he attended a funeral, and, on his way to Church in the afternoon, he was seized with a fit of apoplexy, and almost instantly expired.

It is to be regretted that so little has been made public respecting Dr. Spark's immediate successor, Dr. Harkness, who seems to have possessed great force of character. One who knew him intimately describes him as " a bold, fearless man, generous and kind-hearted in the extreme."

Another monumental tablet within the Church reads thus, "Sacred to the memory of the Rev. James Harkness, D.D., late Minister of this Church. He was born in the parish of Sanquhar, Scotland, called to the St. Andrew's Church in Quebec, and ordained by the Presbytery of Ayr on the 7th of March, 1820. He died on the 25th February, 1835, in the 46th year of his age, and 15th of his Ministry. This monument is erected by his congregation in token of their respect for his character, gratitude for his services and instructions as their Minister, and for his great exertions to promote the interests of the Church of Scotland in Canada."

The Rev. John Cook, D.D.,—the present Minister, is also a native of Sanquhar, Dumfriesshire. He was educated at the University of Edinburgh, and was for three years assistant to the late Mr. Wilson of Cardross. Having received ordination from the

Presbytery of Dunbarton in 1835, he arrived in Quebec early in 1836. In 1838 he received the Degree of Doctor in Divinity from the University of Glasgow. Dr. Cook's services to the Church at large have been numerous and valuable. During the session of 1858 and 1859 he filled, with distinguished ability, the office of Principal and Professor of Divinity in Queen's College, and, since its opening in 1862, has occupied a similar position in Morrin College, Quebec.

St. Andrew's Church having undergone enlargement and repairs is now seated for about 1000. Adjoining it there is an excellent manse, and also on the Church property a commodious school house in which the classes are conducted by Mr. McQuarrie, a licentiate of the Church, who is also superintendent of the Sabbath School.

St. John's Congregation, in Quebec, was first formed in the year 1800. It was originally "Independent" in its constitution, but was for several years supplied by a Minister from the United States, and for their use a Church was erected in 1816. In 1829 this Congregation resolved to connect themselves with the Church of Scotland. Application having been made to the Glasgow Colonial Society, the Rev. John Clugston, a licentiate of the Presbytery of Glasgow, and who was ordained by the Presbytery of Forfar, was appointed to the charge, and commenced his public labours in October, 1830. He continued to be their Minister until 1844, when he resigned, and returned to Scotland, where, it is said, he connected himself with the Free Church. At this time also the Congregation seceded, and, so far as appears, retained possession of the Church property.

121. POINT LEVI.

Point Levi is a village on the south side of the St. Lawrence, opposite Quebec. Since having become the terminus of the Grand Trunk Railway it has rapidly increased in population ; the English speaking inhabitants, however, are few in number. The members of the Church residing here were formerly connected with St. Andrew's Congregation, Quebec ; and here Dr. Cook held occasional services. The Rev. Duncan Anderson, a native of the Parish of Monymusk, Aberdeenshire, was ordained and inducted to the charge in Decem-

ber, 1854. Then, there was neither Church nor manse, and but a
small number of adherents. A grant of 5½ acres of land on the
height, overlooking the river, and whence there is one of the finest
views in Canada, was given by government a number of years ago
for Church purposes. On this site has been erected a tasteful and
commodious Church, at a cost of £800, towards which the Colonial
Committee contributed £100 sterling. An excellent manse has
also been built, and there is now no debt on the property. Their
progress has been very satisfactory. The Congregation is yet small,
numbering only thirty-five families.

122. VALCARTIER.

This is a most interesting little Congregation. The small village
of that name, near to which are the Church and Manse, is distant,
in a northerly direction, eighteen miles from Quebec. Forty years
ago certain parties having received a large grant of land induced
a few hardy Scotchmen from Roxboroshire to pass beyond the lines
of French settlement, and to carve out for themselves homes and
farms here at the foot of the Laurentian Hills. Roman Catholic
French to the east of them, to the west of them, in front of them,
the everlasting hills to the north of them, the little Colony was in a
manner shut out from the world. For six years they laboured on
clearing their farms without scarcely ever seeing a Minister of
the gospel. In 1833 the Rev. David Brown, from Sanquhar, was
sent to them, who remained four years. After he left, Mr. Neill,
now of Seymour, visited them for a short time. In 1841 the Rev.
James Geggie was inducted and remained till the division of 1844,
when he left the Church. The Rev. David Shanks, formerly of St.
Eustache, succeeded in May, 1847, and is still Minister. A native
of Lanarkshire, he came to Canada in 1832, served as a Missionary for one year in Montreal, was fourteen years Minister at
St. Eustache in connection with the U. P. Church, and was
received by the Synod in the year 1841. The log Church built
during Mr. Brown's ministry, was in 1859 supplanted by a
stone edifice, erected on a beautiful site and finished with much
taste. There are very few country Churches to compare with it.
It cost $2000. The Colonial Committee gave £50 stg. There is

a wooden manse, built after the manner of the French Canadian houses, and four acres of land attached. The congregation is indebted to the Manse and Glebe Fund for a grant of £150.

123. Leeds and Inverness.

Mr. Alexander Buchan, now Minister of Stirling, Ont., a licentiate of Dalkeith, was ordained to the charge of Leeds and St. Sylvestre in 1842. He returned to Scotland in 1844 (64). The Rev. Simon C. Fraser from the Greenock Auxiliary Society also officiated for a short time. The Rev. Alex. Forbes, the present Minister, formerly of Dalhousie, New Brunswick, was inducted in January, 1859. Mr. Forbes was sent to New Brunswick as a Missionary by the Colonial Committee in 1854. He was licensed by the Presbytery of Garioch, Aberdeenshire, in 1839. A small frame Church was erected at Inverness in 1840. The charge consists of only sixteen families, who are quite unable to support a Minister. No manse, no glebe, " no nothing !" The Free Church claim one hundred and four families, and one hundred and eighty-one communicants. Would it not be better for these sixteen families to cast in their lot with the others, and for Mr. Forbes to find a more extensive sphere of usefulness ? The case demands the consideration of the Church Courts.

124. Three Rivers.

The City of Three Rivers, so called from the three mouths of the St. Maurice River, has a population of about 6000, of whom 5500 are Roman Catholic : 230 belong to the Church of England ; 150 to the Church of Scotland : 65 are Methodists. It is on the north side of the St. Lawrence, about equi-distant, 90 miles, from Montreal and Quebec. It is noted for its iron works which have been in operation for about 100 years. The lumber business on the St. Maurice and its tributaries is also very extensive. The Rev. James Thom, now of Woolwich (24), was the first Minister of our Church settled here in 1844. He remained ten years, and was succeded by Mr. George D. Ferguson, now of L'Orignal (119), who was ordained to the charge in May, 1855, and remained five years. Through his instrumentality the Church was built. It is a well finished stone edifice and cost $6800. There is a debt of about $3000 upon it. There is neither manse nor glebe. The Rev. Robert G. McLaren, a native of Caithness, was inducted to the charge, 14th of August, 1862. The number of families in the Congregation is only 27.

125. MELBOURNE.

This is rather a group of Congregations than a charge properly so called, there being four stations where services are regularly conducted, viz:—Melbourne village, Brompton Gore, Windsor, and Oak Hill, numbering together 120 families and 90 Communicants. There are good Churches at each of these places. There is a manse and a glebe of 8½ acres near the village of Melbourne, which is beautifully situated on the St. Francis River. The surrounding country is undulating, picturesque and very healthy. Before St. Andrew's Church was erected, the Congregation worshipped in an old wooden edifice which for many years had served all the Protestant denominations in the neighbourhood.

The Rev. Thomas McPherson, now of Lancaster (91), officiated here for a short time in 1836, and in the autumn of that year accepted a call to Beechridge. The Rev. John McMorine (103) was inducted in 1839 and remained four years. The Rev. Robert McFarlane, a Minister of the Church of Scotland, was inducted November, 1852, and remained little more than a year, when he ceased to be a Minister of the Church. The Rev. Thomas Morrison, a missionary from the Colonial Committee, came in March, 1853. Remaining not quite two years he returned to Scotland. Mr. Sciveright, now of Chelsea (114), was ordained in 1857, and was largely instrumental in furthering the interests of the Congregation, and the Mission cause generally, in the Eastern Townships. After a ministry of five years he was translated to Ormstown (76). In October 1862, the Rev. T. G. Smith, formerly Minister of Kintyre, Illinois, was inducted to Melbourne. He resigned in December, 1866, having accepted a call from Fond du Lac, Wisconsin. There is ample material for the formation of two good self-sustaining congregations. The field of labour is too extensive for one Minister longer to do justice to the work.

Since the above was written, the Rev. James McCaul, formerly of Roslin and Thurlow, has been inducted to the charge.

126. SHERBROOKE.

The town of this name is the capital of the Eastern Townships, with a population of 5000, and rapidly increasing. It is finely situated at the confluence of the Rivers St. Francis and Magog, which furnish an unlimited amount of water power. Mr. Charles I. Cameron, a native of Lochiel, Scotland, and a graduate of Queen's College, who, having been licensed and ordained in Scotland, went to India in 1865, and is now one of the Church of Scotland's Missionaries at Bombay, was sent here as a catechist in the fall of 1865, and during eleven months of the most self-denying labours so far advanced the mission work that the adherents at Sherbrooke and Brampton Falls were soon organized into a charge. The Rev. Joseph Evans, formerly of Litchfield, was inducted 27th October, 1864. At that time there was neither Church, manse, nor property of any kind. Soon after his settlement a purchase was made of a building then used as a theatre, and which was formerly a Congregational Church. This was remodelled and fitted up to accommodate comfortably 300 persons. Close to the Church a commodious and a tasteful manse has just been completed. The expense attending the whole, including the land (1 acre), the Church, and manse, has been about $4000. The people of the town, of all denominations, contributed liberally, thus testifying their approval of the good work begun, and their satisfaction on seeing the old Church rescued from desecration. A debt of $1100 has been incurred in carrying out these improvements, which it were a graceful thing that the friends of the Church should liquidate. Up to the close of 1866 Mr. Evans has been in part supported by the Eastern Townships Mission Fund. Henceforth his Congregation have resolved to rely entirely on their own resources ; though respectable in point of numbers, the Congregation is widely scattered, and by no means wealthy.

·   EASTERN TOWNSHIPS MISSION.

There is a large mission field in the Eastern Townships, which includes that part of Canada East lying on the South side of the

St. Lawrence, bounded by the Chambly River on the West, the State of Maine on the South, and extending easterly to the Chaudière River.

Irrespective of that part of it which borders on the St. Lawrence, and which is exclusively French, this interesting District includes 14 or 15 counties, each county averaging eight or nine Townships. The total population is about 160,000, of whom about 70,000 are English-speaking. In all this section of country we have only two organized Congregations, viz, Sherbrooke, and Melbourne : without trenching on ground already occupied by other Churches there is ample room, and, indeed, great need for at least three or four additional Ministers of our Church. There are a great many scattered over this wide section of country who, though nominally Protestants, are connected with no Church. And, yet, it is a country highly favoured by nature, beautiful for situation, rich in agricultural and mineral resources, irrigated by numerous noble rivers, abounding in water power, and with a climate agreeable and salubrious. Gold is found on the Chaudière and its tributaries. At Acton, and elsewhere, copper mines have been worked to advantage for many years. Slate of the finest quality—rivalling the Welsh, is found near Melbourne. The most extensive saw mills in the Province are to be found at Brompton Falls ; woollen factories on a large scale at Sherbrooke : vast tracts of swampy lands, long considered useless, through the enterprize and inventive genius of Mr. Hodges, have been invested with a value almost fabulous, and are becoming highly important sources of wealth and industry by the manufacture of peat fuel, which is destined to supply the place of coal, almost the only economic mineral denied to Canada. But the latest discovery of all, and certainly not the least surprising, as tending to shew that nothing made by the Creator is without its use, is the fact that paper of excellent quality may be produced from Poplar wood, the meanest, and, hitherto, the most useless of all woods. At Windsor a large manufactory has been established, which it is estimated will turn out a thousand tons of paper yearly, chiefly from Poplar pulp !

STATISTICS

OF THE

CHURCH OF SCOTLAND IN CANADA

FOR THE YEAR 1866.

Statistics of the Church of Scotland in Canada for the Year 1866.

No.	Names of Charges.	Names of Ministers.	Ministers where educated.	Date of Ordination.	SALARIES. Temp. Board.	People promise.	Additional.	Total.	Arrears.	Families.	Communicants.	Scholars.	Teachers.	Bible Classes.	Prayer Meet'gs.
	NIAGARA.				$	$	$	$	$						
1	Dundas	James Herald	Aberdeen	1857	150	650	...	800	...	70	106	45	6	...	...
2	Niagara	Charles Campbell	Edin. and St. And.	...	150	400	25	575	...	45	100	60	6	...	W
3	Clifton	George Bell, B.A.	Queen's College	30 May, 1844	450	400	...	850	...	48	54	110	16	1	
4	Saltfleet and Binbrooke	Hugh Niven	Edinburgh	17 Feb., 1857	150	...	...	150	...						
					900	1450	25	2375	899 99	163	260	215	27	2	1
	HAMILTON.														
5	Hamilton	Robert Burnet	Edin. and Aber.	1853	450	1009	...	1450	180	266	250	245	23	1	W
6	Waterdown and Nelson	Vacant	...	...	...	...	...	...	...	60	100	...	...		
7	Hornby and Trafalgar	William Stewart	Glasgow	...	150	400	50	530	...	36	64	15	3		M
8	Nimroe	Martin W. Livingstone	Glas Un. and U.P. Hall	...	150	400	50	600	...	45	70	30	3		
9	Brantford	Vacant	...	...	...	...	...	...	...	20	22				
					750	1809	50	2600	180	417	506	290	29	1	2
	LONDON.														
10	London	Francis Nicol	Glasgow	...	150	400	50	600	...	55	80	55	8	1	W
11	Glencoe	Vacant	...	...	...	...	...	...	...	65					M
12	Chatham	John Rannie, M.A.	Aberdeen	1857	150	600	50	800	...	60	130	16	4	1	
13	North Easthope	William Bell, M.A.	Belfast	May, 1848	450	230	...	649	...	42	80	49	4		
14	Stratford	James George, D.D.	Glasgow	1831	450	470	...	920	...	102	160	40	6		
15	Goderich	Alex. McKid	Edinburgh	1842	450	Re-ir ned in May, 1866				92	80	30	4		
16	Bayfield	Hamilton Gibson	Glasgow	1850	450	300	...	750	...	60	70	60	4	1	

STATISTICS OF THE CHURCH OF SCOTLAND IN CANADA FOR THE YEAR 1866.—*Continued.*

No.	CONTRIBUTIONS								Churches when built.	Churches seated for.	PROPERTY		
	Ordinary Sabbath Collections.	Synod's Home Mission.	Widow's and Orphan's.	Bursary.	French Mission.	Other purposes.	Total Contributions.	Report.			Manses.	Glebes.	Debt on Property.
1	150 00					28 00	374 00		Stone 1832	200	Brick	2 acres	100 00
2	140 00	8 00	20 00			78 00	671 00		Brick 1831	450	Brick	No Glebe	No.
3	121 00	50 00	20 00	4 00		189 00	731 00	Yes.	Brick 1856	450	No...	No Glebe	200 00
4									2 Frame.........	300	Frame	5 acres	No.
	411 00	58 00	40 00	4 00		295 00	1776 00	1	5	1400	3	7 acres.	300 00
5	347 77	28 45	52 00			400 00	1712 75	Yes.	Stone 1857	900	Stone	No...	30,000 00
6		10 00					Not stated		2 Frame 1832–53	400	Frame	3 acres	No.
7	40 00		12 00				491 00		3 Frame 1848	350	Frame	1 acre	No.
8	23 30	16 00				5 50			Brick 1849	250	Brick	2 acres	2000 00
9	150 00								Frame	220	No...		No.
	561 07	54 45	64 00		10 00	405 50	2203 75		8	2120	4	13 acres.	32,000 00
10	199 60		12 00			497 84	1159 44	Yes.	Stone 1860	425	No...	No...	3000 00
11		15 00	12 00	7 00		154 00	561 00		Brick 1862	300	No...	No...	No.
12	161 00	30 00	4 00			22 80	313 80		Brick 1841	300	Frame	10 acres.	No.
13	20 00	14 00				148 52	755 70		Brick 1851	200	No...	No...	No.
14	111 18	6 00	18 50			49 00	152 50		Frame 1851	220	Small Brick...	No...	No.
15	70 00		12 00			280 00	467 00		Frame 1846	280	No...	No...	No.
16	25 00								Brick 1862	240	No...	No...	No.

STATISTICS OF THE CHURCH OF SCOTLAND IN CANADA FOR THE YEAR 1866.—*Continued.*

No.	Names of Charges.	Names of Ministers.	Ministers where educated.	Date of Ordination.	Temp. Board.	People pro. misc.	Additional.	Total.	Arrears.	Families.	Communicants.	Scholars.	Teachers.	Bible Classes.	Prayer Meetings.
	LONDON.—*Continued.*				$	$	$	$	$						
17	Wawanosh	William Darr	Belfast	15 June, 1847	450	50	...	500	...	30	25	...	...	...	...
18	Williams	Vacant	...	...	...	...	...	...	...	100	50	...	...	...	...
19	Dorchester	James Gordon, M.A.	Queen's College	26 Sept., 1854	400	240	...	640	...	40	60	36	4	...	...
20	Westminster	James McEwen, M.A.	Queen's College	12 Oct., 1854	400	200	...	600	...	44	110	...	...	d	d
21	Southwold	Ewan McAulay	Queen's College	Oct., 1866	150	400	...	550	...	35	40	recently	recently	...	...
22	Woolstock and Norwich	Vacant	...	...	...	...	...	...	...	20	...	...	...	...	...
					3500	2890	100	6040	n. st'd	723	885	277	34	3	2
	GUELPH.														
23	Guelph	John Hogg	Glas. Un. and U. P. Hall	13 Oct., 1844	150	600	50	800	...	118	218	122	14	1	W
24	Woolwich	James Thom	Glasgow	...	450	130	...	580	...	40	56	100	11	1	...
25	Fergus	George Macdonnell	...	1850	450	400	...	850	...	125	185	130	10	1	W
26	Arthur	John Whyte	Edinburgh	...	450	200	...	650	...	40	76	70	3	1	...
27	Mount Forest	Vacant	...	...	...	...	...	...	...	40	...	40	4	1	...
28	Priceville	Vacant	...	...	...	...	...	...	...	140	...	...	...	...	...
29	Owen Sound	Vacant	...	...	...	...	...	...	...	60	...	...	...	...	...
30	Leith and Johnson	Alex. Hunter, B.A.	Queen's College	27 Oct., 1854	150	400	50	600	...	80	110	74	10	1	W
31	Kilcurtine	Alex. Dawson, B.A.	Queen's College	23 Sept., 1863	150	400	...	550	...	100	75	60	12	1	W
32	Paisley	Matthew W. McLean	Glas. Q. Col. and Princeton	15 Aug., 1866	150	400	50	600	...	60	30	30	13	1	W
33	Galt	Robert Campbell, M.A.	Queen's College	10 April 1862	150	600	50	800	...	138	234	130	15	1	W
					2100	3130	200	5430	n. st'd	941	984	736	82	9	6

STATISTICS OF THE CHURCH OF SCOTLAND IN CANADA FOR THE YEAR 1866.—*Continued.*

No.	Ordinary Sabbath Collections.	Synod's Home Mission.	Widow's and Orphans.	Bursary.	French Mission.	Other purposes.	Total Contributions.	Reports.	Churches when built.	Churches seated for.	Manses.	Glebes.	Debt on Property.
	$	$	$	$	$	$	$						
17		8 00	5 00	7 00	10 00	20 00	83 00		Frame 1862	200	No.	10 acres swamp	No.
18	22 00						612 00		Frame 1810	220	Brick	5 acres	No.
19	53 00					350 00	495 00		Frame 1856	200	Building	10 acres	No.
20						242 00			Brick 1856	250	No.	No.	No.
21									Brick 1865	300	Frame	10 acres	1200 00
22									2 Frame	450	No.	1 acre (valuable)	500 00
	670 78	145 00	75 50	7 00	10 00	1764 16	4599 44	1	14	3585	4	46 acres.	4700 00
23	268 37		25 00	17 68	15 16	68 79	1045 00		Stone 1858	350	Stone	8 acres and 42 in Lots.	4100 00
24	31 20	10 00	10 00	15 20	2 00	112 00	295 20	Yes.	Frame 1838	200	Stone	3½ acres	No.
25	170 06	70 00	24 00			293 68	972 94		Stone 1862	400	Stone	No.	2000 00
26	18 00	10 00	6 00				134 00		Brick 1854	336	No.	2 acres Church site.	200 00
27									Frame 1859	200	No.	5½ acres	250 00
28									Frame 1865	160	No.	4 acres	No.
29				10 00					Frame 1861	200	No.	No.	No.
30	78 00		7 00	7 00		100 00	638 00		2 Brick and Frame ...1865	430	No.	2 acres	554 00
31	60 00	5 00					479 00		Frame 1859	200	No.	No.	200 00
32	Newly settled								Frame 1859	180	No.	12 acres.	No.
33	200 03		20 00	15 00	15 00	446 00	1346 00	Yes.	Frame 1834	600	Stone	7½ acres	No.
	795 63	95 00	92 00	54 88	32 16	1020 47	4910 14	2	12	3256	4	41¾ acres.	7600 00

H

Statistics of the Church of Scotland in Canada for the Year 1866.—Continued.

No.	Names of Charges	Names of Ministers	Ministers where educated	Date of Ordination	SALARIES. Temp. Board	People promise	Additional	Total	Arrears	Families	Communicants	Scholars	Teachers	Bible Classes	Prayer Meetings
	TORONTO.				$	$	$	$	$						
34	Port Hope	David Camelon	Queen's College	12 Dec., 1859	150	450	30	630		71	158	99	7	2	
35	Peterboro'	D. J. Macdonnell, B.D.	Q. Col. Glas. Ed. and Berlin	14 June, 1866	150	600	50	800		50	66	recently	recently	1	
36	Lindsay	J. B. Muir, B.A.	Edin. and Glas.	3 April, 1863	150	400	50	600		60	36	120	8	1	
37	Brock	Vacant			180					90	180	75	7	1	
38	Eldon	John MacMurchy	Glas. and Edin.	19 Jan., 1842	450	300		750		100	140	35	2	1	
39	Thorah	David Watson, M.A.	Queen's College	30 Aug., 1853	450	400		850		120	170	105	4	1	W
40	Georgina	John Gordon, B.A.	Queen's College	21 Feb., 1865	150	400		550		50	49	35	2	1	
41	Uxbridge	William Cleland	Belfast	1850	400	272		672		75	170	20	3	1	W
42	Scarboro'	James Bain			400	500		900		126	270	30	3	1	
43	Markham	John Campbell, M.A.	Cobourg and Auburn, U.S.	1854	150	368	50	568		81	96	80	3	1	
44	Pickering	Walter R. Ross, M.A.	Aberdeen	1858	150	450		600		66	110	30	3	1	
45	Whitby	Kenneth MacLennan, B.A.	Queen's College	8 Mar., 1853	450	600		1050		60	65	110	14	1	
46	Bowmanville	John H. MacKerras, M.A.	Queen's College	20 Sept., 1863	450	227		677		50	90	40		1	
47	Clarke	James S. Mullan, B.A.	Queen's College	31 Dec., 1861	150	400		550		77	134	40	12	1	W
48	Toronto	John Barclay, D.D.	Glasgow and Edinburgh	1842	450	691		1141		115	125	105	12	1	
49	Chinguacousy	Vacant		George Law.—Since settled						32					
50	Caledon and Mono	William Hamilton	Queen's College	31 July, 1866	150	400		550		100	60	80	9	1	W
51	Orangeville	William E. MacKay	Knox and Queen's Col.	29 Oct., 1866	150	412		562		60	82	70	15	1	
52	Erin	Vacant (Donald Strachan)		Catechist for 6 mon	150	300				60	76	30	4	1	W
53	Tosorontio and Mulmur	Alex. MacLennan, B.A.	Queen's College	2 July, 1862	150	400	50	600		55	77	110	10	1	
54	Nottawasaga	Alex. MacDonald, B.A.	Edin. and Queen's College	31 Jan., 1866	150	500	50	700		200	250	166	18	1	W
55	Innisfil and Gwillimbury	William McKee	Belfast	1852	150	400	50	600		95	80	60		1	
56	Newmarket	John Brown	Edinburgh		400	140		640		32	46	a U. Sch.			
57	King	John Thwne	Aberdeen	8 Mar., 1837	450	60		510		25	40	61	6	1	
58	West King	James Carmichael	Queen's Col. and Glasgow	2 Oct., 1860	140	500	60	700		100	153	74	5	1	
59	Vaughan	William Aitken	Edinburgh		140	500	60	700		116	140	a U. Sch.			
					6000	9670	430	16100	2086	2064	2881	1605	167	15	5

Statistics of the Church of Scotland in Canada for the Year 1866.—*Continued.*

No.	Ordinary Sabbath Collections. ($)	Synod's Home Mission. ($)	Widow's and Orphan's. ($)	Bursary. ($)	French Mission. ($)	Other purposes. ($)	Total Contributions. ($)	Reports.	Churches when built.	Churches seated for.	Manses.	Glebes.	Debt on Property. ($)
34	230 00		9 00		10 00	77 00	539 00	2	2 Brick and Frame..1860	480	Brick	No.	800 00
35	226 55	15 00	6 00	4 00	2 00	77 00	708 77		Stone 1835	450	No.	2 acres in lots	No.
36			6 00			165 00	171 00		Brick 1864	300	No.	No.	700 00
37	78 00	15 00	14 00		6 00	365 00	743 00		Frame 1847	230	Frame	20 acres	No.
38	148 00	25 00	14 00		8 00	18 00	613 00	2	2 Frame 1846	500	Frame	200 acres	No.
39	70 00	10 75			6 00	85 00	565 00		Stone 1840	450	Brick	100 acres	No.
40	No.	32 00	4 00			240 00	426 00		2 Brick and Frame..1863	180	No.	200 acres	No.
41	140 00	50 00	26 00			200 00	730 00	3	Frame 1840	700	Frame	No.	400 00
42	40 00		12 00			103 00	510 00		3 Br. and Frame. 1849-54	400	Brick	7½ acres	No.
43	50 00		12 00			50 00	512 00		Frame 1842	450	Brick	No.	No.
44	200 00	25 00	3 50			196 50	800 00		Stone 1859	450	Frame	125 ac. and $800 invested	1200 00
45	43 00	50 00			5 50	33 00	266 00		Brick	200	Brick	No.	No.
46	332 92		4 00	48 00	13 00	383 00	495 50		2 Frame 1830	300	Brick	5 ac. and $1360 invested	120 00
47			36 00				1503 92	Yes.	1 Brick 1862	1000	$40 in lieu of.	5½ acres	1454 00
48										250	Frame	200 acres	No.
49									2 Log and 1 Stone..	500	No.	No.	No.
50	No.	recently settled	settled			36 00	276 00		Stone 1850	300	Frame	No.	No.
51	40 00	10 00				16 00	316 00		Frame (Union)....	200	No.	100 acres	No.
52	40 00		5 00		5 00	35 00	510 00		2 Frame 1859-64	400	No.	No.	No.
53	60 00				12 00	144 00	766 00		Frame 1853-55	420	No.	100 acres	No.
54							450 00		3 Frame	550	No.	18 acres=$1800	No.
55	No.					23 00	227 00		Brick 1836	180	Frame	40 acres	No.
56	28 00	20 00	12 00	4 00	4 00		77 00		Brick 1848	220	No.	No.	No.
57	30 00	12 00	8 00	32 00	3 00	640 00	1283 00		2 Stone and Frame..	430	Frame	No.	No.
58	46 00		7 00		8 00	34 00	702 00		2 Frame 1863	500	Frame	8½ acres	No.
59	96 00	10 00	12 00										No.
	1968 47	274 75	190 50	88 00	82 50	3125 50	13200 19	1	41	10535	15	1331¼ acres,	4674 00

STATISTICS OF THE CHURCH OF SCOTLAND IN CANADA FOR THE YEAR 1866.—Continued.

No.	Names of Charges	Names of Ministers	Ministers where educated	Date of Ordination	SALARIES					Families	Communicants	Scholars	Teachers	Bible Classes	Prayer Meetings
					Temp. Board	People pro-mise	Additional	Total	Arrears						
	KINGSTON.				$	$	$	$	$						
60	Pittsburgh	William Dell, M.A.	Queen's Col. and Glasgow	5 Oct., 1863	150	400	50	600		45	44	174	17	1	W
61	Kingston	Wm. M. Inglis, M.A.	Aberdeen and Edinburgh	24 Aug., 1844	150	1400	50	1600		266	442	450	53	1	W
62	Roslin and Thurlow	James McCaul, B.A.	Queen's College	10 May, 1854	150	400	50	600		60	70	189	26	1	W
63	Belleville	Archibald Walker	Glasgow		400	400		800		86	104	93	7	1	:
64	Stirling	Alexander Buchan	Edinburgh		150	250		400		30	80	36	3	1	:
65	Seymour	Robert Neill	Glasgow	20 Jan., 1840	400	400		850		135	235	100	8	1	:
66	Wolfe Island	George Porteous	Queen's College	22 Aug., 1860	150	400		550		40	42	73	8	1	W
					1600	3650	150	5400	1443	662	987	1114	122	6	
	MONTREAL.														
67	Hemmingford	James Patterson	Glasgow	1857	150	400	50	600		60	106	24	3	1	:
68	Russeltown	William Masson	Aberdeen and St. Andrews	15 Sept., 1858	150	400	9	559		43	71	26	3	1	:
69	Beechridge	John McDonald	Glasgow	31 Mar., 1854	400	220		620		63	70	25	3	1	:
70	Beauharnois	Frederick P. Sym	Glasgow and Queen's College	29 Sept., 1832	400	440		890		44	54	48	7	1	:
71	St. Louis de Gonzague	Vacant			450	400		850		32	48				
72	Lachine	William Simpson	St. Andrews	16 Mar., 1840	150	500		650		33	68	16	2	1	:
73	Dundee	Donald Ross	Queen's College	20 July, 1859	150	400		550		90	150	78	8	1	W
74	Elgin	William Cochrane	Glasgow	13 Nov., 1862	450	470		920		38	73				
75	Huntingdon	Alex. Wallace, B.A.	Glasgow and Queen's College	1 Oct., 1845	450	600		800		130	180	85	8	1	:
76	Ormstown	W. C. Clarke	Queen's College	28 Oct., 1858	150	600	50	800		119	297	100	11	1	W
77	Georgetown	James C. Muir, D.D	Edinburgh	29 Sept., 1836	450	396		846		120	308	70	7	2	:
78	Laprairie	Vacant	John Barr	Mission'y		200		(400)		21	43	12	2	1	W
79	St. Gabriel, Montreal	Vacant			450	1600		(1600)		80	95	15	1	1	:
80	{ St. Andrew's, Montreal	Alex. Mathieson, D.D.	Glasgow and Edinburgh	19 Oct., 1826	450	2000		2050		260	632	245	28	1	:
	Assistant and Successor	Andrew Paton	Edinburgh	17 Aug., 1865											
81	St. Paul's, Montreal	John Jenkins, D.D.	Hoxton Th. Col. London	1837	150	2300	60	2000		238	450	158	28	1	:
82	St. Matthew's, Montreal	Joshua Fraser, B.A.	Queen's College	21 Sept., 1865	150	400	50	2700		80	110	180	23	1	W
83	Chatham	Donald Ross, B.D.	Queen's College	3 Oct., 1865	160	400		600		125	155	45	7	1	:
					3850	11326	200	15585	1044	1596	2785	1166	154	12	3

STATISTICS OF THE CHURCH OF SCOTLAND IN CANADA FOR THE YEAR 1866.—Continued.

No.	Ordinary Sabbath Collections	Synod's Home Mission	Widow's and Orphan's	Bursary	French Mission	Other purposes	Total Contributions	Reports	Churches when built	Churches seated for	Manses	Glebes	Debt on Property
60	80 00		5 00	5 00	5 00	38 00	413 00	Yes	Stone ...1863	200	Stone	2 acres of site	$ 850 00
61	530 00	2 00	80 00	21 80	46 96	2137 6	4268 42		Stone ...1822	800	Stone	No.	No.
62	50 00		15 00	6 00			541 00		Brick ...1861	250	No.	No.	No.
63	148 91	50 03	15 00	13 00	5 00	175 00	806 91		Frame ...1830	290	Brick	No.	800 00
64	44 00			5 00		230 00	395 00		Brick ...1857	180	Brick	No.	No.
65	51 00	27 00	14 00	6 00	12 00	111 00	621 00		Stone ...1866	450	Stone	12 acres	2000 00
66	30 00		12 00	34 00	6 00	145 00	527 00		Frame ...1856	200	Frame	No.	No.
	933 91	79 00	136 00	99 80	64 96	2070 66	7572 33	1	7	2370	6	14 acres	3650 00
67	53 85		17 42			269 00	789 27	Yes	Stone ...1818	250	Brick	56 arpents	No.
68	45 75	3 00	12 00			174 00	462 75		Frame ...1826	200	Building	40 do	No.
69	63 00	9 25	20 85			7 86	302 86		Stone ...1831	250	Frame	50 do	No.
70	138 92			8 00		98 13	715 15	Yes	2 Stone and Brick ...1835	403	Frame	No.	No.
71									Log ...1842	140	Stone	50 arpents	No.
72	150 00	30 73	32 00		16 00	392 00	920 73		Stone ...1832	300	Stone	No.	No.
73	45 00		12 00		15 00	213 00	783 00		Frame ...1845	230	Stone	50 arpents	No.
74	30 00	4 62				584 83	759 95		Stone ...1839	200	Brick	No.	No.
75	136 00	42 00	12 00		8 00	280 44	954 44	2	2 Stone and Frame ...1862	400	No.	50 arpents	No.
76	88 00		12 00	6 00	18 50	191 50	972 00		Frame ...1834	350	Brick	50 do	No.
77	102 00	53 00	15 50	12 00		460 00	1026 50	Yes	Stone ...1851	400	Brick	75 do	No.
78	29 32	settled.				5 00	205 00		Brick ...1792	250	No.	No.	2200 00
79	Since								Stone	600	Stone	No.	8200 00
80	1139 12	576 00	160 00			8837 00	10312 00		Stone ...1831	900	No.	50 arpents	No.
81	584 15	635 50	218 00	120 75	211 00	3006 50	6741 84	Yes	Stone ...1834	700	$2600 invested for.	No.	5798 00
82	168 39		12 42	10 00	5 00	219 50	835 31		Brick ...1860	300	No.	No.	500 00
83	77 80	8 80	7 50		4 50	576 00	1074 60		2 Stone ...1835	600	Brick	42 arpents	1200 00
	2836 28	1362 90	540 69	156 75	278 00	15313 03	26877 40	4	20	6490	12	513 arpents	17898 00

STATISTICS OF THE CHURCH OF SCOTLAND IN CANADA FOR THE YEAR 1866.—*Continued.*

No.	Names of Charges	Names of Ministers	Ministers where educated	Date of Ordination	Temp. Board	People pro-mine.	Additional.	Total.	Arrears.	Families.	Communicants.	Scholars.	Teachers.	Bible Classes.	Prayer Meetings.
	GLENGARY.				$	$	$	$	$						
84	Matilda	John S. Lochead, M.A.	Queen's Col. and Princeton	21 Sept., 1866	150	370	..	520		75	60	80	8	1	..
85	N. Williamsburg	John Davidson	Glasgow	Sept., 1844	450	210	..	660	..	46	65	80	6	1	..
86	Finch	Hugh Lamont	Edinburgh and Queen's College	22 Feb., 1865	130	400	..	560	..	82	131	64	4	1	..
87	Osnabruck	Robert Dobie	Glasgow and St. Andrews	7 Oct., 1853	450	280	..	730	..	70	120	32	7	1	..
88	Cornwall	Hugh Urquhart, D.D.	King's College Aberdeen	5 Aug., 1822	450	800	..	1250	..	115	200	70	16	1	..
89	Martintown	James Mair, M.A.	Mar. College, Aberdeen & Glas.	1 Oct., 1856	150	600	6.63	756	..	162	269	137	2	1	..
90	Williamstown	Peter Watson, B.A.	Queen's College	4 Sept., 1856	150	400	..	550	..	200	280	36	11	1	..
91	Lancaster	Thomas McPherson, M.A.	King's College, Aberdeen	28 Dec., 1836	450	480	..	930	..	120	138	73	3	1	..
92	Cote St. George	Archibald Currie, M.A.	Queen's College	23 Oct., 1861	150	400	36	586	..	50	120	30	..	1	..
93	Dalhousie Mills	Vacant								40	80				
94	Lochiel	Vacant								150	180				
95	Indian Lands & Roxboro'	Vacant	Neil MacDougall	Mar., 1862	450	200	Missionary of C. C.	650		86	57	10	5	..	..
96	Plantagenet	Thomas Scott	Belfast	12 Jan., 1844						60	32	10			
					3000	4140	42.63	7182	596 33	1256	1732	532	62	7	..
	PERTH.														
97	Brockville	Duncan Morrison, B.A.	Queen's College	22 Oct., 1851	450	500	..	950	..	60	108	80	8	1	..
98	Kitley	William White	Belfast	Mar., 1853	150	300	50	500	..	50	80			1	..
99	Smith's Falls	Solomon Mylne	Belfast	16 Oct., 1850	450	240	..	690	..	80	138	60	9	1	..
100	Perth	William Bain, M.A.	Queen's College	29 Oct., 1845	450	490	..	940	..	213	325	133	21	1	W
101	Lanark	James Wilson, M.A.	Aberdeen	14 July, 1856	150	400	15	565	..	85	130	55	8	1	..
102	Middleville and Dalhousie	Donald J. McLean, B.A.	Queen's College	11 Feb., 1863	150	400	50	600	..	140	208	130	15	1	..
103	Ramsay	John McMorine, D.D.	Edinburgh	29 June, 1839	450	320	..	770	..	102	174	60	7	1	..
104	Beckwith	Walter Ross, M.A.	Queen's College	15 Oct., 1862	150	400	50	600	..	60	158	108	12	..	..
					2400	3050	165	5615	none.	790	1321	626	80	4	1

119

STATISTICS OF THE CHURCH OF SCOTLAND IN CANADA FOR THE YEAR 1866.—*Continued.*

No.	Ordinary Sabbath Collections.	Synod's Home Mission.	Widow's and Orphan's.	Bursary.	French Mission.	Other purposes.	Total Contributions.	Reports.	Churches when built.	Churches seated for.	Manses.	Glebes.	Debt on Property.
	$	$	$	$	$	$	$						$
84	15 00	4 00	4 00	recently settled	recently settled	1694 00	1931 00		Frame 1859	180	No....	No....	No.
85	57 50		12 00			74 50	547 28		Stone 1866	200	Brick	12 acres.....	No.
86	54 00	7 00		4 00	4 28	77 70	431 45		Frame 1836	400	Frame	200 do	No.
87	184 00	15 00	12 00			28 15	762 15	Yes.	2 Brick and Frame.. 1857	290	Brick	25 do	No.
88	81 08	50 00	20 00	40 00	20 00	186 00	894 54		Frame 1826	420	2 lots—site for....	100 do	No.
89	55 84		12 64		8 37	744 45	1267 23		Stone 1836	800	Stone	50 do	No.
90	88 00	25 10	12 50	12 62	16 72	800 00	1239 20		2 Stone and Frame.. 1812	800	Frame	125 do	No.
91	27 00	40 00	24 50		7 20	138 00	614 00		2 Stone and Frame.. 1855	800	Frame	200 do	No.
92			8 00	2 00	3 00				Frame 1830	220	Brick	75 do	No.
93									Stone 1847	140	Brick	No.....	No.
94	20 16					144 50	161 66		Stone 1865	803	Brick	55 acres.....	2000 00
95	20 00	6 00	4 00			7 00	179 00		Frame 1836	500	Frame (small)	170 do	No.
96									Log	140	No....	No.....	No.
	602 59	147 10	109 04	58 62	59 57	3894 30	8030 51	1	16	5730	10	1012 acres.	2000 00
97	125 45	50 00	17 77		15 30	203 00	908 52	tl'd	Stone 1837	300	Stone	No.....	50 00
98	14 00		5 00			300 00	recently se	recently se	Stone 1849	200	Frame	50 acres.....	200 00
99	50 33	34 00	4 00		20 00	227 75	576 10	Yes.	Frame 1836	230	Site for manse	No.....	No.
100	171 76	135 05	24 00	20 00	51 20	293 02	1185 03		Stone 1832	600	Stone	200 acres.....	No.
101	95 00	15 27	4 25		8 00	186 00	723 00		Stone 1860	378	Stone	116 do	No.
102	71 40		7 00	20 00	22 00	260 00	860 40		2 Log and Frame.... 1863	350	Frame	No.....	450 00
103	80 00	50 00	15 00	8 00	24 00	11 50	520 50		Stone 1861	400	$700 invested for	Sold for 700 dollars.....	No.
104	65 00	10 00	10 00		6 00	25 00	574 00		Stone 1832	300	Stone	100 acres	No.
	672 96	294 32	87 02	48 00	146 50	1603 27	5345 55	1	9	2778	6	466 acres.	700 00

STATISTICS OF THE CHURCH OF SCOTLAND IN CANADA FOR THE YEAR 1866.—Continued.

No.	Names of Charges.	Names of Ministers.	Ministers where educated.	Date of Ordination.	Temp. Board.	People promise.	Additional.	Total.	Arrears.	Families.	Communicants.	Scholars.	Teachers.	Bible Classes.	Prayer Meetings.
	RENFREW.				$	$	$	$	$						
105	Pakenham	Alexander Mann, M.A.	King's College, Aberdeen	14 May, 1840	450	240		690		83	144	87	4		
106	Arnprior	Peter Linsay, B.A.	Queen's College	12 Oct., 1853	450	400		850		80	117	115	16	1	W
107	MacNab & Horton	George Thompson, M.A.	King's College, Aberdeen	5 Sept., 1851	450	400		850		113	249	120	18		
108	Douglas	J. K. MacMorine, M.A.	Queen's College	16 June, 1864	450	Resigned.		in 18 66.		110	120				
109	Ross and Westmeath	Hugh Cameron	Queen's College	8 Oct., 1862	150	400		550		91	122	150	14	1	
110	Litchfield	Duncan MacDonald, M.A.	Queen's College	11 Jan., 1865	150	400		550		98	97	102	12	1	
					1650	1840		3490	855 00	575	849	524	64	3	1
	OTTAWA.														
111	Huntley	James Sinclair	Belfast	1854	400	108		508		50	100				
112	Richmond	Vacant								60	80				W
113	Ottawa	Alex. Spence, D.D.	Aberdeen and Edinburgh	22 Feb., 1841	450	600		1050		159	197	222	24	2	W
	Assistant	H. J. McLardy, B.A.	Un. N. B. and Edinburgh	23 June, 1858											
114	Chelsea	James Sieveright	Aberdeen and Queen's College	30 July, 1857	150	400	50	600		42	30	54	4	1	W
115	Buckingham & Cumberl'd	James C. Smith, M.A.	Queen's College	24 July, 1864	150	530	50	730		120	225	118	13	1	W
116	Oxford	Wm. T. Canning	Belfast and Edinburgh	1 May, 1849	150	286	30	466		122	90	125	9	1	M
117	S. Gower and Mountain	Joseph Anderson, retired	Joseph Anderson, retired	1830						80	117				
118	Spencerville	James B. Mullan	Queen's College	23 July, 1862	150	400	50	600		80	110	160	20	1	W
119	L'Orignal	George D. Ferguson, B.A.	Q. Col. Edin. and Halle, Saxony.	16 May, 1855	400	400		800		90	72	88	7		
					1850	3364	180	5394	213 72	803	1021	767	77	4	5
	QUEBEC.														
120	Quebec	John Cook, D.D.	Edinburgh	1835	450	1600		2050		250	250	320	35		
121	Pointe Levi	Duncan Anderson, M.A.	King's College, Aberdeen	26 Dec., 1854	400	400		800		39	35	25	5	3	W
122	Valcartier	David Shanks	Glasgow and U. P. Hall	27 May, 1833	450	120		570		51	118	27	3	1	
123	Inverness	Alexander Forbes	Mar. Col. Aberdeen	1845	150	200		350		16	37	25	2	1	
124	Three Rivers	R. G. MacLaren, B.A.	St. Andrews.	1857	150	400	50	600		27	40	25	6		
125	Melbourne	Thomas G. Smith	Queen's Col. and Princeton	1861	150	600	50	800		120	90	219	24	1	W
126	Sherbrooke	Joseph Evans	Queen's College	3 Nov., 1858	150	500		650		130	69	80	8	1	W
					1900	3820	100	5820	434 00	633	639	721	83	3	2

Statistics of the Church of Scotland in Canada for the Year 1866.—*Continued.*

No.	CONTRIBUTIONS							Reports	Churches when built.	Churches seated for.	PROPERTY		
	Ordinary Sabbath Collections.	Synod's Home Mission.	Widow's and Orphan's.	Bursary.	French Mission.	Other purposes.	Total Contributions.				Manses.	Glebes.	Debt on Property.
105	40 00	5 00		5 00	5 00	130 00	395 00	....	Stone 1847	220	No....	25 acres....	No.
106	100 00	50 00	12 00	6 00		382 50	950 50	....	Frame 1859	250	No....	No....	90 00
107	77 94	25 00	12 00	13 00		1102 58	1575 50	....	2 Stone and Frame .1853	450	Frame	2 acres	No.
108								....	Log at Lake Dore.....	140	No....	No....	No.
109	48 43	5 15	14 00		6 00	347 50	720 08	....	2 Frame 1862-3	440	No....	10 acres....	No.
110	40 00	8 15	2 90	4 60	6 50	400 00	711 15	....	3 Frame	500	Log (old)	3 do	No.
	216 37	93 30	52 90	28 60	15 50	2362 58	4352 23		10	2010	1	40 acres	90 00
111	20 00	50 50	8 00		4 00	118 23	308 73	....	2 Log.....	703	No....	No....	No.
112				31 10	25 59	1048 17	2262 83	Yes.	Frame 1860	220	Frame	10 acres.....	No.
113	447 82	80 41	29 74					....	Stone 1828	650	Stone	178 acres=$600 per an	No.
114	46 00		12 00		5 17	176 00	699 17	....	Frame 1858	200	Frame	No....	No.
115	78 00		12 00	10 00	9 00	92 00	807 00	....	2 Stone and Frame .1846	360	Frame	200 acres.....	600 00
116	28 00	6 00	2 50		2 50	157 00	361 21	....	2 Stone and Frame.	300	Log	5 do	86 00
117								....	2 Stone and Fr. ..1845-7	320	No....	10 do	No.
118	27 00		12 00		6 07	326 75	821 82	....	2 Stone 1865	250	Frame	No....	650 00
119	83 00	50 00	15 82		10 50	589 00	885 32	....	2 Stone and Frame.	380	Stone	¼ acre.	600 00
	729 82	140 91	98 06	41 10	62 83	2507 15	6146 08	1	14	2980	7	40¾ acres.	1936 00
120	1000 00	500 00	64 00	60 00		1000 00	4224 00	....	Stone 1810	1000	Stone	No....	3200 00
121	120 00		12 00		7 00		532 00	....	Frame 1858	250	Frame	No....	No.
122	38 40		2 00	2 00		32 10	206 50	....	Stone 1859	160	Frame	4 acres...	180 00
123	15 00	5 00					75 00	....	Frame 1840	200	No....	No....	No.
124	60 00	6 00	29 42		33 77	142 00	514 00	Yes.	Stone 1856	280	No....	No....	3000 00
125	80 00		4 00		8 00	767 00	1550 19	....	1 Brick 3 Frame .	900	Frame	5½ acres	400 00
126	60 00					605 00	977 00	....	Frame	300	Frame	No....	1100 00
	1373 40	511 00	123 42	62 00	48 77	2536 10	8078 69	1	10	3090	5	12½ acres.	7880 00

SUMMARY.

No.	PRESBYTERIES.	No. of Congregations.	No. of Ministers.	Q.C.	Glasgow.	Edinburgh.	St. A'drew.	Aberdeen.	England.	Ireland.	SALARY. Temp. Board.	People promise.	Additional.	Total salary promised.	Arrears.	Families.	Communicants.	Sabbath School Scholars.	Sabbath School Teachers.	Bible Classes.	Prayer Meetings.
1	Niagara	4	4	1		2*	1	1			$900	$1450	$25 00	$2375	$899 99	163	260	215	27	2	1
2	Hamilton	5	3		2	1*		1*			750	1800	50 00	2600	180 00	447	506	290	29	1	2
3	London	13	10	3	3	1		1		2	3500	2890	100 00	6040	n. sta'd	723	885	277	34	3	2
4	Guelph	11	8	4	2	1					3130	2100	200 00	5430	n. sta'd	941	984	756	82	9	6
5	Toronto	26	23	11*	4*	5*		2		2	6000	9670	430 00	16100	2683 00	2064	2881	1605	167	15	5
6	Kingston	7	7	3*	3*	2	2	1			1600	3650	150 00	5400	1413 00	662	987	1114	122	6	4
7	Montreal	17	15	6*	6*	3*	1	1	1		3850	11326	209 00	15586	1044 00	1596	2735	1166	154	12	3
8	Glengary	13	10	4*	2	1*		3		1	2000	4140	42 63	7182	596 33	1256	1732	532	62	7	
9	Perth	8	8	4		1		1		2	2400	3050	165 00	5615	None.	790	1321	626	80	4	1
10	Renfrew	6	6	4				2			1650	1840		3490	855 00	575	849	524	64	3	1
11	Ottawa	9	8	4*		3*		2*		1	1850	3364	180 00	5394	233 72	803	1021	767	77	4	5
12	Quebec	7	7	2	1	1	1	2			1900	3820	100 00	5820	434 00	633	639	721	83	3	2
		126	109								29500	50130	1651 63	81031	8371 04	10653	14850	8393	981	69	32

MINISTERS WHERE EDUCATED. When attending two or more Universities they are returned in both, such being marked * thus.

SUMMARY.—Continued.

No.	DEBT — Amount of debt on Property.	DEBT — Without	DEBT — With	GLEBES — Number of Acres.	GLEBES — Without	GLEBES — With	MANSES — Stone	MANSES — Brick	MANSES — Wooden	MANSES — Number of	CHURCHES — Seated for	CHURCHES — Stone	CHURCHES — Brick	CHURCHES — Wooden	CHURCHES — Number of	Print Reports.	Total contributed for all purposes.	Other purposes.	SCHEMES — French Mission.	SCHEMES — Bursary.	SCHEMES — Widow's and Orphan's.	SCHEMES — Home Mission.	Ordinary Sabbath Collections.
1	$300	2	2	7	2	2	…	2	1	3	1400	1	2	2	5	1	$1776 00	$295 00	$ …	$4 00	$40 00	$58 00	$411 00
2	32000	3	2	13	3	2	1	1	2	4	2120	1	1	6	8	…	2203 75	405 50	…	…	61 00	54 45	561 07
3	4700	10	3	46	8	5	…	2	2	4	3585	1	6	7	14	1	4599 44	1764 16	10 00	7 00	75 50	145 00	670 78
4	7600	6	5	44¾	5	6	4	…	…	4	3256	2	2	8	12	2	4910 14	1020 47	32 16	54 88	92 00	95 03	795 63
5	4674	10	6	1331½	9	17	…	6	9	15	10535	9	7	25	41	1	13200 19	3125 50	82 50	88 00	190 50	274 75	1968 47
6	3650	4	3	14	6	1	3	2	1	6	2370	3	2	2	7	1	7572 33	2970 66	64 96	90 80	136 00	79 00	933 91
7	17898	12	5	436	8	9	5	5	2	12	6490	12	3	5	20	4	26877 40	13313 03	278 00	156 75	540 69	1362 90	2896 28
8	2000	12	1	1012	3	10	1	5	4	10	5730	6	1	9	16	1	8030 51	3894 30	59 57	58 62	109 04	147 10	602 59
9	700	5	3	466	4	4	4	0	2	6	2778	7	0	2	9	1	5345 55	1503 27	146 50	48 00	87 02	294 32	672 96
10	90	5	1	40	2	4	…	…	1	1	2010	2	…	8	10	…	4352 23	2362 58	15 50	28 60	52 90	93 30	216 37
11	1936	5	4	403	4	5	2	…	5	7	2980	6	…	8	14	1	6146 08	2507 15	62 83	41 10	98 06	140 91	729 82
12	7880	2	5	12½	5	2	1	…	4	5	3090	3	1	6	10	1	8078 69	2336 10	48 77	62 00	123 42	511 00	1378 40
	83426	10 86	10 86	3625½	59	67	21	23	33	77	46344	53	25	88	166	14	93092 31	37697 72	800 79	639 75	1600 13	3255 73	11772 28

GENERAL REMARKS.

From the foregoing notices of the several Congregations, we gather that the history of the Church of Scotland in Canada, begins in the year 1765, with the ministry of the Rev. George Henry, at Quebec, and that his immediate successor, Dr. Spark, was ordained for that charge by the Presbytery of Ellon, in 1784.

The Rev. John Bethune two years afterwards began to organize a Congregation in Montreal, and in 1787, removed to Glengary, where he was instrumental in forming a number of Congregations, and building several Churches. Niagara was the third Congregation formed. The Rev. William Smart came to Brockville in 1811, from the London Missionary Society, and officiated in all the settlements from Cornwall to Kingston. A petition to the associate Presbytery of Edinburgh, by a number of Presbyterians settled at Perth, resulted in the appointment of the Rev. William Bell to that place. It is worthy of record as shewing the difference in travelling facilities, betwixt now and then, that he sailed from London on the 5th of April, and arrived at Quebec on the 2nd of June, 1817 : that the passage from Quebec to Montreal, by steamer, occupied 36 hours ; the fare was £3 : and that leaving Montreal on the 11th June, he reached Prescott on the 18th, by the only mode of communication then existing, having been seven days on the voyage ! Mr. Kirkland was settled at Lachine the following year. The Rev. John McLauren was settled at Lochiel, in 1819 : Mr. Bryning at Mount Pleasant, in 1820. The Rev. Robert Boyd was ordained to the charge of Prescott in 1821. St. Andrew's Congregation in Kingston, was organized in 1822, under the Rev. John Barclay. In 1826, Mr. Sheed came to Dundas ; in 1827, Dr. Urquhart, to Cornwall ; in 1829, Mr. Cruickshank, to Bytown. At St. Thomas, in the West, the Rev. Alex. Ross was settled about 1829, and the Rev. Geo. Cheyne, at Amherstburgh, about the same time.

The Synod was first constituted in St. Andrew's Church, Kingston, on the 8th of June, 1831. There were present eleven Ministers and two elders. The Rev. John McKenzie, of Williamston, was chosen Moderator. The earliest Roll of Synod preserved, is that of 1833, containing the names of 25 Ministers. The following table shews the number of ministers and missionaries on the roll, and the vacancies in each year since 1831.

Year	Number of Presbyteries	Number of Ministers on Roll	Moderators	Vacancies	Missionaries	Retired Minister
1831	4	....	John McKenzie			
1832	4	....	Alex. Mathieson, D.D.			
1833	4	25	John Machar, D.D.			
1834	5	41	Archibald Connel	4		
1835	5	43	John Cruickshank	4		
1836	6	49	W. Rintoul	2		
1837	6	52	Alex. Galo	4		
1838	6	54	John Cook, D.D.	3		
1839	6	55	Robert McGill, D.D.	4		
1840	6	76	Hugh Urquhart, D.D.	7		
1841	6	82	James George, D.D.	10		
1842	7	84	Henry Esson	4		
1843	8	86	John Clugston	5		
1844	7	91	M. Y. Stark	3		
1844	7	54	John Cook, D.D.	22		
1845	6	53	William Bell	36		
1846	6	57	George Romanes	29		
1847	6	57	Walter Ronch			
1848	6	59	John Barclay, D.D	34	6	
1849	6	60	James Muir, D.D.	41	5	..
1850	6	62	J. M. Smith	39	5	..
1851	6	62	Robert Niell	39	5	..
1852	6	65	John McMorine, D.D.	41	5	..
1853	6	68	Alex. Spence, D.D.	37	4	3
1854	6	75	James Williamson, D.D	33	4	2
1855	6	79	Alex. McKid	31	2	2
1856	7	76	Alex. Mann	33	3	3
1857	8	81	Geo. McDonnell	30	4	2
1858	8	83	Geo. Bell	39	8	3
1859	8	93	John McMurchy	20	13	2
1860	8	96	Alex. Mathieson, D.D.	21	7	3
1861	8	99	Wm. Bain	31	7	3
1862	9	95	William Leitch, D.D.	21	7	7
1863	10	100	John Campbell	18	5	9
1864	12	105	Archibald Walker	21	7	10
1865	12	103	Geo. Thompson	28	13	12
1866	12	107	Prin. Snodgrass	27	12	12
1867	12	108	Kenneth McLennan	26	8	9

From the first, the Ministers of the Scotch Church in Canada were recognized by the Government, and received a small annual grant from the public chest. In 1836, we find a Committee of Synod reporting as follows, "that there are in Upper Canada, 36 Ministers of this Church: that 24 of these receive £57 10s. Stg. each, annually, from the monies granted for the support of Ministers of the Church of Scotland in Upper Canada, that two receive out of the grant to the United Synod: that one, Mr. William Bell, receives £100 Stg. on a special grant, and that nine are without any pecuniary assistance from Government. That the sum at present granted to this Synod, is £1350 Stg., and that each Minister has hitherto received £57 10s. annually."

It further appears that in addition to grants of lands for Church purposes, in 1833, £900, and in 1834, £550 were granted by Government to the Synod to aid in erecting Churches, and that these sums were divided among a number of Congregations in sums varying from £25 to £80.

In 1840, after nine years of negotiation, eighteen Ministers of the United Synod of Upper Canada were received into connection with this Church.

From 1831 until 1840, memorials, petitions and remonstrancee, followed by deputations, had been sent to the Imperial Government, in relation to the Clergy Reserves, setting forth the right of the

Church of Scotland to participate in the fund arising from the sale of these lands, on equal terms with the Church of England in Canada. In 1840 this vexed question was, for the time being, settled. One-half of all the Reserves unsold was retained by Government to satisfy different claimants: the Church of England to receive two-thirds, and the Church of Scotland one-third of the proceeds of the other half as they were disposed of—a balance on hand from past sales being subject to a like division.

In 1839, subscriptions began to be received for the establishing of a theological school, and Queen's College was constituted by Royal Charter in 1841.

On the 3rd of July, 1844, the Synod met at Kingston; on the 10th of July in that year, Mr. Bayne, of Galt, on behalf of himself and those adhering to him, laid on the table of the Synod a document containing their reasons of dissent from the decision of the Synod of the previous day to continue their connection with the Church of Scotland, and protesting that they could no longer hold office in this Church; twenty Ministers of the Synod subscribed this document, and two others dissented separately. Messrs. Smart and Boyd withdrew before the next meeting of Synod, making in all 24 who at that time ceased to be Ministers of the Church. In the summer of 1845 the Churches in the British Provinces of North America were visited by a deputation, appointed by the General Assembly of the Church of Scotland, consisting of the Revds. Dr. Simpson, Dr. John McLeod of Morven, and Dr. Norman McLeod. A second deputation, similarly appointed, visited the Provinces in 1847, the Revds. J. C. Fowler, Robert Stevenson, and Simon Macintosh being at that time charged into the embassy. It is true that allusion to these does not *necessarily* come under remark, yet, to leave them altogether unnoticed were an unpardonable omission. The lapse of twenty years has not effaced the pleasurable remembrances associated with the mention of these visits. None who listened to the kind words then spoken are likely to forget the earnest and affectionate addresses of the various members of the deputations, the lucid and satisfactory explanations given, their wise counsels, and, more than all, that total absence of recrimination, and of every thing calculated to offend even those who differed from them, which invested the sentiments expressed with an abiding charm.

In December, 1854, the Clergy Reserves were secularized by the Government of Canada. On the 10th of January, 1855, a *pro re nata* meeting of Synod was held in Montreal for the purpose of taking such steps as the circumstances might render necessary. The mode of commutation will be explained under the heading of the Home Mission Fund. At this meeting commissioners were appointed to negotiate with the Government. Out of these negotions are sethe " Temporalities Board," who held their first meeting in Quebec on the 22nd February, 1855.

OF STATISTICS.

It is hoped that no arguments are needed to prove the value of carefully collated statistics. In secular matters they have come to rank as a science, and, marking a new era in political economy, they serve as data for all the civilized governments of the world to found laws, regulate commerce, and determine foreign and domestic policy and relationships. Their value in ecclesiastical institutions cannot be over-estimated. Our branch of the Church in Canada has hitherto signally failed in her attempt to obtain them. Did each Minister, Session, and Presbytery, resolve *to do their duty* in this matter, there were no difficulty in procuring every year, at least as full returns as those now submitted. By a subdivision of labour, each Presbytery doing its share, the work, confessedly not a small one, could be easily accomplished.

The returns in the accompanying tables are for the calendar year 1866, though from this cause there may be a seeming discrepancy when compared with the statements of the treasurers of the different Schemes, and which embrace the *Synodical year*, it will yet be found that they so nearly approximate as to substantiate their correctness in the main.

It is respectfully represented that the business of the Church would be greatly simplified by each Congregation making up all its accounts for *the Calendar year*. By so doing, ample time would be obtained for making up full annual returns to be presented to Synod. Some Congregations have already acted on this suggestion, to which it is hoped that the Synod will give practical effect.

There are 126 charges enumerated in this Report: of these, 19 were vacant in 1866: 42 of them are double charges; in five instances the Ministers officiate regularly in three different places, and some were found having four and even five stations separated by long distances. In addition to these most of the country Ministers have occasional preaching stations. A considerable number preach three times each Sabbath. Those officiating in Gaelic not unfrequently have two double services, implying the delivery of four sermons. One Minister was met with who not unfrequently preached two Gaelic, and three English sermons in one day!

The number of Ministers in charges in 1866, was 107. If we include the assistant Ministers of St. Andrew's Churches, Montreal, and Ottawa, three Ministers, Professors in Queen's College, and one in Morrin College, we have 113; to which may be added 14 ordained Missionaries, making in all 127. Of the 12 Ministers retired on their commutation allowance, four were found to be engaged in ministerial work; these were, the Rev. Thomas Fraser, whose services have been frequent and most useful in Montreal, Mr. Johnson of Norval, since deceased, who may be said to have died in the harness, Mr. Anderson, of South Gower, who officiates nearly every Sabbath, and Mr. Paul, at Ormstown. The following table shews the number of Ministers in the several Presbyteries in 1866 : their allowances from the Temporalities Board : where they were educated ; and distinguishing those who have come to us directly or indirectly—as through the Lower Provinces—from the Colonial Committee of the Church of Scotland, as well as through other channels.

PRESBYTERIES.	Number of Ministers	Receiving from Temporalities Board.			Educated in Scotland for		Educ'ed in whole or in pt. in C'da	Educated in Ireland	Came through Col. Com.	Came through Glasgow Col. So.	From Free Ch'ch	From Presb. Ch. of England.	Natives of Nova Scotia.
		$ 450	$ 400	$ 150	Ch. of Scotl'd.	U. P. Church.							
Niagara	4	1	....	3	3	..	1	....	2	..	..	..	..
Hamilton	3	1	....	2	2	1	..	....	2	..	..	..	..
London	10	5	2	3	4	1	3	2	3	..	..	..	..
Guelph	8	3	....	5	3	1	4	....	2	..	..	..	..
Toronto	23	6	3	14	7	1	12	2	3	1	1	..	1
Kingston	10	1	1	5	6	..	4	....	3	1	..	..	..
Montreal	15	5	1	8	8	..	5	....	4	1	..	1	1
Glengary	10	5	....	5	5	..	4	1	2	..	..	..	..
Perth	8	4	....	4	2	..	4	2	1	..	..	..	1
Renfrew	6	3	....	3	2	..	4	..	..	..	..	..	1
Ottawa	8	1	2	4	2	..	3	2	2	..	..	..	..
Quebec	8	2	1	4	5	1	2	..	3	..	..	..	..
	113	37	10	60	49	5	46	9	27	3	1	1	4

Of the 25 Ministers composing the Roll of Synod in 1833, there remain only three in connection with our Church alive. These are, Dr. Mathieson, Dr. Urquhart, and Mr. Colquhoun. Seven of them joined the Free Church. Three, Messrs. Cruikshank, Clugston, and Ketchan, returned to Scotland, and are believed to be still living there, 16 are known to have died; of the 68 Ministers on the Roll of our Church in January, 1855, when the commutation with the Government was effected, 35 only remain in active ministerial work, 12 have retired on their commutation allowance of $450 per annum. One, the Rev. Peter McNaughton, formerly of Pickering, withdrew from the Church in November, 1855. Two, the Rev. John McMurchy, and Dr. McMorine, included in the statistics, have since died, making in all 22 deaths of commuting Ministers since 1855. Of the eleven " Privileged Ministers " on the Roll of Synod in 1854, ten are still in charges. One, the Rev. John Lindsay of Litchfield, died in 1857. The remaining 60 Ministers receiving $150 per annum from the Board, have been inducted to charges since 1855. The number of Ministers educated in whole or part in Queen's College, and in charges, is 46.

Of the 18 Ministers belonging to the United Synod of Upper Canada, and who were received into the Church in 1840, Messrs. Anderson and Porter, are now the only representatives, and both have retired from active duty. Some of them joined the Free Church, the rest have gone the way of all the earth.

OF STIPEND.

The total amount of salary promised to 108 Ministers (including two assistant Ministers), in 1866, was $31,031; of this sum $29,350 came from the Temporalities Fund—rather more than one-third of the whole. The average salary *promised* to each Minister, from all sources, was $750. The average sum promised by the Congregations themselves was about $484 each. The largest salary paid from all sources, was $2700 (81). The smallest salary from all sources (promised) was $350 (123). The largest sum paid *by a Congregation* to one Minister is $2550 (81). The largest sum paid for ministerial services by one Congregation, $3600 (80).

I

The smallest sum offered by a Congregation to a Minister in the shape of salary, is, $50 per annum, from 30 families! and it is not believed that its members are in the slightest degree ashamed of themselves. Another Congregation returning 100 communicants paid their Minister $108. It is supposable that each member of it may have paid as much in taxes for the keeping of a *dog!* as for the support of the Minister. For convenience of reference the salaries promised by the people appear in tabular form thus.

$ 50	$ 100	$ 150	$ 200	$ 250	$ 300	$ 350	$ 400	$ 450	$ 500	$ 550	$ 600	$ 650	$ 700	$ 750	$ 800	$ 850	$ 900	$ 1000
& over.	& over.	& over.	& over.	& over.	& over.	& over.	& over.	& over.	& over.	& over.	& over.	& over.	& over.	& over.	& over.	& over.	& over.	& over.
2	3	1	12	3	5	3	30	22	4	3	5	8	....	....	1	....	....	6

Before passing from these figures, let the intelligent reader be entreated to pause and reflect. It appears that there are fifty-nine Congregations whose promises for stipend do not exceed $400, the *minimum* required by Synod. Twenty-two range between that sum and $450; twenty-seven only are found promising $500 and upwards, and, of these, but six exceed $1000! Granted that these salaries were all duly paid, and even supplemented to the fullest extent of our Home Mission Fund, what do we find? Simply this, that the incomes of a large number of Christian Ministers are less than that accorded to a good mechanic, and that the highest salary is not more than is given to a competent clerk in a merchant's office. And yet it is required that a candidate for the Ministry shall present evidence of his having spent at least seven years in the study of Classical Literature and Theology at a University. Having obtained the object of his studies, he is expected to keep abreast of the scientific and literary accomplishments of the day, to dress and comport himself like a gentleman, to be a leader of thought, and to give tone to society. Need we wonder if the first talent of the country is diverted into other channels, or, that some of those who have embraced the Christian Ministry as a profession, become a disappointment to themselves and to their Congregations.

In referring to Stipend, the word *promised* occurs with significant frequency. It is less with regret than deep humiliation that the acknowledgement is made that Stipend *promised* and Stipend actually *paid*, are two very different things. Why not speak the truth ? " 'Tis true—and pity 'tis, 'tis true," that of all kinds of promises known among men, promises for Stipend are the most unreliable. 'Tis a pity to dispel the *dream* that these 108 Ministers, who, after many long years of hard study, fitted themselves for the noblest and best work in which man can engage, are receiving a decent competence for themselves and their families ; honesty compels the admission that they are not.

OF ARREARS OF STIPEND.

Would that they could be written off with a dash of the pen, hidden under a bushel, or otherwise consigned to the sea of oblivion ; to deal with them is painful, yet, they must be dealt with, honestly, and fearlessly. For reasons, which, it is hoped, will be satisfactory to the Synod, defaulting Congregations shall not be particularised in this Report. And it is also hoped that Congregations *not* in arrears to their Minister, will kindly forgive us for not doing them the justice which is their due by pointedly distinguishing them irom others. Reticence on this point will enable us better to grapple with an evil rankling at the very core of our Church's prosperity, an evil that all have an interest in having remedied, and one, which, if allowed to continue, will grow upon us rapidly, and soon sap the foundations of the Church of Scotland in Canada. Impressed with the importance of this subject, your Agent has given it much time and consideration, and omitted no opportunity of procuring as full and reliable information respecting it as was possible. This part of his duty was at once difficult and delicate. Difficult, inasmuch as the managers of many Congregations have been in the habit of keeping correct accounts neither with their Minister, nor those who profess to support him : any statement of arrearages in such cases, being at best but a rough guess. In some instances these had become literally *unaccountable !* It were strange had defaulting Congregations no feeling of repugnance in exposing their own shame in this matter ; the natural desire of every Minister is that the state of his Congregation should appear as favourably as possible ; hence the delicacy of unveiling these spots and blemishes, and probing these sores. Even those Ministers with the largest amount of arrears offered no complaint. It cannot but be that some of them are suffering worse than inconvenience, but they are suffering silently ; hoping, year by year, for better times.

The following table, the result of much time and anxious thought, embodies all the information received under this head. The sum of arrears stated is $8371, and is distributed over 25 Congregations, in sums varying from $50—the smallest noted—to $1281 the largest sum acknowledged. In addition to these are 30 Congregations admitting arrears, more or less, without giving them a name. After careful analysis of the information derived on the spot, and with every desire to give Congregations in all cases the benefit of a doubt, the smallest value that can be assigned to the class, " not stated " is $5550 as appears in the second column. There are thus 55, rather more than one-half of the Congregations, in arrears to their Ministers ! the total estimated amount being $13,921. Of the 30 " not stated" fourteen were given vaguely ; these are described in the table as 4 large, 5 considerable, 5 small : 16 were stated *approximately*.

The remaining 54 Congregations are equally divided into two classes of 27 each, that in the last column but one, includes all the Congregations newly settled, in which there *has not been time* to accumulate arrears, a few others are also included in this column, in which there is a reasonable *doubt* that arrears to a small extent *may* exist, though not acknowledged. The last column shews that there are 27—exactly one-fourth part of the Congregations, under notice—who have, *certainly*, no arrears.

Total Arrears stated.	Arrears estimated.	Total stated and estimated.	No. of Congregations in Arrear.	No. who state their Arrears.	No. who do not state their Arrears.	Those not stated classed thus:			New charges and doubtful.	No Arrears.
						Large.	Considerable.	Small.		
$8371.04	$5550	$13,921.04	55	25	30	4	5	5	27	27

These figures speak for themselves. Your Agent is of opinion that he has sufficiently discharged his duty in thus dragging to light these humiliating *facts*. It is for the Synod to devise such measures as in its wisdom shall seem best calculated to bring about a change for the better. The publishing of full statistics, and recourse to annual " Presbyterial visitation" in each Congregation, appear to be at once the most effective and constitutional modes of action required.

OF FAMILIES.

Much difficulty was experienced in ascertaining the exact number of families in the several Congregations, and this from two causes : first, the difficulty of deciding what is meant by a family. If one member of a family, for instance, belong to the Church of Scotland, and the remainder to some other Church, difficulty seems to present itself. It is submitted that, for this purpose, that one *does* constitute a family. It is presumed that he contributes for the Minister's support, and that the Minister visits that one officially as he does other families. The second cause, however, is less satisfactory, arising from the fact that comparatively few Ministers have the names of their adherents enrolled in visiting books. Were this practice universally followed there were no difficulty in ascertaining the number of families in each Congregation. In several instances it was observed that the Minister kept a correct list, not only of the heads of families, but of every child, stating their names and ages, so that the actual number could at any time be easily given. Such exactitude cannot be too highly commended. It is valuable to the pastor while he remains in a charge, and, when he removes, especially in the case of a large Congregation, to his successor such a catalogue is invaluable. The total number of families stated in the return of organized Congregations is 10,553 to which may be added families in mission stations which have been regularly supplied, say 447 more, making in all 11,000. It is proper to state that none but Communicants and *bonâ fide* contributors to the support of ordinances are included in this return. The number of " dead heads" is very large, as may be gathered from the returns of the Census taken in 1861 when 132,651 were given to the Church of Scotland in Canada, which, counting five to a family, made 26,521 families, six years ago. The same discrepancy occurs in the statistical return of the C. P. Church, who, claiming to have 25,000 families in 1866, had accorded to them by the census enumerators 214,540, equal to 42,868 families.

OF COMMUNICANTS.

The total number reported is 14,850. A number of vacant Congregations are not included in the returns, these, with what have come under notice in mission stations, may be set down at 600 more, making in all 15,450 Communicants. Comparatively few sessions are in possession of proper Communion rolls. With a view to supply this deficiency, arrangements have been made with Mr. Creighton of Kingston who has kindly consented to furnish as many Communion Roll books as may be required—after the pattern used in the Church of Scotland, at the price of $1 each.

In 1860 the number of Communicants reported was 11,337, but, comparison utterly fails, as in that year no returns were received from 24 Congregations, and six of those reporting did not give the number of Communicants.

OF SABBATH SCHOOLS.

There is room for congratulation in regard to the increasing interest manifested in this direction. Returns from 98 Congregations give an aggregate of 8393 scholars, and 981 Sabbath School teachers for the year 1866, an increase on the published returns of 1865 of 2256 scholars and 320 teachers, and, since this time last year, an increase of 587 scholars and 112 teachers. It is pleasing to notice a very considerable improvement in the efficiency of our Sabbath Schools, which may be attributed in some measure to the suggestions during a number of years past of different Committees of the Synod. A more general use of the Scheme of lessons furnished by the present convener of the Sabbath School Committee, has induced greater uniformity and system in conducting the classes. The general introduction of Hymn books, and the attention given to singing, have been productive of results most interesting and satisfactory. In the most distant settlements, in the back woods of Canada, may be heard every Sabbath day the voices of many children joyfully singing together their Maker's praise in hymns

and melodies the most beautiful known in the English language.
There is no music so sweet as that of children's voices, and, as there
is no better way to seek a much needed improvement in the psalmody of the Church than to begin with the children, every effort
should be made to create and cultivate a taste for singing in the
Sabbath School.

Nearly all the Schools are supplied with libraries. In this
way a vast amount of interesting and instructive literature
is in circulation, and the good seed of Gospel truth is being
scattered broadcast over the length and breadth of the land. A
large number of religious books, too, are annually distributed
among the scholars in the shape of presents. Competitive examina-
tions for *prizes* are being discontinued, and wisely so. A considerable number and variety of periodicals are read by the
scholars. Among these are,—" the Sabbath School Messenger",
" the Children's Paper", " the Band of Hope Review", " the British Workman", published in England: " The Child's Paper", in
the United States, and the " Juvenile Presbyterian" in Montreal.
All of these are profusely illustrated, the wood cuts in the British
Workman are indeed *Chef d'œuvres*. A Sunday School Magazine
for the Dominion is yet a disideratum, one, which, combining the
attractive features of the English publications with their cheapness,
would also be possessed of local interest and be a medium of
missionary intelligence for the young. * In most cases, the
Minister superintends in person the Sabbath School of his Congregation. It is a work few can do so well as he, and though
a considerable tax on his time, it is of a kind more likely to be
amply rewarded and blessed than any other part of his ministerial
labours. Nearly every School has an annual Soiree, excursion
party, or pic-nic, which serves the double purpose of amusing
the children and interesting parents and others in the work. St.
Andrew's Sabbath School, Montreal, is the oldest in connection

* This want is likely to be supplied very soon. Mr. John L. Morris of Montreal, who has for many years conducted the publication of the " Juvenile Presbyterian," has taken the matter in hand, and our Sabbath School friends may
rest assured that the new Monthly Magazine which is announced to make its
appearance in January next, will be such as to commend itself to all who have
the interests of the rising generation at heart.

with the Church. St. Andrew's in Kingston is the largest. The Presbytery of Kingston seems to have taken the Key Note from the City, for we find them with 1114 scholars and 122 teachers on the Rolls of their Sabbath Schools—by far the largest in proportion to the number of families, of any Presbytery in the Church. Though there are difficulties in the way of maintaining Sabbath Schools in scattered country Congregations, instances have been met with which go to show that they are not insurmountable.

Of the 28 Congregations from whom no returns on this head were received, the greater part were vacant. In a few cases the existence of " Union Schools " in the neighbourhood, accounted for the omission. Most of the Sabbath Schools take up collections ; some do so every Sabbath, others but once a month. In Clifton Sunday School, and some others, it was observed that each class had a separate collecting box ; at the end of the year the boxes are opened and the contents counted in the presence of the Scholars, who enjoy the process much. Besides paying for their books and Magazines, a considerable amount is annually devoted to Missionary purposes : the children thus put us to shame with their Indian Juvenile Mission. For this purpose there was acknowledged by the treasurer for the year ending May, 1866, the sum of $676.47, from which 33 orphan children were supported, clothed, and educated in India, and a certain sum besides sent to the Canadian School at Calcutta.

Of the 69 Bible Classes reported, the greater part are senior classes of the Sabbath School taught by the Minister. In Ottawa city two Bible classes have been conducted by Mrs. Spence for many years with marked efficiency and success. There are also a number of infant classes in connection with our Sabbath Schools in which children from two to five years of age, or until they can read, are taught orally to repeat short passages of Scripture, and the Mother's Catechism. Singing, too, forms a prominent and most interesting feature in these infant classes. That in St. Andrew's School, Montreal, conducted by Mrs. Morris, has 60 infants on the Roll.

While the aspect of our Sabbath School system is thus on the whole encouraging, there is yet room for expansion. The number of scholars might be greatly increased did each Minister realize the importance of the School as a nursery of the Church : each parent, as a valuable supplement to home instruction : were there no feeling among the rich that their children were too good to associate in the Sunday School with children of the poor, and, did more young men and young women evidence a willingness to offer their services as teachers.

OF PRAYER MEETINGS.

Thirty-two Congregations report the holding of weekly Prayer Meetings. The attendance is, usually, very discouraging, and many Ministers, after years of persevering effort, have been forced to discontinue them. It surely cannot be that Christian people are losing faith in the efficacy of prayer. Surely it cannot be that they are so wholly engrossed with worldly business as to be unable, by a little judicious management, to spare one hour of a week-day evening for Christian intercourse. It may be that our prayer Meetings are *uninteresting*. The people, in Presbyterian Churches, are not accustomed to take a public part in them : the whole duty of conducting them devolves upon the Minister, and the exercises vary little from the ordinary Sabbath Services. What a valuable *School*, to take no higher view of it, might not the weekly Prayer Meeting become ! Were members of the Congregation accustomed in turn to take a part, what a company of *assistants* to the Minister were created. Many a Congregation has met of a Sabbath Morning and separated without engaging in devotional exercises at all, because disappointed of a Minister : they themselves being wholly wanting either in the " Gift of Prayer," or in moral courage. Had it not been for the late Mr. Fordyce—an elder of the Church—who himself conducted, regularly, the weekly services of the Lord's day, and for years, in the absence of a Minister, it is more than likely we should have had no Congregation in Fergus to-day.

ORDINARY SABBATH COLLECTIONS.

The total amount reported for 1866, is $11,772.28. We have 166 Churches, seated for 46,344 persons : say that on an average there is one service in each, every Sabbath in the year, and that the attendance averages only one-half of the capacity of the Churches, we have 23,172 contributing *less* than one cent each per Sabbath. But $5206, nearly one-half of the whole, was contributed by 11 Congregations, as appears in the following table :

S. Contributions of 11 Cities and Towns.	Communicants.	Churches seated for.	Estimated average attendance	Sabbath Collections 1856.
				$
Hamilton	250	900	690	348
London	89	425	284	200
Guelph..............................	218	350	240	268
Toronto..............................	125	10·0	866	333
Kingston............................	442	800	540	530
St. Andrews, Montreal.	534	900	600	1139
St. Pauls, Montreal...............	450	700	466	584
Cornwall...........................	200	420	280	184
Ottawa	197	650	440	448
Quebec	250	1000	666	1000
Perth................................	325	600	400	172
	3069	7745	5182	5206
Lindsay	36	....	120	$226 50

Deducting these eleven congregational contributions, we have $6466 left as from 11,781 Communicants, but as Communicants to the number of 1081 are returned in the table from vacant congregations making no Sabbath collection, the *net* number of contributing Communicants is 10,700, giving $6466, that is, an aggregate of $124 per Sabbath—exactly *one-half cent* to each Communicant per Sabbath. Or if we estimate the probable average attendance in the country charges at one-half of the capacity of the Churches, we arrive at the conclusion that each individual gives 30 cents per annum— $\frac{2}{3}$ of a cent each Sabbath, but as we have no smaller coin in the realm than one cent, and as a considerable number give a small silver coin, the number who give absolutely nothing must be very great.

To return to the cities and towns, having 3069 Communicants, Churches seated for 7745, and contributing $5206. We shall suppose that the actual average attendance is two-thirds of the capacity of the Churches, 5182 on daily Sabbath attendance. Then each Communicant in these gives $1.69 per annum, as nearly as possible 3 cents per Sabbath : each worshipper gives $1 per annum ; but there are two services in these Churches each Sabbath, therefore, it follows that *one cent* is the average contribution per worshipper, at each Sabbath Service in the cities and towns. It would be interesting to know how many of these citizens give one cent each morning to the little ragged boy who sweeps the crossing that lies between his residence and his place of business.

There is no easier nor better way of increasing the revenue of congregations than by members enlarging their Sabbath-day contributions; a well directed and united effort in this direction would easily quadruple the amount at present received from this source—and nobody would miss it! That this is no visionary idea, a case in point is selected from the Statistical Returns—that of Lindsay, which, according to numbers, stands at the head of the list of ordinary Sabbath Collections. Numbering 60 families, 36 Communicants, and having an average attendance of 120, their Sabbath Collections amount to $226,50, being $6.29 to each Communicant per annum, and $1.88 cents for each worshipper. In this case the contribution *per Sabbath* from each Communicant is, after all, but 12½ cents, and for each individual 3⅖ cents. Were each congregation to give in the same proportion, based on Communicants, our revenue would be $93,406, or if that were too much to expect, taking the standard of attendance, we should have $46,024 per annum, instead of the paltry sum of $11,772.

Three Congregations were met with who make no Sabbath Collections. In one case enquiry was instituted as to the reason. *Conscientious scruples* were assigned by an old elder, who submitted that he and others thought it *sinful* to collect money on the Lord's day which might be applied to secular purposes " such as digging post holes around a minister's garden." The fallacy is plausible : but, " facts are stubborn chiels ; " the fact fatal to our elder's argument in this case, being, that there happened to be no minister's manse, nor garden, belonging to that Congregation!

THE HOME MISSION SCHEME.

The Synodical Schemes of the Church are four in number, viz., the Home Mission Scheme, the Ministers Widows' and Orphan's Fund, the Bursary, and the French Mission Schemes, for each of them a collection is appointed by Synod to be taken in all the Congregations once a year. Before referring to the figures in the return it may be well to explain fully the nature of our Home Mission Fund which will best be done by reference to its history. In the year 1763, Canada was formally ceded to Britain, when it was stipulated that its inhabitants, then nearly all French Roman Catholics, should remain in possession of all their Church property and endowments. These were large, and have since become immensely valuable. At the same time it was thought but a simple act of justice to place the Protestant population, who might subsequently people the Province, in as favourable a position with regard to the maintenance of *their* religion. Accordingly, the Imperial act of 1791, commonly called the Constitutional Act, provided, among other things, that one-seventh part of all the Crown lands in Canada should be reserved for the benefit of ". a Protestant Clergy." At that time, and for many years after, Crown lands in Canada were of small value, and the revenue accruing from the Reserves was very insignificant, but, as time went on, their value increased. Up to the year 1820 the Church of England in Canada had received whatever emoluments arose from the sale of these lands. In that year, however, for the first time, they asserted a claim as of *right*, to monopolize the Reserves, upon the principle that, being the established Church in England, they should be so regarded in Canada. An advertisement which appeared in the Quebec Gazette about that time, aroused the indignation of Presbyterians generally throughout the Province. It commenced as follows :—

" CLERGY RESERVES. — His Majesty having been graciously " pleased to erect and constitute a corporation, consisting of the " Bishop of this Diocese and the Clergy of the Church of England, " holding benefices within this Province, for the superintending, " managing, and conducting the Reserves made, or to be made, for " the support of a Protestant Clergy within the Province, public " notice is hereby given, that all leases of such Reserves will in " future be granted by the said Corporation ; and that applications " for the same are to be made, either to the Secretary of the Cor- " poration at Quebec, or to the Clergyman of the Church of Eng- " land residing nearest to the lot to be applied for," &c., &c.

From the first, the Church of Scotland in Canada protested

against the avarice and injustice of the representatives of the Anglican Church, and their indignation was greatly increased by the establishment of 57 Rectories, by Sir John Colborne, in 1836. In that year we find the Synod petitioning the King to revoke the Act.

The late Dr. Black, of Montreal, the late Hon. William Morris, of Perth, and the late Hon. Chief Justice McLean, were among the foremost of the Church of Scotland's friends and advocates during the long continued and bitter controversy that ensued ere the Presbyterians of Canada were recognized as having a rightful claim to any share of the Reserves.

By the Imperial Act of 1840—uniting Upper and Lower Canada —the claim of the Church of Scotland was at last conceded, and after making provision for certain other denominations to a limited extent, it was arranged that the remaining proceeds should be divided, two-thirds to go to the Church of England; one-third to the Church of Scotland. Dissatisfaction still prevailed. Appeals, protests, petitions, followed: the Church and the Country alike became agitated, and the secularization of the Reserves became the political topic of the day. Yielding to public pressure, the Canadian Government applied to the British Parliament for power to deal with the Reserves. This was granted in 1853, and authority given "to vary or repeal all or any of the existing provisions for the distribution of the Reserves' Fund, and to apply the proceeds to any purpose they may see fit, *provided, that it shall not be lawful for the said Legislature to amend, suspend, or reduce, any of the annual stipends or allowances, which have already been give to the Clergy of the Churches of England and Scotland, or to any other religious bodies or denominations of Christians in Canada, (and to which the faith of the Crown is pledged), during the natural lives or incumbencies of the parties now receiving the same.*" The Canadian Government considered it advisable, by one decisive blow, FOR EVER, to remove all semblance of connection between Church and State in Canada, which could only be done by buying off the claims of existing ministers. " Be it therefore enacted," says the Statute of 1854, " that the Governor in Council may, whenever he may deem it expedient, with the consent of the parties and bodies severally interested, commute with the said parties such annual stipends or allowances thereof, to be calculated at the rate of 6 per cent. per annum, upon the probable life of each individual, and, in case of the bodies specified (namely the Churches of England and Scotland, and others to whom the faith of the Crown was pledged), at the actual value of the said allowances received at the time of commutation, to be calculated at the rate aforesaid."

Each of our Ministers during the year immediately preceding the commutation, had been in receipt of the sum of £150 per annum and there were 68 Ministers on the Roll who were recognized by Government as entitled to commutation. A calculation based on their ages and probable lives, having been made, the result was, that the sum of £127,448 2s.10d. was placed at the credit of these 68 Ministers. This money they agreed to invest in a common Fund for the benefit of the Church in all time to come. They did more than this. Between the passing of the Imperial Act of 1853, and the Canadian Act of 1854, there had been added to the Roll of Synod, eleven Ministers : these were refused commutation by the Government, and it is evident, that had the commuting Ministers insisted on receiving each £150 annually, from the Fund, these eleven could receive nothing from it. The Synod regarded their claim as valid for commutation, but, as the Government did not, its members resolved to surrender £37 10s. per annum—accepting £112 10s. as their annual allowance—in order that the others—hence known as " privileged Ministers"— might participate in the Fund, to the extent of, at least, £100 per annum. The Revds. Dr. Mathieson and Dr. Cook, and Messrs. John Thompson, Quebec, and Hugh Allan, Montreal, with the Hon. Thomas McKay, were appointed by the Synod, in January, 1855, to effect the commutation and to manage the Fund, and on the 4th of October following, Dr. Cook reported that the negotiations had been completed on the terms above mentioned.

This, then, is the nucleus of the Synod's Home Mission Fund. Previous to this arrangement, the proceeds of the Reserves had been managed by a Board of nine Commissioners. At the time that these changes were effected, they had a balance on hand of about $29,-100, of which $12,000 was handed over to the new management, who became known as the Temporalities Board, and which was by them mostly expended in meeting the annual payments of the commuting

Ministers, until such time as the Government Debentures received for commutation could be sold in England, and the proceeds invested in Canada began to yield interest. $12,000 was appropriated as a Manse and Glebe Fund ; nearly all of the congregations of that time receiving £150 on condition that this sum should be supplemented by £50 from the congregations receiving it, each Minister binding himself to see the money faithfully applied for the purpose intended. By this means a large number of manses were built and glebes purchased throughout the Province. The remaining $5,000 was divided amongst the commuting Ministers in order of seniority.

Under the new arrangement, the commuting Ministers were thenceforth to receive £112 10s. per annum ; the eleven privileged Ministers, £100 ; and all others, not so provided for, £100 a year, " *if the funds admit of it.*" In 1858 the ministers on the roll had increased to 85, and in the following year to 93, and the funds at the disposal of the Board, after paying the commuting and privileged ministers, proved insufficient to pay even £50, to the rest. In 1860-1,the congregations of the Church, from Quebec to Toronto inclusive, were visited by deputations, and efforts made to supplement the invested fund so as to ensure regularity of payments. The result of this, spread over several years, was the total receipt of about £7000 ; only a part of which, however, was permanently invested, the remainder, with the consent of the subscribers, being employed by the Board to relieve the increasing pressure on their exchequer, caused by the continued increase of ministers, who in 1863 numbered 100. In November of that year the Board were compelled to adopt the following by-law, which received the sanction of the Synod:

1. " That it shall be a condition of any minister, other than commuters, receiving £50 from the Board, that he shall obtain from his congregation, a subscription of $50 per annum to the fund.

2. "That such subscription shall, in every case, be returned to the minister to whom the Board is not able to give the allowance of £50 per annum."

From that date, all Ministers inducted since 1854, received from the Board, only $150. It being expressly understood that the congregation should make up to them the $50. On reference to the third column of figures in the statistical sheet, it will be seen that in 1866, thirty congregations are reported as contributing $50 *additional* for this purpose ; seven met this demand in part ; twenty-three contributed nothing towards refunding the minister the $50 deducted by the Board.

The sequel is told in few words : " The funds of the Board were insufficient to meet even the $150 payments in July, 1864, when fourteen Ministers' names were struck off from the list of recipients altogether. In January, 1865, fifteen, and in July following, nineteen, shared a similar fate. At the Synod of 1865, your committee was appointed to manage the Schemes of the Church ; the congregations in Montreal and Quebec nobly responded to your appeal for aid to replace these ministers on the roll of recipients. In January, 1866, and each half year since then, the salaries of all the ministers were supplemented from the Temporalities Board, and there is reason to hope for such an increased and sustained interest in this important mission as shall place the ability of the Board to meet future demands—at least for some time to come, beyond peradventure." The contributions for 1866 amounted to $3255.75.

The following is a statement of monies invested and held by the Temporalities Board on the 30th of May, 1866 :—

	Cost.	Par Value.
1264 Shares Commercial Bank Stock.........	$142101.82	$ 126,400
590 " City " "	52120.07	47,200
620 " Bank of Montreal "	144546.00	124,000
Montreal Harbour Debentures.	16336.44	16,000
City of Montreal Debentures................	164455.16	183,000
Un.Counties of Peterboro &Victoria Debentures	4413.16	4800
Mortgage investments	6294.21	6294.21
Legacy from Mr. Michie.....................		2000
Legacy from Miss Fisher...................		800
	$530,266.86	$510494.21

An Act of Parliament, incorporating the Temporalities Board, was assented to on the 24th July, 1858. By this act the Board is always to consist of twelve members, of whom five are to be Ministers, and seven laymen, all in full communion with the Church ; two Ministers and two laymen to retire annually in rotation, their places being supplied by the Synod. Of this board, Mr. Thomas Paton, manager of the Bank of British North America, is now the Chairman, and Mr. William R. Croil the Secretary and Treasurer.

THE MINISTERS' WIDOW'S AND ORPHAN'S FUND.

The Managers of this Fund received an Act of Incorporation on the 28th of July, 1847, and commenced operations immediately afterwards. The Act provides for the maintenance of a Board of twelve Managers — four Ministers and eight laymen : one Minister and two laymen retiring annually in rotation, their places being supplied yearly by the Synod. It is supported by contributions from the Ministers and the Congregations ; the fund being divided into two distinct branches for the purpose of distribution. The annuities from the Minister's contribution being uniform—$50 per annum ; those from the congregational contributions fluctuating in proportion to the sums paid by the several congregations in the ratio exhibited in the accompanying schedule. Each Minister contributes to the fund $12 annually, and a collection is expected to be taken up once a year in each congregation. Only 53 congregations, however, out of 126, are returned in the statistical sheet as having contributed in 1866. Of these 19 were vacant. This still leaves 48 congregations—34 of which have Ministers settled over them—that made no collection for this deserving fund. Why this short-sighted policy in regard to a scheme most worthy of support, does not admit of satisfactory explanation, unless it arises from utter carelessness or want of method. In 1865 there were 35 delinquent congregations : this year, *one less*. The total amount reported for the calendar year is $1609. During the same period the Ministers contributed $1308. Upon the whole, however, the fund, which has been exceedingly well managed, is now in a prosperous condition. The amount invested has reached the respectable sum of $44982. The number of annuitants on the list in 1866 was 23. It has since been increased to 26.

The following is the scale of annuities paid:

From the Ministers' contribution a uniform sum of $50.

From Congregational sources *under* $12, at the discretion of the Board, not to exceed $60 annually.

	Congregational.	From Min. contrib.	Total.
$12 and under $24	$80	$50	$130
24 " " 36	100	50	150
36 " " 48	120	50	170
48 " " 60	140	50	190
60 " " 72	160	50	210
72 " " 84	180	50	230
84 " " 96	200	50	250
96 " " 108	220	50	270
108 " " 120	*240	50	290

THE BURSARY SCHEME.

The idea of a Bursary scheme, first brought under the notice of Synod by an overture from the Presbytery of Toronto in 1847, was soon afterwards carried into effect, the avowed object being to aid deserving students having the ministry in view in defraying the expenses attendant upon a collegiate course. The sum of $140 is estimated to be the smallest that will cover the necessary expenditure during a session at Queen's College. Few candidates for the ministry come from the wealthy classes, and, unless aid from some source is provided, the expenses of a seven years' course of study, which is required by the Synod, amounts almost to a prohibition. Not unfrequently those who commence with a view to the ministry are compelled, before completing their curriculum, to abandon their purpose, and, accepting appointments as Grammar school teachers, or engaging in other avocations, their services are lost to the Church.

It is a fact too well known to be dwelt upon here, that the number of theological students attending our University at Kingston is discouraging to the College authorities, and much too small to supply the yearly increasing demand for Ministers. This is a

* No annuity to exceed $240 from the congregational source. A bonus of 30 per cent was added for 1866-7 to all receiving under $120 a year, and 20 per cent. to those receiving above that sum.

The Treasurer of this fund is Mr. Archibald Ferguson, Montreal, whose zeal and assiduity in the discharge of his office entitle him to the approbation and gratitude of the whole Church.

matter of complaint with other Churches in Canada as well as in the old country; more especially it is felt and acknowledged by all Voluntary Churches, and, we need not try to hide the truth, *ours* is a Voluntary Church. This Scheme, if well supported, is calculated, in some degree, to add to the number of students and Ministers. We cannot much longer expect to receive reinforcements from Scotland. The spirit of self-reliance that is rapidly pervading the minds of the people of this great and growing colony, suggests the necessity of a like spirit in regard to the equipment of the Church. The condition of any Church, that, beyond a reasonable term of probation, relies on external aid, is an abnormal one. The natural source to which we should now look for the supply of Ministers for the New Dominion is, undoubtedly, the Provinces confederated. During the calendar year 1866 there is reported the sum of $639.75, contributed by 38 Congregations, leaving 69 Congregations, having Ministers, who made no contributions to this important Scheme. The Colonial Committee of the Church of Scotland bestows an annual grant of £50 sterling for Bursaries in Queen's College ; should not this put to the blush those among us who contribute nothing for this purpose ?

THE FRENCH MISSION.

The history of this Mission is a record of disappointments and discouragements. These, however, from its very nature, were to be looked for, and it is not on this account to be lightly esteemed, still less abandoned. Having put our hand to the plough, we dare not look back. It commenced in 1841. On the 2nd of September in that year, Mr. Emile Lapelletrie, who came to Canada as a colporteur from the London Missionary Society, was ordained to the office of the ministry with the customary solemnities. The services on that interesting occasion were ably conducted in the French language by Professor Campbell, now Principal of the University of Aberdeen. About the same time a small frame Church was purchased, in which Mr. Lapelletrie continued to officiate until 1850, when, in impaired health, he returned to the south of France, his native country, and, after engaging in Missionary work for a few years, he died there. Two Swiss Mission-

aries, Messrs. Baridon and Jacquemart, were engaged in 1850.
Mr. Baridon resigned from ill-health in 1853, but resumed work in
1859, under the Presbytery of Montreal, who were appointed by
Synod to the management of the Mission. For some years it was
under a cloud, and the operations in Montreal were suspended,
Mr. Baridon and Mr. Charbonelle meanwhile labouring in the Townships. In November, 1861, the Rev. J. Emmanuel Tanner, pastor
of the French Reformed Church in Montreal, along with 26 communicants, made application to be embraced in the operations of
the Mission, and were received accordingly. In 1862 steps were
taken for the erection of a new Church, and a very neat brick edifice, built in Dorchester Street, at a cost of about $4,000, was
opened for worship during the sitting of Synod in Montreal in
1863. Soon after this, Mr. Tanner having become incapacitated
from ill-health, the late Rev. Mr. Doudiet supplied the Congregation with services. The Rev. J. Goepp, from France, was
next engaged for a term of one year, at the expiration of which
he removed to Western Canada to take charge of a German
Congregation, and our Mission Church is now without a Minister.
The Committee seem, however, to be warranted in their hope
that a brighter day is about to dawn upon the mission. Mr.
Charles Doudiet, a son of the above named French Missionary,
has entered Queen's College with a view to the ministry, and
his success at the University has been such as to afford all interested in the cause the highest gratification. This young man,
who possesses qualifications that render him peculiarly fitted for
the work, having it in his heart to devote himself to the preaching
of the Gospel to French Canadians, it may be hoped that the
efforts of the Committee will receive a more generous and united
support from all the Congregations of the Church than has hitherto
been accorded them. Mr. Doudiet has been employed by the
Committee as a Catechist to the Dorchester street Congregation
during the last summer (1867). His labours have been unremit-
ting, his aptitude for the work undoubted, and his success propor-
tionate to both the one and the other. The contributions for 1866
amounted only to $809.75. This sum was given by 54 Congre-
gations. Fifty-three Congregations having Ministers gave nothing.
Two entire Presbyteries are reported blank under this heading.

One Presbytery, having 13 congregations, and in these 723 families, with 885 communicants, gave only $10. Dr. Jenkins, of Montreal, is convener of the French Mission Committee, and Mr. Archibald Ferguson is the Treasurer.

CONTRIBUTIONS.

The column headed "other purposes," is intended to include everything contributed for Church purposes not otherwise enumerated in the statistical sheet. As for example, the Presbytery's Home Mission Fund, the building and repairing of Churches and manses, taxes, insurance, Presbytery and Synod fees, Minister's travelling expenses—though there is not much of that—Sabbath School contributions for the Juvenile Mission, &c., &c. The whole sum reported for these is $36,997.72, which added to the sums paid for stipend, and the Schemes of the Church, make our contributions for all purposes $92,002.31. Much more has been given that could not easily be ascertained: in every congregation there were items "forgotten to be mentioned," and, besides, where any doubt existed as to the precise amount for any purpose the *lowest* estimate was adopted. Hence, we may with safety add ten per cent. to the sums contributed for all purposes, and, in round numbers, accept $100,000, as the measure of our liberality for the year 1866.

The number of families who contributed this sum is 9108 : allowing 5 to a family—each individual—man, woman and child, gave $2.10. At the same time, the number of communicants contributing was 13,743, being an average to each communicant of * $7.27, which, on the whole, exhibits a creditable degree of liberality.

REPORTS.

Only 14 congregations in the whole Church have been met with who are in the habit of printing and circulating annual reports respecting their finances and general management. It is proper to state that in each case they have proved of immense advantage to these congregations, and, indeed, more than one dates the commencement of its prosperity, from the time when full and accurate

* The C. P. Church in 1866 report $7.50 from each communicant.

statements of the receipts and disbursements were placed in the
hands of every member of the congregation. The principle is unde-
niably right that all who pay money should know how their money
is expended. Besides, it is expedient : people who pay their obligations punctually, have, generally, no objections to see their names
in print, while the publishing the names of those who do not, soon
shames them into better habits. The cost involved is trifling.
Though to some, it may seem a small matter, it is yet important, as
affording an index of exact business habits worthy of commendation.
Every congregation ought to adopt the practice, and, along with
it, such a systematic plan of collecting all revenues of the Church
and contributions for the Schemes, as would insure prompt and
regular payments. The want of SYSTEM and machinery is *the*
great want in the Church. The use of printed schedules, it is
thought, would be productive of good results. In Scotland, where
such have been in use for some time, the value has been tested
in a most satisfactory manner. There is no longer any doubt in
the minds of those who have studied this subject, that monthly
or quarterly collections, gathered by visitors going from house
to house, is of all other modes, the best for obtaining the means
needed to carry on Christian work. The schedule system has
many advantages : 1. It prevents loss arising from the absence of
members of a congregation. 2. It demolishes the plea of bad
weather and bad roads so often urged in extenuation of small
meetings and small collections. 3. There can be no mistake as to
the *day* appointed for taking up a particular collection. 4. Christian people would be led to give the matter *deliberation*, and in
course of time become habituated to regular giving, " as God has
prospered them." And, besides, this lay agency going out and in
frequently among the members of a congregation, would unite
them more closely in the bonds of brotherhood, and lead to greater
pleasure and cordiality in the work of contribution. The Synod is
earnestly entreated to sanction the use of collection cards or schedules in every congregation. A sample of such a schedule as is
deemed suitable for our Church, is herewith submitted. They can
be furnished at the rate of $2.50 per 1000.

SCHEMES OF THE CHURCH.

ANNUAL CONTRIBUTIONS.

The undersigned desires to contribute for the Schemes the sums herein specified, and authorizes the duly appointed Collector to call quarterly for the amount mentioned in the last column.

SYNOD'S HOME MISSION.		WIDOWS' AND ORPHANS.		BURSARY SCHEME.		FRENCH MISSION.		TOTAL.		QUARTERLY.	
$	Cts.	$	Cts.	$	Cts.	$	Cts.	$	Cts.	$	Cts.

Dated   186

The Synod has appointed collections for THE SCHEMES to be made as follows in all the Churches on the first Sabbath of each month named:

 I. JANUARY —THE MINISTERS' WIDOWS' AND ORPHANS' FUND.
 II. MARCH —THE BURSARY SCHEME.
 III. JULY —THE FRENCH MISSION
 IV. OCTOBER THE HOME MISSION.

The *First* is for the benefit of the Widows and Children of Ministers who die in the service of the Church. As Ministers' salaries seldom exceed a bare competency, this Fund has strong claims upon our practical sympathy and support. At present there are 26 annuitants.

The *Second* is for the assistance and encouragement of deserving students having the Ministry in view. The Synod prescribes a long course of study, and presents no hope of worldly gains. It is therefore highly proper to facilitate by such a fund the preparatory training of those who devote themselves to the service of the Church.

The *Third* contemplates the provision of religious instruction to those of our countrymen speaking the French language—to whom our influence extends.

The *Fourth* is designed to supplement the ordinary support of the means of grace, especially in new settlements and in weak and scattered congregations. The Divine precept—*Go ye into all the world and preach the Gospel to every creature*—at once describes the privilege and dictates the duty of giving our influence and means along with our prayers, for the extension of the Redeemer's Kingdom.

☞ To these Schemes our Church is committed. Each has a distinct claim on every one of us. To each, "every man, according as he purposeth in his heart, so let him give; not grudgingly, or of necessity for God loveth a cheerful giver."

CHRISTIAN FRIEND: Remember the words of the Lord Jesus, how he said,

 IT IS MORE BLESSED TO GIVE THAN TO RECEIVE.

CHURCHES.

The total number of Churches is 166: of these nine are built of "logs," 79 are frame buildings, 25 brick, 53 stone. Together, they are seated for 46,344 persons. Two of these—St. Andrew's Churches in Montreal and Hamilton—may be called splendid specimens of Christian architecture. They cost respectively, $64,000, and $56,000. About a dozen are entitled to rank as fine Churches, 60 are good, comfortable and substantial, 57 are passable—without any pretension to architectural beauty, 35 belong to the "Barn" order of architecture. Of those now building that of St. Paul's in Montreal, will equal, if it does not surpass, any of the existing ones. There is great room for improvement in the style of our Church building. Such edifices should not only be decent, commodious and comfortable, but they should also be beautiful and attractive. This could be attained without extravagance. A book of designs for Churches and manses, placed in the keeping of the Synod clerk, or other public officer—and to which parties intending to build should have access—might be of great service in promoting correct taste in this important matter.

And here a question naturally arises: is our Church accommodation sufficient? The statistical facts embodied in the returns of the several congregations bear concurrent testimony that it is not. The want in this respect is most apparent in the cities and towns. In Hamilton, Toronto, Kingston, Ottawa and Montreal, there is not only room, but pressing need, for Church extension. From this cause, many warm friends of our Church have connected themselves—some of them temporarily—with other denominations, and others will, doubtless, soon follow their example, if adequate provision is not made for them by their own.

MANSES, GLEBES, AND DEBT.

Of the 126 congregations enumerated, 77 only are possessed of Manses, and 67 of Glebes; 49 have no Manse; 59 no Glebe. It has been mentioned that most of the older congregations have received assistance to procure Manses and Glebes. There is no source from which the more recently formed congregations can receive like aid. Assistance received in this way may be said to have been simply an accident—not because of any particular *merit* in the recipients—and others are now as needful as ever they were. It would seem to be a simple act of justice that those who have been thus favoured should now, in turn, taste the blessedness of *giving*, and institute a Manse and Glebe fund, for those new congregations who, struggling under difficulties to support ordinances, are not in a position to possess themselves of these indispensable requisites to a well ordered congregation.

Of Glebe lands we have 3,265 acres. The revenue of a few of them is applied to Ministers' salaries. As a general rule, however, the Glebe is, as it ought to be, the Minister's perquisite. Seven Congregations have Glebes of 200 acres : eleven, of 100 acres : nine, of 50 acres. The remainder have from two to forty acres each. In country congregations, no Ministers should have less than ten acres of good land. Large Glebes are not profitable.

Our Churches, Manses and Glebes are encumbered with debt to the aggregate amount of $83,426, spread over forty congregations. Eighty-six congregations have no debt on their Church property. $54,148 of the debt lies against 8 Churches in the cities of London, Hamilton, Toronto, Montreal, Three Rivers, and Quebec ; the largest amount on one Church, being $30,000. The remaining $28,780, is distributed over 32 congregations, of which eleven are in towns, leaving only 21 country congregations burdened with a small amount of debt.

WORSHIP AND PSALMODY.

In respect of the form of worship in our Churches, there is little to note. It varies in no important particular from the usages and practices of the Church of Scotland. Instrumental music has been introduced in twelve Congregations, St. Andrew's Congregation, Montreal, having recently procured a very fine organ built in Canada, at a cost of $5000. The Congregations usually sit while singing : a standing position, however, during this part of the service, has been adopted by two or three congregations. In very few cases was it observed that the collection of Hymns prepared by the Synod's Committee, is used in public worship. The *prose version* of a psalm, or portion thereof, is chaunted during the service, in one congregation, and with excellent effect. In two or three country Churches was noticed the unnatural custom—now nearly obsolete—of the male portion of the Congregation occupying one side of the Church, and the female the other side. In one, the whole congregation stood with their backs turned towards the Minister during prayer. Congregational singing, upon the whole, is very imperfectly conducted. As was well remarked by one at a congregational meeting, " it would be a good thing to have a *Psalmody Scheme*." In many Churches only a fractional part of the Congregation audibly join in the singing, while in others it cannot always be said

> " They chaunt their artless notes in simple guise;
> They tune their hearts, by far the noblest aim :
> Perhaps Dundee's wild warbling measures rise,
> Or plaintive Martyrs, worthy of the name."

In too many cases there is a want at once of harmony and heartiness. It is rare in Presbyterian Churches to hear the voices of a whole Congregation swelling the loud chorus, or uniting in sweet melody " with heart strings reverberating to every note." Than this there is no grander or more effective music on earth. It remains to be seen whether the introduction of instrumental music will help to bring about the much needed change. While there is no small danger of being thus carried to the opposite extreme—a style of music quite above the capacities of the masses—there is yet no doubt that the organ and melodeon are admirable *accompaniments* to the human voice, and, when used *only as such*, are calculated to render important services in the improvement of Church Psalmody.. There are other methods worthy of consideration. In nearly every Congregation there are some endowed by nature with " the gift of song." Were they to take the matter up, and by weekly *praise-meetings* endeavour to communicate a share of this enviable gift to others, the result would be surprising. Many accustomed to call themselves " *timmer tuned* " would find ere long that they can sing. Among children, especially, the task would be an easy and delightful one. Were each Minister to recommend and encourage, in every household, singing at family worship, in this way, improvement might be expected.

QUEEN'S UNIVERSITY AND COLLEGE.

This Report would be incomplete without some allusion to Queen's College, the origin and foundation of which form no inconsiderable part of the history of the Church. Very soon after the formation of the Synod, the importance to the Church in Canada of a theological school began to be felt and acted upon, and, from the first, it was considered advisable, that it should embrace the general objects of a Collegiate institution, and, thus, be the means of affording a liberal education to the youth of Canada. Donations for this purpose began to be received in December, 1839, and ultimately amounted to $34,955 in money. In 1840 the College was incorporated by an act of the Parliament of Upper Canada as " the University at Kingston." This act was afterwards *pro forma* disallowed in order that the College might be constituted by Royal Charter, which was granted in the following year, and bears date at Westminster the 16th day of October. The Charter constitutes all the Ministers and members in full communion with the Presbyterian Church of Canada, in connection with the Church of Scotland, one body corporate by the name and style of " Queen's College at Kingston," and provides that this Corporation shall have perpetual succession " with the style and privileges of an University." The Charter names eleven Ministers, the Principal for the time being, and fifteen laymen to be Trustees of the Corporation, and provides for their succession. To this Board the conveyances of estate made to the University at Kingston, as originally established were transferred by authority of an act of Parliament passed in 1846, and the Board found that they then held 2,264 acres of land granted by various owners, and situated in Upper Canada, with several lots in the City of Toronto. These lands were valued at $6,928, but sales have shewn this estimate to have been in excess of the real value. Classes in Arts and Divinity were opened in 1842, and were taught for a number of years in buildings rented for the purpose. In 1853 purchase was made of the Summer-Hill property in the city of Kingston, consisting of six acres of land, with a large and substantial stone edifice, to which the classes were forthwith transferred. Shortly, thereafter, a building fund was formed which, in April, 1858, amounted to $12,622. With this sum and reserved funds of the original foundation, the property was entirely relieved from debt, the whole cost being $35,993. Additional accomodation having been found necessary, another building was erected at an expenditure of upwards of $10,000. The faculty of medicine was constituted, and medical classes opened in 1854. In 1861 an attempt was made to organize a faculty of the Law. Three lecturers were appointed, but as it was found impossible to provide salaries from the funds of the College, after a year or two, it was discontinued. Hitherto Students for the Ministry in connection with the Church of Scotland have been exempted from Class fees. It has, however, been found that Students who, at the commencement of their course, avowed their intention of studying for the Ministry, changed their minds, and though under written obligation to pay fees, should they do so, failed in the fulfilment of this promise, with but few exceptions. On this state of things continually becoming more unsatisfactory, the Trustees asked and obtained the permission of the Synod, in 1865, to charge class fees, from all students alike, and to return the fees to Students for the Ministry by instalment during their attendance at the Theological Hall. This arrangement will come into force next session. During the past session fifteen Students of Divinity were registered, four of whom appear before the present meeting of Synod as Candidates for license. There were also 34 Students in Arts registered, making a total of 49. The Register also shows 72 Undergraduates in Medicine, attending the Royal College of Physicians and Surgeons, an Institution incorporated by act of Parliament, and affiliated to the University in 1866, when the teaching department of the Faculty of Medicine in Queen's College was discontinued. Since the opening of the College in 1842 there have been registered 676 Students in the various faculties, and the Senate has conferred 573 degrees, viz: 174 in Arts ; 175 in Medicine ; 15 in Theology, and 9 in Law. In order to convey some idea of the services rendered to the Church by this Institution, a list is appended shewing that 67 Ministers and Licentiates of this Synod have here received their education, in whole or in part. It also shews that 19 of its Students have been, or now are, engaged in the work of the Ministry in other Churches.

The ordinary revenue of the University for last year was as follows :—

Government Grant.................	$5000 00
Grant from the Colonial Committee of £300 stg.......	1463 34
From the Temporalities Fund.......................	2000 00
Interest from Investments.........................	2765 17
Fees...	870 40
Rent of Medical Hall 9 months.....................	187 50
	$12,286 41

The expenditure for the year was :—

Salaries of six Professors....	$9600 00
Salaries of Secretary, Janitor, and other officers.......	922 50
Contingencies.....................................	1539 49
	$12,061 99

The Principal receives a Salary of $2200 with house accommodation. The Salaries of the other Professors range from $1200 to $1600.

The Library contains over 8000 volumes, a descriptive catalogue of which is in preparation. There is a very fine collection of mineralogical and other specimens, but the want of necessary accommodation and *funds* has hitherto prevented its proper arrangement in the Museum.

List of Ministers and Licentiates of the Presbyterian Church of Canada in connection with Church of Scotland, who have studied at Queen's College, Kingston.

No.	NAME.	First Session.	Last Session.	REMARKS.
1	George Bell, B. A......	1842 1st Ses.	1842 2nd Ses.	Now at Clifton. Formerly at Cumberland, and Simcoe.
2	John B. Mowat, M.A.....	1842	1845	Now at Q. C. Kingston. Formerly at Niagara.
3	William Bain, M.A.....	1843	1844	At Perth.
4	James T. Paul	1843	1844	Formerly of St. Louis de Gonzague. Now retired.
5	Alexander Wallace, B.A.	1844	1844	At Huntingdon.
6	John Campbell, M.A....	1844	1851	Died at Nottawasaga, August 22, 1864.
7	Kenneth Maclennan,B.A.	1845	1850	At Whitby Formerly at Dundas, and Paisley.
8	William Johnson, M.A..	1846	1851	For. at Saltfleet, L'Orig., A'prior, L'say. Now retired.
9	John H. Mackerras, M.A.	1847	1852	At. Q. C. Kingston. Formerly at Bowmanville.
10	David Watson, M.A.....	1847	1852	At Thorah.
11	Duncan Morrison, B.A...	1848	1850	At Owen Sound. For. at Beckwith, and Brockville.
12	Frederick P. Sym........	1848	1851	At Beauharnois. Formerly at Woodstock.
13	George D. Ferguson, B.A.	1848	1851	At L'Orignal. Formerly at Three Rivers.
14	James Gordon, M.A.....	1848	1853	At Dorchester. Formerly at Markham.
15	Peter Lindsay, B.A......	1849	1852	At Arnprior. For. at Richmond, and Cumberland.
16	John Lindsay, B.A......	1849	1853	Died at Litchfield, July 13, 1857.
17	James McEwen, M.A....	1849	1853	At Westminster.
18	Peter Watson, B.A......	1849	1855	At Williamstown.
19	Donald Macdonald, B.A.	1851	1855	Formerly at Lochiel. Now at Sleat, Skye, Scotland.
20	George Weir, M.A......	1853	1853	For. Q. C. Kingston. Now at Morrin College, Quebec.
21	William E. MacKay, B.A.	1855	1855	At Orangeville. Formerly at Camden.
22	William Bell, M.A	1852	1855	At Pittsburgh. Now in Scotland.
23	Joseph Evans, M.A......	1855	1857	At Sherbrooke. Formerly at Litchfield, and Oxford.
24	William C. Clark	1852	1857	At Ormstown. Formerly at Middleville.
25	Alex. Maclennan, B.A...	1854	1861	At Mulmur.
26	Donald J. McLean, B.A.	1852	1861	At Middleville. Formerly at Kitley.
27	Donald Ross............	1853	1858	At Dundee. Formerly at Vaughan, and Southwold.
28	John Livingston, B.A....	1853	1858	Died at Dundee, August 15, 1860.
29	David Camelon.........	1853	1858	At Goderich. Formerly at Port Hope.
30	Robert Campbell, M.A...	1853	1858	At St. Gabriel's, Montreal. Formerly at Galt.
31	James Carmichael	1854	1858	At West King.
32	George Porteous........	1854	1860	At Wolfe Island.
33	James Sieveright, B.A...	1855	1856	At Chelsea. Formerly at Melbourne, and Ormstown.
34	James Douglas, B.A.. ...	1856	1858	Licentiate residing at Quebec.
35	Prosper C. Leger........	1856	1857	Died at Beauharnois, November 22, 1859.
36	Hugh J. Borthwick, B.A.	1855	1857	Teaching at Ottawa. Formerly at Chelsea.
37	James S. Mullan.........	1854	1861	At Clarke.
38	D. J. Macdonnell, B.D..	1855	1860	At Peterboro'.
39	Joshua Fraser, B.A.....	1855	1862	At St. Matthew's, Montreal.
40	Archibald Currie, M.A..	1856	1861	At Brock.
41	James McCaul, B.A.....	1856	1862	At Melbourne. Formerly at Roslin.
42	William Darrach........	1858	1861	Died at Montreal, June 13, 1865.
43	Hugh Cameron	1856	1861	At Ross and Westmeath.
44	James B. Mullan........	1856	1861	At Spencerville.
45	Walter Ross, M.A.	1856	1861	At Beckwith.
46	Alex. Dawson, B.A......	1855	1862	At Kincardine.
47	Duncan Macdonald, M.A.	1856	1862	At Litchfield.
48	Donald Ross, B.D.......	1857	1862	At Chatham, C. E.
49	Thomas Hart, B.A......	1857	1862	Teaching at Perth.
50	John Barr...............	1857	1862	At Laprairie.
51	John D. Robertson......	1859	1862	In Australia.
52	John Gordon, B.A.......	1858	1863	At Georgina.
53	William Hamilton.......	1858	1863	At Caledon and Mono.
54	Alex. Hunter, B.A......	1858	1863	At Leith and Johnson.
55	John S. Lochead, B.A...	1858	1864	At Matilda.
56	Alex. Macdonald, B.A...	1858	1864	At Nottawasaga.
57	James C. Smith, M.A...	1858	1863	At Cumberland and Buckingham.
58	John McMillan, B.D.....	1859	1864	At Musquodoboit, Nova Scotia.
59	Alex. N. McQuarrie,B.A.	1859	1863	Teaching at Quebec.
60	Hugh Lamont	1861	1863	At Finch.
61	John R. Ross, B.A......	1857	1864	Missionary in Toronto Presbytery.
62	Robert Jardine, B.D....	1860	1865	At University of New Brunswick.
63	Matthew W. Maclean....	1863	1864	At Paisley.
64	William T. Wilkins.....	1863	1864	At Woodstock, New Brunswick.
65	Ewan Macaulay, B.A....	1860	1865	At Southwold.
66	Henry Edmison, M.A....	1860	1865	At Nelson and Waterdown.
67	Alex. Jamieson, B.A....	1860	1864	Teaching at Williamstown.

N. B.—There were *two* Sessions in the year 1842.

LIST of Ministers of other Churches who have studied at Queen's College, Kingston.

No.	NAME.	First Session.	Last Session.	REMARKS.
1	Thomas Wardrope.....	1842 1st Ses.	1842 2nd Ses.	Now Can. Presbyterian Minister at Ottawa.
2	John G. Carruthers......	1842	1842	Now Can. Presbyterian Minister without a charge.
3	Lachlan Macpherson.....	1842	1843	Now Free Church Minister at Williams.
4	Angus McColl............	1842	1843	Now Can. Presbyterian Minister at Chatham, C. W.
5	John MacKinnon........	1842	1843	Deceased. Formerly C. P. Minister at Owen Sound.
6	Robert Wallace.........	1842	1843	Now Can. Presbyterian Minister at Drummondville.
7	William S. Ball, B.A....	1842	1843	Now Can. Presbyterian Minister at Guelph.
8	Peter Gray..............	1843	1843	Now Can. Presbyterian Minister at Kingston.
9	David Barr.............	1843	1843	Now Episcopal Minister in Southern States.
10	John Corbett...........	1842	1843	Now a Minister of Wesleyan Methodist Church.
11	W. B. Curran, B.A......	1856	1858	Now Episcopal Minister at Montreal.
12	John May, M.A..........	1854	1856	Now Episcopal Minister at March.
13	Thomas G. Smith........	1847	1848	Now P. Min. at Fond-du-lac, U.S., for. of Melbourne.
14	George McNutt	1858	1859	Formerly an Episcopal, now a Baptist Min. in Toronto.
15	John K. McMorine, M.A.	1856	1862	Formerly of Douglas, now an Episcopal Deacon.
16	George J. Caie, B.A	1858	1860	Now Ch. of Scot. Min. at Portland, St. John's, N. B.
17	John Goodwill..........	1858	1863	Now Ch. of Scotland Minister at Roger's Hill, N. S.
18	Charles I. Cameron, M.A.	1858	1862	Now Ch. of Scotland Missionary at Bombay, India.
19	George Milligan, B.A....	1859	1863	Now a Licentiate of the O. S. Pres. Church of U. S.

159

PROFESSORS, IN ARTS AND THEOLOGY, OF QUEEN'S COLLEGE, KINGSTON, SINCE 1841.

Date of appoint.	NAME.	WHERE FROM.	REMOVAL.	DATE OF.
1841. Oct. 27	Rev. Thomas Liddell, D.D., Principal and Primarius Professor of Divinity.	Lady Glenorchy's Ch., Edinburgh	Resigned. Went to Scotland, and was presented to the Parish of Lochmaben of which he is still minister.	1846. July 14
1846. July 14	Rev. John Machar, D.D., Interim Principal and Primarius Professor of Divinity.	St. Andrew's Church, Kingston	Resigned. Continued as Minister of St. Andrew's Church, Kingston, till his death, in 1863.	1853. July 20
1854. 1846. July 14	Rev. James George, Vico Principal and Interim Lecturer of Systematic Theology	Scarborough, C. W.	Resigned	1857. Sept. 30
1858. Jan. 14	Rev. John Cook, D.D., Temporarily Principal and Professor of Divinity	St. Andrew's Church, Quebec.	Resigned	1859. Nov. 9
1859. Nov. 9	Rev. Wm. Leitch, D.D., Principal and Primarius Professor of Divinity	Parish of Monimail, Scotland.	Died at Kingston, 9th May 1864.	1864. May 9
1864. Aug. 3	Rev. William Snodgrass, D.D., Principal and Primarius Professor of Divinity.	St. Paul's Church, Montreal.		
1840. May 22	Rev. Peter C. Campbell, A.M., Professor of Classical Literature.	St. John's Ch., Brockville	Resignation accepted. Now Principal of the University of Aberdeen.	1845. Oct. 10
1842. Oct. 26	Rev. James Williamson, L.L.D., Professor of Mathematics and Natural Philosophy.			
1850. July 11	Rev. John Malcolm Smith, M.A., Professor of Classical Literature.	Galt, C. W.	Died at Gairloch Head	1856. Oct. 8
1853. July 20	The same: Professor of Eccles. Hist. Bib. Crit. and Hebrew.			
1853. July 20	Rev. James George, Prof. of Logic and Mental and Moral Philosophy.	Scarborough.	Resigned but acted till close of Session.	1861. Dec. 12
1853.	Rev. George Weir, M.A., Professor of Classical Literature.	Scotland.	Removed	1864. Feb. 10
1857. Aug. 5	Rev. J. B. Mowat, M.A., Professor of Oriental Languages, Bib. Crit. and Church History	Niagara.		
1846. July 14	Rev. Geo. Romanes, M.A., Interim Professor of Classical Literature.	Smith's Falls	Resigned	1850. May 7
1847. June 10 / 1855. June 2	The same: permanently appointed. Geo. Lawson, Ph. D., L.L.D., Prof. of Chemistry and Natural History.	Edinburgh	Resignation accepted 19th Oct. 1863. Now Professor of Chemistry and Mineralogy in Dalhousie College, N.S.	
1846. Sept. 1	Rev. Hugh Urquhart, D.D., Interim Prof. Bib. Crit. and Ch. History			
1862. Oct. 9	John C. Murray, Professor of Rhetoric, Logic, Metaphysics, & Ethics	Scotland.		
1864. Feb. 9	Robt. Bell, C.E., F.G.S., F.C.S., Prof. of Chemistry and Natural History.			
1866. April 26	Rev. John H. McKerras, M.A., Professor of Classical Literature.	Bowmanville.		

MORRIN COLLEGE, QUEBEC.

This Institution owes its existence to the late Dr. Joseph Morrin of Quebec, who in September, 1860, executed a Deed of Trust, making over to parties therein named certain immoveable properties and sums of money, " for the establishment of a University or College within the city of Quebec, for the instruction of youth in the higher branches of learning, and especially for young men for the Ministry for the Church of Scotland, in the Province of Canada." In conformity with the views of its benevolent founder, and with the Act of Incorporation passed in 1861, this College was opened on the 6th of November, 1862. The Rev. John Cook, D.D., of St. Andrew's Church, Quebec, having been named by the testator as its first Principal, now occupies that position and is Primarius Professor of Divinity. The Rev. George Weir, A.M., formerly of Queen's College, is Professor of Hebrew, Church History and Classics. The Board of Governors consists of twelve members.

During the four years that have elapsed since its commencement, six of its students have taken the degree of B.A. in McGill University, with which the College is affiliated. There are at present three Students of Divinity.

The number of general students has varied from twelve to twenty. It is in contemplation to erect a College Building.

Concluding Remarks.

In reviewing the history and present position of the Church, attention is first arrested by the advantages that have been derived at various times and from different sources, and, chiefly, through our connection with the Church of Scotland. It has been shewn that from the Imperial and Canadian Governments, in addition to grants of lands for sites and glebes, we have received pecuniary aid to build Churches and to support Ministers. By virtue of our connection with the Church of Scotland we became participators in the Clergy Reserve Fund, and, when that was abrogated, though we may not have got all we then thought we were entitled to, we yet received a sum of money large enough to be the nucleus of a valuable sustentation fund. To the Canada Company, the Seigneur of

Beauharnois, and other kind friends, we have also been placed under obligations.

What has the Colonial Committee of the Church of Scotland *not* done for us ? How many Ministers have come to Canada through that agency cannot now be easily ascertained : the names of 67, at least, occur in connection with the History of these Congregations * Twenty-seven of our present Ministers were sent to us by the Colonial Committee. Nor can it be stated how much aid, in all, has been received for Church building ; 23 cases, however, incidentally appear to have received $7,900. The truth is that ever since our Church began, the prayers and practical sympathies of the good old Mother Church have been unceasingly wafted to us across the ocean. During the last five years alone, as the following table shews, there has been expended for the benefit of the Church and College by the Colonial Committee, no less than $32,425.

Year.	For Missionaries.	Outfits.	Grants to Churches.	To Queen's College.	120 copies of Record.	Totals.
1862	£620 10 4	£77 18 0	£90	£350	£8	£1146 8 2
1863	446 9 2	119 12 0	115	350	8	1039 1 2
1864	571 19 5	85 13 0	75	350	8	1090 12 5
1865	853 14 2	141 0 0	315	350	8	1667 14 2
1866	1052 15 10	51 0 0	80	350	8	1541 15 10
Totals	£3545 8 9	£475 3 0	£675	£1750	£40	£6485 11 9

It is not for us to boast of this connection nor these advantages, but rather to endeavour to realize the responsibilities arising from them. There is yet ample scope in Canada for the united efforts of all our Congregations in the support of HOME MISSIONS. Though not at present committed to the support of a FOREIGN MISSION, there is no reason why our Church should not in some way—other than through the Sabbath Schools—engage heartily in this work.

> " Shall we whose souls are lighted
> With wisdom from on high :
> Shall we to men benighted
> The Lamp of Life deny ? "

(*) Besides these, 28 came under the auspices of " the Glasgow Society for promoting the religious interest of Scottish settlers in British North America." This Society was organized in 1825, Dr. Burns of Paisley, and now of Toronto, was one of its most active and useful Secretaries. It was the forerunner of the Assembly's Colonial Committee with which it united in 1840.

This we can do, and not leave the other undone : other Churches are setting us a worthy example. The growth of the population of these Provinces—perhaps the most remarkable on record—is of itself a sufficient incentive for us, as a Church, to be up and doing. The rapid extension of another system of Religion amongst us presents also a stimulus to work and watchfulness : while we would speak and judge of it charitably, we are bound as Protestants to resist its encroachments. Never was there a time when greater need existed for vigilance and active co-operation ; and our Church, to occupy a position of honour and usefulness, must avail itself of every appliance that may be found conducive to success in Christian work.

While some, with plausible ingenuity, are sedulously endeavouring to shew the points of *agreement* existing between Protestants and the system against which they protested, with a view to a reunion, and others treat the points on which we *differ* as mere trifling matters of form, let us " hold fast the profession of our faith "—" putting on the whole armour of God, that we may be able to stand in the evil day, and having done all, TO STAND."

Some, nowadays, would magnify the Sacraments into means of Salvation. Some seek for a revival of Religion in the restoration of Church Architecture ; some in a gorgeous ritual and an elaborate and decorous liturgy ; some in posture at praise and prayer. Some would even seem to pin their faith upon " mediæval millinery." Others, calling themselves Protestants, advocate the restoral of the confessional, of bodily mortifications, of penance, of invocation of saints, of monkish seclusion, morbid asceticism, and clerical celibacy. While it is not to be denied that a certain importance may attach to some of these, it were evidence of a weak mind unduly to trust to mere externals : and yet, it *is* incumbent on all true friends of the Church to enquire into the means of rendering our worship as instructive, as impressive, as edifying, and as interesting as possible. Slow to admit of *innovations*, we should seek to divest ourselves of narrow-minded prejudices and bigotry.

It is expected, perhaps, that something should be said in this Report on the subject of " Union with other Presbyterians." In respect of this, your Agent, in his public addresses, has studiously avoided any attempt to influence the members of our Church in one direction or in the other. Of the desirableness of such a union, there cannot be two opinions : with regard to its practicability, we are not at all agreed. This being the case, wisdom and sound policy alike dictate that, for the present, the proposition be held in abeyance, and that with united energies we, one and all, apply ourselves to the work of developing and utilizing the untold resources and power that yet lie dormant in our congregations.

Sooner or later a union with the Synods of the Lower Provinces must follow in the wake of Confederation. It is worthy of the consideration of this Synod, whether it were not wise *now* to give some consideration to the proposition of establishing a General Assembly for the Dominion of Canada.

Though other matters, interesting and important, might have been touched upon, the length to which this Report has already extended forbids the attempt. It is hoped that the remarks submitted will be received in the like friendly spirit which suggested them. If the weak points of our Church have been exposed it has been from no desire to disparage, or to place us in an unfavourable light as compared with others. All that has been observed—and that is not a little—of the state of other Protestant Churches throughout Canada, leads to the belief that in nearly every matter here alluded to they are as needful of reformation as we are. There is work for us all to do, and it is to be hoped that with them we may be enabled to cultivate, increasingly, feelings of friendly relationship and co-operation.

Words more appropriate to the conclusion of this Report cannot be found than those contained in the following few sentences, quoted from the Church of Scotland Magazine for 1853, page 645 :

" The battle of the Church is not to be fought in General Assemblies or other Church Courts ; nor in the High Court of Parliament ; but it is to be fought and won in our parishes, and at the firesides of the humblest of our country's population. The sooner our Clergy know this and act upon it the better. If any amongst them are not willing to become laborious workmen in the vineyard of God, to spend and be spent in the Church's service ; always at their post and always working ; let them know that they are traitors to their Church and a disgrace to their profession. These are not the days when the Church can contemplate with patience the case even of a single individual eating her bread and not doing her work, or doing it superficially. . . . . Let every one who has the status of a Minister make it a matter of conscience to do a Minister's work. By the great oath which he registered in Heaven on his ordination day, by the undoubted commandment of God's word, by the present exigences of the Church, he is bound to give himself up exclusively to the duties of his profession."

Whether or not the labour of these fifteen months may have been productive of good results, or have been like water spilled upon the ground, remains to be seen. Whether or not your Committee will have it in their power to point in future years to a marked and satisfactory increase of liberality among our adherents, depends not on feeble human agency, but on Him " who giveth the increase." It will be something for us at least to say, "we have done what we could."

All which is respectfully submitted.

JAMES CROIL.

ALPHABETICAL LIST OF MINISTERS AND LICENTIATES

Connected with the Church of Scotland in Canada from the year
. 1765 to 1867.

ABBREVIATIONS USED IN THIS TABLE:—*Q. C.* denotes Queen's College, Kingston, Canada; *Col. Com.* stands for Colonial Committee of the Church of Scotland; *Glas. So.* for the Glasgow Society for promoting the religious interests of Scottish settlers in British North America; *U. S. U. C.* for the United Synod of Upper Canada; *Ass. S. S.* for the Associate Synod of Scotland; *U. S.* for United States; *I. Pr. Ch.* the Presbyterian Church of Ireland; *Ch. of S.* for the Church of Scotland. An asterisk placed over the date of ordination denotes the year in which the minister became connected with the Church in Canada, the date of ordination not having been ascertained.

NAMES.	Native of	Educated.	From	Date of Ordination.	Charges held.	REMARKS.
Aitken, William............	Scot..	Edinburgh..	Col Com	1864	Vaughan....	Now Minister of.
Alexander, Thomas, M.A....	Scot..	....	Glas. So.	1835	Coburg......	Seceded 1844.
Allan, Daniel,.............	Scot..	Aberdeen ...	Glas. So.	1838	Stratford ...	Seceded 1844.
Anderson, Duncan, M.A.....	Scot..	Aberdeen ...	Col Com	1854	Point Levi..	Now Minister of.
Anderson, James............	Scot..	Aberdeen ...	....	1835	Ormstown ..	Died there 1861.
Anderson, Joseph, M.A.....	Irel'd.	Glasgow	U.S.U.C	1830	South Gower	Retired 1864.
Bain, James...............	Scot..	....	U. P.Ch.	1826	Scarboro.....	Now Minister of.
Bain, William, M.A........	Scot..	Q. C.......		1845	Perth.......	Now Minister of.
Balmain, John.............	Scot..	....			Licentinte ..	Resides in Montreal.
Barclay, John.............	Scot..	Edinburgh..	Ch. of S.	1821	Kingston ...	Died there 1826.
Barclay, John, D.D.........	Scot..	Glas. & Ed..	Ch. of S.	1842	Toronto	Now Minister of.
Baridon, Louis.............	Switz.	....	....		Missionary...	Resigned 1864.
Barr, John................	Scot..	Q. C.......	....	1867	Laprairie...	Now Minister of.
Barr, William..............	Irel'd.	Belfast	I.Pr. Ch.	1847	Trafalgar, Wawanosh..	Now Minister of.
Bayne, John, D.D...........	Scot..	....	Glas. So.	1834	Galt.........	Seceded '44, died '59.
Baynes, John William.......	U. S..	....	....		Missionary...	Returned to U.S. '49.
Bell, Andrew..............	Engl..	Glasgow	U.S.U.C	1828	Toronto Township, Dundas, L'Orignal ...	Died there 1856.
Bell, George, B.A..........	Can....	Q. C........	....	1844	Cumberland, Simcoe, Clifton	Now Minister of.
Bell, Peter................	Scot..	....	Ch. of S.		Licentiate.	
Bell, William, M.A.........	Scot..	Glasgow	Ass. S.S.	1817	Perth	Died there 1857.
Bell, William, M.A.........	Can....	Q. C. & Glasg		1863	Pittsburg...	Resigned 1867.
Bell, William, M.A.........	Irel'd.	Belfast	I.Pr.Ch.	1848	Stratford, Easthope ...	Now Minister of.
Bethune, John.............	Scot..	....	About..	1771	Montreal, Williamst'n.	Died there 1815.
Black, Edward, D.D.........	Scot..	Edinburgh..	Ch. of S.	1823	St. Gabriel's & St. Paul's, Montreal ..	Died there 1845.
Black, William M...........	Can....	Edinburgh..	....		Licentiate ..	Resides in Montreal
Black, David..............	Scot✝	Edinburgh..	Ch. of S.	1837	Laprairie, St. Thérèse..	Seceded 1844.
Black, James, M.A..........	Scot..	Glasgow	Col Com	1860	Chatham ...	Resigned 1864.
Blair, Andrew.............	Scot..	....	Col Com	1851	Missionary...	Died in Scotland.
Blair, George, M.A.........	Scot..	St. Andrews.	Ch. of S.	1843	Licentiate ..	Super. of Schools.
Blood, William............	Irel'd.	....	Pr. Ch..	1840	Lachute	Drowned at sea.
Borthwick, Hugh J., M.A....	Scot..	Ed. & Q. C..	....	1862	Chelsea	Resigned 1864.
Boyd, Robert, D.D..........	Irel'd.	....	U.S.U.C	1821	Prescott.....	Seceded 1844.
Brown, David..............	Scot..	Edinburgh..	Ch. of S.	1833	Valcartier ..	Resigned 1837.
Brown, John...............	Scot..	Edinburgh..	Ch. of S.	1852	Newmarket.	Now Minister of.
Brown, William............	Irel'd.	....	U.P.Ch.	1846	Uxbridge...	Died there 1853.
Bruce, John...............	Scot..	....	....		Missionary...	Returned to Scotl'd.
Brunton, William..........	Scot..	Aberdeen ...	Ch. of S.	1820	Lachine	Resigned 1822.
Bryning, John	Engl..	....	U.S.U.C	1830	Mt. Pleasant	Died there 1853.
Buchan, Alexander.........	Scot..	Edinburgh..	Col Com	1842	Inv.,Stirling	Now Minister of.
Buchanan, George..........	Scot..	....	Ass. S.S.	1822	Beckwith.	
Burnet, John S............	Scot..	Edinburgh..	Col Com	1863	At Cornwall.	Now assistant Min.
Burnet, Robert............	Scot..	Ed. & Ab...	Col Com	1853	Hamilton ..	Now Minister of.

ALPHABETICAL LIST OF MINISTERS, &c.—*Continued.*

NAMES.	Native of	Educated.	From	Date of Ordination.	Charges held.	REMARKS.
Burns, John...............	Scot..	....	U. S....	1810	Niagara	Died there 1824.
Burns, John, M.A..........	Scot..	Glasgow	Ch. of S.	1824	St. An. Mon.	Returned to S. 1826.
Cairns, James, M.D........	Scot..	....	....		Missionary...	Seceded 1814.
Calhoun, James............	Irel'd.	....	Col Com	1846	Missionary...	Dismissed 1847.
Camelon, David............	Scot...	Q. C.		1859	Port Hope, Goderich ...	Now Minister of.
Cameron, Charles I.B.A.....	Scot..	Q. C.	....	1865	Missionary ..	Now in India.
Cameron, Hugh.............	Scot..	Q. C.	....	1862	Ross & Westmeath	Now Minister of.
Cameron, John, M.A.........	N. S.	Glasgow....	Col Com	1861	Dundee.....	Now Min. of Campbeltown, Scotl'd.
Campbell, Charles..........	Scot..	Ed. & St. An.	Col Com	1858	Niagara	Now Minister of.
Campbell, John, M.A........	Scot..	Q. C.	....	1853	Nottawasaga	Died there 1864.
Campbell, John, M.A........	Can...	U. S.	....	1854	Brock, Markham ...	Now Minister of.
Campbell, Peter Colin, D.D..	Scot..	Edinburgh..	Glas. So.	1836	Brockville ..	Now Principal of University of Aberdeen.
Campbell, Robert, M.A......	Can....	Q. C.	....	1862	Galt, St. Gabriel's, Montreal..	Now Minister of.
Canning, William T........	Irel'd.	Belfast	....	1849	Douglas, Oxford......	Now Minister of.
Carmichael, James, M.A.....	Scot..	Q. C. & Glas.	....	1860	West King..	Now Minister of.
Carruthers, J.............	Scot..	....	....	....	Catechist....	Died 1866.
Chambers, John Park........	Irel'd.	....	....	....	Licentiate ..	Dismissed 1847.
Charbonell, M.............		....	....	....	French Missionary.	
Cheyne, George, M.A........	Scot..	....	Ch. of S.	1831	Amherstbg', Saltfleet	Seceded 1814.
Clark, William C...........	Scot..	Q. C.	....	1858	Middleville, Ormstown ..	Now Minister of.
Clark, Daniel.............	Scot..	Aberdeen ...	Col Com	1839	Indian Lands	Seceded 1844.
Cleland, William..........	Irel'd.	Belfast	U. S....	1850	Uxbridge....	Now, Minister of.
Clugston, John............	Scot..	Glasgow....	Glas. So.	1820	Quebec	Seceded 1844.
Cochrane, William.........	Scot..	Glasgow....	Col Com	1862	Elgin, Q.C..	Now Minister of.
Colquhoun, Archibald.......	Scot..	....	Glas. So.	1832	Georgetown, Dummer, Mulmur	Retired 1861.
Connell, Archibald, M.A.....	Scot..	Glasgow....	Ch. of S.	1825	Martintown	Died there 1836.
Cook, John, D.D...........	Scot..	Edinburgh..	Ch. of S.	1835	Quebec	Now Minister of.
Creen, Thomas.............	Irel'd.	....	U.S.U.C	1819	Niagara.....	Sec. to Ch. of Engl'd
Cruickshank, John, D.D.....	Scot..	Aberdeen ...	Ch. of S.	1828	Bytown, Brockville, Niagara.	Now Minister of Turriff, Scotland.
Currie, Archibald, M.A.....	Scot..	Q. C.	....	1861	Côte St.Geo., Brock	Now Minister of.
Cuthbertson, Samuel........	Irel'd.	....	....	1810	Missionary ..	Seceded 1843.
Darrach, William..........	Scot..	Q. C.	....	1861	Pt. St Charles	Died there 1865.
Darroch, John, M.A.........	Scot..	Princeton...	U. S....	1861	Lochiel	Now Minister of Portree, Scotland.
Davidson, John............	Scot..	Glasgow....	....	1844	Laprairie, NewCarlisle, NewRichmd, Williamsb'g.	Now Minister of.
Dawson, Alex., B.A.........	Can....	Q. C.	....	1863	Kincardine ..	Seceded 1867.
Dickie, John..............	Irel'd.	....	U.S.U.C	1841	Williamsb'g.	Died there 1851.
Dobie, Robert.............	Scot..	Gl. & St. An.	Col.Com	1853	Osnabruck..	Now Minister of.
Douglas, James, B.A........	Can....	Q. C.	....	....	Licentiate ..	Resides in Quebec.
Douglass, James...........	Irel'd.	....	....	1823	Cavan.......	Seceded 1844.
Douglas, James S., M.A.....	Scot..	....	Col Com	1858	Peterboro ..	Resigned 1864.
Dunbar, William..........	Scot..	....	Col Com	1847	Missionary ..	Dismissed 1848.
Duncan, Robert...........	Scot..	....	Ch. of S.	....	Missionary ..	Resigned in 1831.
Dunn, John...............	Scot..	Glasgow....	U. S....	1794	Niagara	Drowned 1803.
Durie, William...........	Scot..	Relief Ch..	Col.Com	1847	Bytown	Died there 1847.
Dyer, John...............		....	....	....	Licentiate ..	Drowned at sea.
Eastman, Daniel W.........		....	U.S.U.C	1840	Grimsby.	

ALPHABETICAL LIST OF MINISTERS, &c.—Continued.

NAMES.	Native of	Educated.	From	Date of Ordination.	Charges held,	REMARKS.
Easton, Robert..............	Scot..	....	Ass. S.S.	1804	St. Gabriel's, St. Andrew's Montreal..	Died in Montreal '51
Edmison, Henry, M.A.......	Can....	Q. C........	....	1866	Nelson and Waterdown	Now Minister of.
Epstein, Ephraim, M.D.... {	Polish A Jew.	{ U. S......	As. mis..	....	Salonica.... Monastir	Sent to, 1861. Resigned at, 1862.
Esson, Henry, M.A..........	Scot..	Aberdeen ...	Ch. of S.	1817	St. Gabriel's.	Seceded 1844.
Evans, David..............	Irel'd.	Glasgow....	U.S.U.C	1815	St. Thérèse, Richmond, Kitley......	Died at Prescott
Evans, Joseph, M.A.........	Can....	Q. C........	....	1858	Oxford, Litchfield, Sherbrooke .	[1864. Now Minister of.
Fairbairn, John..............	Scot..	Edinburgh ...	Glas. So.	1833	Ramsay.....	Seceded 1843.
Ferguson, George D., B.A....	Can....	Q. C. Ed. & Halle.	....	1855	Three Rivers L'Orignal...	Now Minister of.
Ferguson, John, B.A..........	Can....	Un. Tor. Q.C	....	....	Licentiate.	
Ferguson, Peter.............	Scot..	....	U.S.U.C	1830	Esquesing ..	Died there 1863.
Ferguson, William, M.A......	Scot..	Aberdeen ..	Ch. of S.	....	Catechist...	Now in Glengary Pr.
Findlay, William..............	Scot..	....	Col Com	1841	Sarnia	Resigned 1842, now Min. W.Ch. Stirling
Findlater, Andrew.............	Scot..	Aberdeen ...	Ch. of S.	....	Licentiate ..	Returned to Scot.
Fletcher, Alexander.........	Scot..	Glasgow....	Sec. Ch..	1819	Martintown	Died at Plantagenet
Forbes, Alexander.............	Scot..	Aberdeen ...	Col Com	1845	Inverness...	Now Minister of.
Forrest, Robert.............	Scot..	....	....	....	St. Gabriel's.	Resigned 1803.
Fraser, Donald, M.A.........	Can....	Q. C........	....	1867	Priceville ..	Now Minister of.
Fraser, Joshua, B.A.........	U. S..	Q. C........	....	1865	Pt.StCharles	Now Minister of.
Fraser, Simon C., M.A.........	Scot..	....	Glas. So.	1844	Leeds	Seceded 1844.
Fraser, Thomas..............	Scot..	Relief Ch...	U. S....	1819	Niagara, Lanark......	Retired 1861.
Gale, Alexander, M.A........	Scot..	Aberdeen ...	Ch. of S.	1828	Amherstburg h, Lachine, Hamilton ...	Seceded 1844.
Galloway, George, M.A......	Scot..	Aberdeen ...	Glas. So.	1840	Markham ...	Died there 1844.
Gardiner, Alexander.........	Scot..	Aberdeen ...	Glas. So.	1837	Markham, Fergus......	Died there 1841.
Geggie, James.............	Scot..	....	U. P. Ch	1841	Valcartier ..	Seceded 1844.
Gemmell, Dr. John...........	Scot..	....	U.S.U.C	1786	Dalhousie ..	Died there 1844.
Geoffry Antoine.............					Missionary t	o French Canadians
George, James, D.D..........	Scot..	Glasgow....	U. S....	1831	Scarboro, Belleville, Scarboro, Queen's Col.. Stratford	Now Minister of.
Gibson, Hamilton............	Scot..	Glasgow....	Col Com	1850	Galt, Bayfield	Now Minister of.
Glen, Andrew................	Scot..	....	....	1817	Terrebonne ..	
Goepp, M., B.D..............	Frnce.	....	....	....	Missionary ..	Resigned 1867.
Gordon, Henry..............	Scot..	Edinburgh ...	Glas. So.	1833	Newmarket, Gananoque ..	Seceded 1844.
Gordon, James, M.A........	Scot..	Q. C........	....	1854	Markham, Dorchester ..	Now Minister of.
Gordon, John, B.A..........	N. S..	Q. C........	....	1865	Georgina ...	Now Minister of.
Gordon, Daniel Miner., B.D...	N. S..	Glasgow....	....	1866	Ottawa......	Now Minister of.
Grigor, Colin..............	Scot..	Glasgow....	U.P.Ch.	1843	L'Orignal, Guelph, Plantagenet	Died there 1861.
Haig, Thomas...............	Scot..	Glasgow....	Col Com	1848	Brockville, Beauharnois	Died 1866.
Hamilton, William..........	Can....	Q. C........	....	1866	Caledon.....	Now Minister of.
Harkness, James, D.D.......	Scot..	Glasgow....	Ch. of S.	1820	Quebec	Died there 1835.
Hart, Thomas, B.A..........	Scot..	Q. C........	....	....	Licentiate ..	Teacher at Perth.
Hay, John.................	Scot..	Ed. & St. An.	Col.Com	1858	Mt. Forest...	Died 1866.
Henry, George..............	Scot..	Military....	Chapl'n.	1759	Quebec	Died there 1795.
Henry, Thomas.............	Scot..	Edinburgh ...	....	1841	Lachute	Seceded 1845.
Herald, James	Scot..	Aberdeen ...	Col Com	1857	Dundas.....	Now Minister of.
Hogg, John.................	Scot..	Glasgow....	U.P. Ch.	1846	Guelph......	Now Minister of.

Alphabetical List of Ministers, &c.—*Continued.*

NAMES.	Native of	Educated.	From	Date of Ordination.	Charges held.	REMARKS.
Hunter, Alexander, B.A......	Scot...	Q. C........	....	1864	Leith and Johnson ..	Now Minister of.
Inglis, Wm. M., M.A.F.R.S.E.	Scot..	Aber. & Ed...	....	1862	Kingston ...	Now Minister of.
Jacquemart, M.............	Switz.	....	....	....	Missionary to	French Canadians.
Jamieson, Alex., B.A........	Can ..	Q. C. & P'ton	....	....	Licentiate.	
Jardine, Robert, M.A., B.D., [Sc.D.	Can ..	Q. C. & Edin.	....	....	Professor of Logic, &c., University of New Brunswick.	
Jenkins, John, D.D.........	Engl.	Hoxton	E. Pr.C.	1837	St. Paul's, Montreal..	Now Minister of.
Johnson, Thomas............	Irel'd.	Belfast	U.S.U.C	1822	Chinguacousy	Died there 1866.
Johnson, William, M.A......	Can ..	Q. C........	....	1852	Salt Fleet, L'Orignal, Arnprior, Lindsay.....	Retired 1865.
Johnston, Joseph...........	Irel'd.	....	I.Pr.Ch.	1817	Cornwall, Osnabruck, Niagara	Died in Texas
Kerr, James, M.A...........	Scot..	Ed. & St. An.	Ch. of S.	1860	Asst. St. An., Montreal ..	Drowned at sea, S.S. 'London.'
Ketcham, James, M.A........	Scot..	Glasgow....	Glas. So.	1831	Belleville...	Seceded 1844.
King, William	Irel'd.	....	U.S.U.C	1824	Nelson and Waterdown	Died there 1859.
Kirkland, Hugh.............	Irel'd.	....	I.Pr.Ch.	1818	Lachine	Resigned 1819.
Lambie, James, M.A.........	Scot..	....	Ch. of S.	1841	Pickering ..	Died there 1847.
Lamont, Hugh.............	Iona..	Ed. & Q. C..	....	1865	Finch......	Now Minister of.
Lapelletrie, Emile...........	Frnce.	France	BibleSo.	1841	Montreal ...	Died in France.
Law, George................	Scot..	Aberdeen ..	Col.Com	1863	Chinguacousy	Now Minister of.
Leach, Wm. T., D.C.L.......	Scot..	Edinburgh..	Glas. So.	1833	Toronto, York Mills..	Sec. to Church of England, 1842.
Leger, Louis Prosper........	Frnce.	Q. C........	....	1859	Beauharnois	Died there 1859.
Leitch, William, D.D........	Scot..	Glasgow....	Ch. of S.	1843	Queen's Col..	Died at Kingston '64
Leith, Harry..............	Scot..	Aberdeen...	Ch. of S.	1822	Cornwall ...	Became Minister of Rothiemay, Scot.
Lewis, Alexander...........	Irel'd.	....	U.S.U.C	1822	Caledon.....	Retired 1863.
Liddell, Thomas, D.D.......	Scot..	Edinburgh..	Ch. of S.	1829	Queen's Col..	Res. 1846, now Min. of Lochmaben.
Lindsay, John, M.A	Scot..	Q. C........	....	1854	Litchfield ..	Died there 1857.
Lindsay, Peter, B.A.........	Scot..	Q. C........	....	1853	Richmond, Cumberland, Arnprior	Now Minister of.
Lindsay, Robert	Scot..	....	Col Com	....	Ayr	Seceded 1844.
Livingston, John, B.A......	N. S..	Q. C........	....	1859	Dundee	Died there 1860.
Livingstone, Martin W......	Scot..	Glasgow....	U.S.U.C	1837	Simcoe	Now Minister of.
Lochead, John, S., M.A......	Can ..	Q. C........	....	1866	Matilda	Now Minister of.
Lyle, Robert...............	Irel'd.	....	U.S.U.C	1822	Finch......	Died there 1841.
Machar, John, D.D.........	Scot..	Aber. & Ed..	Ch. of S.	1827	Kingston ...	Died there 1863.
Mair, Hugh, D.D...........	Scot..	Glasgow.....	U.P.Ch.	1828	Fergus	Died there 1854.
Mair, James,...............	Scot..	Aberdeen ...	Col.Com	1856	Martintown	Now Minister of.
Mair, William.............	Scot..	Glasgow....	Cb. of S.	1833	Chatham	Died there 1860.
Mann, Alexander, M.A......	Scot..	Aberdeen ...	Col Com	1840	Pakenham..	Now Minister of.
Marshall, Alex. Porter......	Scot..	....	Col Com	1858	Missionary ..	Retur'd to Scot. 1858
Masson, William...........	Scot..	Ab. & St. An.	Col Com	1858	St John's Hamilton, Russeltown .	Now Minister of.
Mathieson, Alexander, D.D..	Scot..	Glas. & Ed..	Ch. of S.	1826	St.Andrew's, Montreal ...	Now Minister of.
M'Allister, William..........	Scot..	....	Glas. So.	1830	Lanark, Sarnia......	Seceded 1844.
Macauley, Duncan..........	Scot..	Glasgow....	Glas. So.	1833	Leeds	Dismissed 1837.
Macauley, Ewan, B.A........	Scot..	Q. C........	....	1866	Southwold..	Now Minister of.
Macauley, James...........	Irel'd.	....	U.S.U.C	....	Missionary ..	Resigned 1841.
M'Caughey, Samuel, M.A....	Irel'd.	Belfast	....	1855	Pickering ..	Resigned 1859.
M'Caul, James, B.A	Irel'd.	Q. C........	....	1861	Roslin, Melbourne..	Now Minister of.

Alphabetical List of Ministers, &c.—*Continued.*

NAMES.	Native of	Educated.	From	Date of Ordination	Charges held	REMARKS.
M'Clatchey, George	Irel'd.		U.S.U.C	1840	Clinton	Died at London 1857
M'Coll, Alexander				1842	Aldboro,	
McCormick, Thomas	Irel'd.				Missionary,	
M'Donald, Alexander, B.A.	Scot.	Q. C.		1866	Nottawasaga	Now Minister of.
M'Donald, Donald, D.A.	Scot.	Ed. & Q. C.		1856	Lochiel	Now Min. of Sleat, Scotland.
M'Donald, Duncan, M.A.	N. S.	Q. C.		1865	Litchfield	Now Minister of.
M'Donald, John	Scot.	Glasgow	Ch. of S.	1854	Lochiel, Beechridge	Now Minister of.
Macdonnell, D. J., B.D.	N. B.	Q. C., Edin., Germany	Col Com	1866	Peterboro	Now Minister of.
Macdonnell, George	Scot.	Edinburgh.	N. Brus. Col Com	1840	Nelson and Waterdown, Fergus	Now Minister of.
McDougall, Daniel	Scot.		Col Com	1864	Missionary	London Pres.
McDougall, Neil	Scot.	Glasgow	Col Com	1863	Eldon	Now Minister of.
McDowall, Robert	Irel'd.		U.S.U.C	1800	Fredricksbg	Died there 1841.
McEwan, James, M.A.	Irel'd.	Q. C.		1854	Westminster	Now Minister of.
McEwan, William, M.A.	Irel'd.		I.Pr.Ch.	1849	Belleville, Dorchester	Retired 1863.
McFarlane, Robert	Scot.		Col Com	1848	Melbourne	Dismissed 1851.
McGill, Robert, D.D.	Scot.	Glasgow	Ch. of S.	1829	Niagara, St. Paul's,Mont.	Died there 1856.
McGillivray, Daniel, B.A.	N. S.	Q. C.		1867	Brockville	Now Minister of.
McHutchison, William	Scot.	Glasgow	Ch. of S.	1857	Beckwith	Resigned 1862.
McIntosh, Angus	Scot.		Glas. So.	1836	Markham, Thorold	Seceded 1844.
McIsaac, John, M.A.	Scot.	Glasgow	Ch. of S.	1835	Lochiel	Became Min., Oban. Scot.,died there1847
McKay, Alexander, M.A.	N. S.	Q.C.&Aberdeen			Lochiel	Now Minister of
McKay, William E., B.A.	Irel'd.	Knox & Q.C.		1856	Camden, Orangeville.	Now Minister of.
McKee, William	Irel'd.	Belfast	C. P. Ch.	1857	Innisfil	Now Minister of.
McKenzie, Donald	Scot.		Ch. of S.	1834	Zorra	Seceded 1844.
McKenzie, John, M.A.	Aber.		Ch. of S.	1818	Williamst'n	Died there 1855.
McKerras, John H., M.A.	Scot.	Q. C.		1853	Darlington, Queen's Col.	Now Prof. Classics.
McKid, Alexander	Scot.	Aberdeen	Col Com	1842	Bytown, Hamilton, Goderich	Retired 1866
McKillican, William	Scot.	Aberdeen	Ch. of S.	1835	Gwillimbury St. Thomas.	Resigned 1842.
McLardy, H. J., B.A.	Scot.	Fred'n & Ed.	Col Com	1858	Asst. Ottawa	Resigned 1867.
McLaren, R. G., B.A.	Scot.	St. Andrews.	Col Com	1857	Three Rivers	Now Minister of.
McLaurin, John	Scot.	St. Andrews.	Ch. of S.	1819	Lochiel, L'Original	Died there 1833.
McLaurin, John, M.A.	Scot.	Glasgow	Col Com	1840	Martintown	Died there 1855.
McLean, Æneas	Scot.		N.Scotia	1847	C. St. George	Died 1856.
McLean, Alexander	Scot.			1844	Picton	Seceded 1844.
McLean, Donald J., B.A.	Can.	Q. C.		1863	Kitley, Middleville	Now Minister of.
McLean, Matthew W.	Can.	Q. C. and Princeton.		1856	Paisley	Now Minister of.
McLennan, Alex., B.A.	Can.	Q. C.		1862	Tossorontio.	Now Minister of.
McLennan, Kenneth, B.A.	Can.	Q. C.		1853	Dundas, Paisley, Whitby	Now Minister of.
McLeod, John, M.	Scot.	Ed. & Glasg.	Ch. of S.	1853	Williams	Now Minister of.
McMillan, Duncan			U.S.U.C	1831	Caledon. Williams	Seceded 1844.
McMillan, John, B.D.	N. S.	Q. C.			Licentiate	Musquodoibit, N. S.
McMorine, John, D.D.	Scot.	Edinburgh	Ch. of S.	1839	Melbourne, Ramsay	Died there 1867.
McMorine, John K., M.A.	Can.	Q. C.		1864	Douglas	Sec. to Ch.of Eng.'67

Alphabetical List of Ministers, &c.—*Continued.*

NAMES.	Native of	Educated.	From	Date of Ordination	Charges held	REMARKS.
McMurchy, John............	Scot..	Glas. & Ed..	Ch. of S.	1842	Bradford, Eldon......	Died there 1866.
McNaughton, Alex.........	Scot..	Glasgow....	Glas. So.	1833	Lancaster...	Trans'd to Colonsay, Scotland 1842.
McNaughton, Peter, M.A....	Scot..	Aberdeen...	Glas. So.	1833	Vaughan, Dores, Scot., Vaughan, Pickering...	Resigned 1855.
McNee, Daniel.............	Scot..	Edinburgh..	Col Com	1850	Hamilton...	Resigned 1853.
McPherson, Thomas, M.A....	Scot..	Aberdeen ...	Ch. of S.	1836	Beechridge, Lancaster...	Now Minister of.
McQuarrie, Alex. N., B.A...	N. S..	Q. C......	....	....	Licentiate ..	Teacher in Quebec.
McVicar, Peter.............	Scot..	Glasgow....	Col Com	1856	Martintown	Now Min. of Manor, Scotland.
Meldrum, William...........	Scot..	....	....	1840	Puslinch....	S.ceded 1844.
Merlin, John..............	Irel'd.	Glasgow....	U.S.U.C	1823	Hemmingf'd	Died there 1866.
Miller, Matthew...........	Scot..	Glasgow....	Ch. of S.	1833	Cobourg....	Drowned 1834.
Miller, William...........	Scot..	....	....	1856	Stratford ...	Resigned 1862.
Milligan, Archd. II.........	Scot..	....	Col Com	1853	Russeltown.	Died 1855.
Moffat, John..............	Scot..	Glasgow....	Col Com	1858	Laprairie & Longueuil ..	Resigned 1860, now in Scotland.
Moody, Duncan.............	Scot..	Glasgow....	Col Com	1832	Dundee	Died there 1855.
Morrison, Duncan, B.A......	Scot..	Q. C......	....	1851	Beckwith, Brockville, Owen Sound.	Now Minister of.
Morrison, Thomas...........	Scot..	Edinburgh..	Col Com	1853	Melbourne..	Resigned 1855.
Mowat, John B., M.A.......	Can....	Q. C. and Ed.	....	1850	Niagara, Queen's Col..	Now Prof. of Oriental languages., Q.C.
Muir, James B., B.A......	Scot..	Edin. & Glas.	P.Ch En'	1863	Lindsay, Galt........	Now Minister of.
Muir, James C., D.D........	Scot..	Edinburgh ..	Glas. So.	1836	Georgetown.	Now Minister of.
Mullan, Elias..........	Can....	Q. C......	....	1867	Richmond ..	Now Minister of.
Mullan, James B..........	Can....	Q. C......	....	1862	Spencerville	Now Minister of.
Mullan, James S., B.A......	Irel'd.	Q. C......	....	1861	Clarke	Now Minister of.
Munro, Donald.............	Scot..	Glas. & Ed..	Col Com	1850	Finch	Died there 1867.
Murray, John C............	Scot..	Glasg. Ed. & Germany.	Free Ch.	....	Licentiate ..	Now Prof. of Logic, &c., Queen's Col.
Murray, J. Allister.........	Scot..	Nova Scotia.	N.Bruns	1858	Mt. Forest...	Now Minister of.
Murray, Robert.............	Scot..	Edinburgh..	U. S....	1836	Oakville, Sup. School Prof. Math.	Died at Goderich. for U. C. Un. Toronto.
Mylne, Solomon............	Irel'd.	Belfast	Pr.Ch.I.	1850	Smith's Falls	Now Minister of.
Neill, Robert..............	Scot..	Glasgow....	Glas. So.	1840	Seymour....	Now Minister of.
Nicol, Francis..............	Scot..	Glasgow....	Col Com	1859	London	Now Minister of.
Nimmo, James.............	Scot..	....	Col Com	1866	Missionary ..	Now in Demerara.
Niven, Hugh............	Scot..	Edinburgh..	Ch. of S.	1857	Saltfleet	Now Minister of.
Paton, Andrew............	Scot..	Edinburgh..	Ch. of S.	1865	Asst. St. An. Montreal ...	Now Asst. Min. of.
Paterson, James............	Scot..	Glasgow....	Col Com	1857	Hemmingf'd	Now Minister of.
Penny, Robert............	Scot..	....	Col Com	1846	Catechist....	Resigned 1847.
Paul, James T..............	Scot..	Q. C......	....	1850	St. Louis de Gonzague .	Retired 1865.
Peden, Robert............	Scot..	Aberdeen ...	Sec. Ch.	1844	Amherstb'rg	Seceded 1844.
Porteous, George...........	Engl..	Q. C......	....	1860	Wolfe Island	Now Minister of.
Porter, Samuel.............	Irel'd.	....	U.S.U.C	1840	Clarke	Retired 1861.
Purkis, Isaac.............	Engl..	....	U.S.U.C	1840	Osnabruck..	Died there 1852.
Rannie, John, M.A.........	Scot..	Aberdeen ..	Col Com	1857	Chatham ...	Now Minister of.
Reid, William, M.A........	Scot..	....	....	1840	Colborne....	Seceded 1844.
Ritchie, William...........	Scot..	Edinburgh..	Ch. of S.	1831	Newmarket.	Sec. to Ch. of E. 1842
Rintoul, David.............	Scot..	Glasgow....	Ch. of S.	1841	St. Catherine	Resigned 1845.

Alphabetical List of Ministers, &c.—*Continued.*

NAMES.	Native of	Educated.	From	Date of Ordination	Charges held.	REMARKS.
Rintoul, William, M.A.......	Scot..	Glasgow....	Glas. So.	1821	Toronto, Streetsville..	Seceded 1844.
Roach, Walter.............	Scot..	Edinburgh..	Glas. So.	1833	Beauharnois	Died there 1849.
Robb, John................	Scot..	....	....	1845	Chambly, Chatham ...	Died there 1858.
Robb, John................	Scot..	U. P. Ch....	U. S....	1846	Dalhousie,	Died there 1851.
Robertson, James...........	Scot..	....	....	....	Licentiate..	Returned to Scot.
Robertson, John D.........	Can....	Q. C........	....	....	Licentiate..	In Australia.
Roger, John M., M.A........	Scot..	....	Glas. So.	1833	Peterboro ..	Seceded 1844.
Rogers James...............	Irel'd.	....	U.S.U.C	1840	Demorest-ville......	Went to U. S.
Romanes, George, LL.D.....	Scot..	Edinburgh..	Glas. So.	1834	Smith's Falls Queen's Col..	Now in England.
Rose, Alexander............	Scot..	Glasgow....	....	....	....	Retur'd to Scot. 1866
Ross, Alexander, M.A........	Scot..	Aberdeen ...	Glas. So.	1829	Aldboro, Woolwich, Innisfil......	Died there 1857.
Ross, Donald...............	N. S..	Q. C........	....	1859	Vaughan, Southwold, Dundee	Now Minister of.
Ross, Donald, B.D...........	Can ..	Q. C..... ♠..	....	1865	Chatham ...	Now Minister of.
Ross, John Reid, B.A.......	Scot..	Q. C........	....	....	Licentiate..	
Ross, Walter, R...........	Scot..	Aberdeen ...	Col Com	1?	Pickering ..	Now Minister of.
Ross, Walter, M.A...........	N. S..	Q. C........	....	1?..	Beckwith...	Now Minister of.
Scott, Thomas..............	Irel'd.	Belfast	Col Com	184?	Simcoe, Camden, Williamsb'g, Matilda, Plantagenet	Now Minister of.
Sieveright, James, B.A......	Scot..	Ab. & Q. C..	....	1857	Ormstown, Melbourne, Chelsea.....	Now Minister of.
Shand, Alexander...........	Irel'd.	....	....	....	Missionary..	Resigned 1852.
Shanks, David..............	Scot..	Glasgow....	U.S.U.C	1833	St. Eustache Valcartier, Cumberland Valcartier ..	Now Minister of.
Sheed, George, M.A.........	Scot..	Aberdeen ...	Ch. of S.	1827	Ancaster ..	Died 1832.
Simpson, William...........	Scot..	St. Andrews.	Col Com	1840	Lachine	Now Minister of.
Sinclair, James.............	Irel'd.	Belfast	U.S.U.C	1849	Huntley....	Now Minister of.
Sinclair, Donald............	Scot..	Gl. & St. An.	....	1843	Côte St. Geo.	Res. 1846, Now Min. of Duror, Scotland.
Skinner, John, D.D..........	Scot..	Glasgow....	U. P.Ch.	1853	London, Waterdown ..	Died there 1864.
Smart, William	Engl..	Gosport.....	U.S.U.C	1810	Brockville ..	Seceded 1844.
Smellie, George............	Scot..	Edinburgh ..	....	1836	Fergus	Seceded 1844.
Smith, James..............	Scot..	Edinburgh..	Ch. of S.	1832	Guelph	Died 1853.
Smith, James C., M.A........	Scot..	Q. C........	....	1862	Cumberland	Now Minister of.
Smith, John................	Scot..	Aberdeen ..	Ch. of S.	1833	Beckwith...	Died there 1851.
Smith, John Malcolm, M.A..	Scot..	....	Col Com	1850	Galt, Queen's Col..	Died in Scotland 1856.
Smith, R. P...............	Scot..	....	Col Com	....	Missionary..	In Quebec Pres.
Smith, Thomas G...........	Scot..	Q.C., St.And. & Princeton.	U. S....	1862	Melbourne...	Resigned 1866.
Snodgrass, William, D.D.....	Scot..	Glasgow....	Col Com	1852	St. Paul's, Montreal, Queen's Col..	Now Principal of.
Somerville, James..........	Scot..	Glasgow....	Relief C.	1803	St. Gabriel's.	Died in Mont. 1837.
Spark, Alexander, D.D......	Scot..	Aberdeen ...	Ch. of S.	1784	Quebec......	Died there 1819.
Spence, Alexander, D.D......	Scot..	Aber. & Ed..	Col Com	1841	Ottawa......	Retired 1867.
Spenser, Adam.............	Scot..	Glasgow....	Col Com	1862	Missionary..	In Toronto Pres.
Stark, Mark Y, M.A........	Scot..	Glasgow....	Glas. So.	1833	Dundas.....	Seceded 1844.
Starke, Wm. D............	Scot..	....	Col Com	....	Missionary..	Seceded 1845.
Stevenson, Robert..........	Scot..	Glasgow....	Col Com	1855	Williams ...	Now a Missionary
Stewart, A.C..............	....	....	U. P.Ch.	....	Missionary..	Resigned 1859.

Alphabetical List of Ministers, &c.—*Continued.*

NAMES.	Native of	Educated.	From	Date of Ordination.	Charges held.	REMARKS.
Stewart, William.............	Scot..	....	Ch. of S.	1832	Galt	Resigned 1835,app'd to Demerara.
Stewart, William.............	Scot..	Glasgow ...	Col Com	1860	Hornby	Now Minister of.
Story, Robert Herbert.......	Scot..	Edin. & Glas.	Ch. of S.	1859	Asst. St. An. Montreal ...	Now Minister of. Roseneath, Scotland
Stott, David.................	Scot..	Edinburgh..	Col Com	1858	Brantford...	Now in Scotland.
Stuart, James................	Irel'd.	....	....	1847	Markham, Wawanosh, Woodstock ..	Retired 1861.
Stuart, James................	Scot..	....	Col Com	1860	Missionary ..	Drowned at sea. S.S. 'Hungarian' 1860
Sym, Frederick, P...........	U. S.	Glas. & Q.C.	....	1852	Woodstock, Russeltown, Beauharnois	Now Minister of.
Tanner, John E.............	Switz.	....	....	....	Missionary..	Resigned 1864.
Tawse, John, M.A..........	Scot..	Aberdeen ...	Glas. So.	1837	King	Now Minister of.
Taylor, Henry, M.A........	Scot..	St. An. & Ed.	Ch. of S.	1841	Missisquoi, Philipsburg.	Now Minister of West Anstruther,S.
Taylor, John................	Scot..	Edinburgh..	Ch. of S.	1834	Lachine	Died in Scot. 1865.
Taylor, William............	Scot..	....	....	1807	Osnabruck..	Went to U. S. 1819.
Thom, James	Scot..	Glas. & Ed.	Ch. of S.	1844	Three Rivers Woolwich...	Now Minister of.
Thomson, George, M.A.......	Scot..	Aberdeen ...	Ch. of S.	1851	Renfrew	Now Minister of.
Thompson, Peter...........	Scot..	Glasgow....	Col Com	1858	Missionary ..	Returned to Scot.
Urquhart, Hugh, D.D........	Scot..	Aberdeen ...	Ch. of S.	1822	Cornwall ...	Now Minister of.
Walker, Archibald...........	Scot..	Glasgow....	Col Com	1854	Belleville ...	Now Minister of.
Walker, Thomas............	Scot..	Glasgow....	Col Com	1865	Missionary ..	Returned to Scot.
Walker, W. Montgomery.....	Scot..	Glasgow....	Glas. So.	1834	Huntingdon	Now Minister of Ochiltree, Scot.
Wallace, Alexander, B.A.....	Scot..	Q. C.......	....	1845	Huntingdon	Now Minister of.
Watson, David, M.A........	Scot..	Q. C.......	....	1853	Thorah	Now Minister of.
Watson, Peter, B.A.........	Scot..	Q. C.......	....	1856	Williamst'n	Now Minister of.
Weir, George, M.A........	Scot..	....	....	....	Licentiate, Queen's Col..	Now Prof. in Morrin College.
Wells John.	Scot ..	Glasgow	Col Com	1861	New Richmond	Now Minister of.
Wilkie, Daniel, L.L.D.......	Scot..	Glasgow....	....	....	Licentiate ..	Died in Quebec.
Williamson, James, L.L.D....	Scot..	Edinburgh..	Ch. of S.	1845	Queen's Col..	Now Prof. Math.
Wilkins, William T., B.A....	N. B..	Fred'n &Q.C.	....	....	Licentiate ..	Now Minister at Woodstock, N. B.
Wilson, James, M.A.........	Scot..	Aberdeen ...	Col Com	1856	Lanark	Now Minister of.
Wilson, Thomas C..........	Scot..	Glasgow....	Ch. of S.	1830	Perth.......	Now Minister of Dunkeld, Scotland
White, William.............	Irel'd.	Belfast	U. S...	1853	Richmond, Kitley......	Now Minister of.
Whyte, John................	Scot..	Edinburgh..	Col Com	1851	Brockville, Arthur	Now Minister of.
Wightman, Thomas..........	Scot..	....	Ch. of S.	1844	Camden	Seceded 1844.
Young John.................	Scot..	Glasgow....	Ch. of S.	1786	St. Gabriel, Niagara	Died at Truro, N.